New Novel, New Wave, New Politics

New Novel, New Wave, New Politics

Fiction and the Representation
of History in Postwar France

LYNN A. HIGGINS

University of Nebraska Press, Lincoln and London

Acknowledgments for
the use of previously
published material
appear on page viii.
© 1996 by the University
of Nebraska Press
First paperback printing: 1998
Most recent printing indicated by
the first digit below:
1 2 3 4 5 6 7 8 9 10
Library of Congress
Cataloging-in-Publication
Data   Higgins, Lynn A.
New novel, new wave,
new politics: fiction and
the representation of
history in postwar France
/ Lynn A. Higgins.
p.   cm.—(Stages)
Includes biblio-
graphical references and index.
ISBN 0-8032-2377-3
(cl: alk. paper)
ISBN 0-8032-7309-6
(pa.: alk. paper)
1. Motion pictures and
literature—France.
2. Film adaptations.
3. French fiction—
20th century—History
and criticism.
4. Experimental fiction
—History and ctiticism.
5. France—Politics and
government—1945–
I. Title.   II. Series.
PN1995.3.H54   1996
791.43'658—dc20
95-15226 CIP

Contents

Illustrations

Preface

This book began with a focus on a series of works from the early heyday of the New Novel and the New Wave, a period coinciding with the French identity crisis over Algeria. But one of the hazards—and one of the thrills—of studying living artists is that they refuse to stand still. The years during which I worked on the book saw an evolution in its subject that could sometimes be dizzying and discouraging. Just as I thought I had figured something out, one of the artists I was studying would come out with a new novel or a new film that would pull the rug out from under me, sending me back to the drawing board. They kept redefining their own projects, defying my attempts to frame them. We grew together through the eighties and early nineties. My desire to gain access to these texts' historical roots grew from my frustration with my training in structuralist and poststructuralist criticism. Although I did not want to abandon these powerful critical tools, I also did not want to turn my back on aspects of the texts that were inaccessible to them. I loved texts like *L'Année dernière à Marienbad* (1961; *Last Year at Marienbad*), crystalline in their internal geometry and their irreverent indifference to outside realities, but at the same time I could not help asking, "So what?" I was stuck, as it were, on the question of "relevance."

Apparently, Robbe-Grillet was experiencing similar discomforts, along with Truffaut, Duras, and many others. After a period of sometimes nearly unintelligible abstraction during the 1960s and early 1970s, many of these authors and filmmakers "returned," some for the first time, to seek the anchors of their practice in contemporary history. My initial project became the first part of the book, one of three moments I distinguished in the evolution of the New Novel and the New Wave. First drafts of those chapters were written before Robbe-Grillet, or Duras, or Malle produced their memoirs. In addition, the Cold War has ended, a *mode rétro* has emerged, and the return to history has become a major preoccupation in France as in the United States. Most of the primary and secondary works consulted here were published after I began working on this project. Even as I write these words, Duras and Robbe-Grillet are still writing. Resnais and Malle and Godard and Varda are still making films. Truffaut is gone, an incalculable loss. It is possible that the next step will be something completely different. I had better pack up and move on before the intermission is over.

Earlier versions of parts of this book have previously appeared in print. "Durasian (Pre)Occupations" appeared in *L'Esprit créateur* 30 (summer 1990). "Problems of Plotting: *La Route des Flandres*" was published as "Language and the Shapes of History in Claude Simon's *The Flanders Road*" in *Studies in Twentieth Century Literature* 10, no. 1 (1985). A version of the chapter on *Au revoir les enfants*, "If Looks Could Kill: Louis Malle's Portraits of Collaboration," appeared in *Fascism, Aesthetics, and Culture,* edited by Richard J. Golsan (Hanover NH: University Press of New England, 1992). Some of my analysis of *L'Année dernière à Marienbad* served a complementary argument in "Screen/Memory: Rape and Its Alibis in *Last Year at Marienbad*," in *Rape and Representation,* edited by Lynn A. Higgins and Brenda R. Silver (New York: Columbia University Press, 1991). Permission to reprint is gratefully acknowledged.

Throughout, where no translator is cited, translations are my own. Photographs were done by Karen A. Vournakis.

The initial sparks of this project were ignited during a National Endowment for the Humanities Summer Seminar led by Victor Brombert at Princeton University. Along the way, financial assistance has also been provided by Dartmouth College's faculty research funds and a Dartmouth senior faculty grant. A Camargo Foundation residency provided a semester's uninterrupted work time. An Oberlin College Haskell Fellowship permitted a research trip to Paris.

The professional dedication of Dartmouth College's staff and academic support offices must surely be unsurpassed. I would like to thank Cecile Thornton and the Instructional Services staff, Nancy Millichap in the Humanities Computing Office, and Patricia Carter, Marianne Hraibi, Gregory Finnegan, and Robert Jaccaud of Baker Library for their invaluable help. I have also relied on Carol Peper, the administrative assistant in the Department of French and Italian and the most even-tempered person I have ever met.

Encouragement and support take many forms, and I am happy to acknowledge the many colleagues and friends who made writing this book a pleasure. I thank my students at Dartmouth College, whose impertinent questions remind me that if I cannot explain something, I probably do not understand it myself. I am grateful to Leah Hewitt at Amherst College, Philippe Carrard at the University of Vermont, the Modern and Classical Languages Department and the Women's Studies Program at Texas A&M University, and Wesleyan University's Romance Languages Department for inviting me to their campuses to present and discuss my work. Many colleagues have provided important feedback, key bibliographic tips, enlightening conversation, and unexpected opportunities at crucial moments: Victor Brombert, Bruce Duncan, Joe Golsan, Mary Jean Green, Marianne Hirsch, Lawrence Kritzman, Pierre Laborie, Albert Lavalley, Amy Lawrence, Ian Lustick, Neal Oxenhandler, Bill Pence, Catherine Portuges, Dina Sherzer, Brenda Silver, Camille Smith, Richard Stamelman, Klaus Theweleit, Steven Ungar, and Kathleen Wine. Edward M. Anthony did some crucial sleuth work on the *Internationale situationiste* and has unselfishly aided and abetted my schemes on many other occasions. Some of the characters in my story generously shared their reflections and insights: Alain Robbe-Grillet, Marcel Ophuls, Jean Ricardou, Jérôme Lindon, and Agnès Varda willingly answered my questions, listened to my ideas, and argued with me.

Thanks to my son Julian, this project took longer and was more fun than I initially expected. I worked best when he was sleeping or drawing or reading quietly beside me. I also owe an incalculable debt of gratitude and admiration to the teachers at the Redwing Preschool in Wilder Vermont, at the Dartmouth College Child Care Center, and at the Hanover After School Program. Through them, I would like to acknowledge, if only in token fashion, all the childcare professionals whose skill and dedication provide, not only for children but also for their parents, the peace of mind in which to work and grow.

Finally, in honor of more than twenty-five years of patient support and engrossing conversations, I wish to dedicate this book to Roland L. Higgins. Historian, Asianist, conscientious objector, humanist, partner, and best friend, he has been a major shaping force in the effort this project represents.

New Novel, New Wave, New Politics

Introduction: The Politics of Style

The internal politics of style (how the elements are put together) is determined by its external politics (its relationship to alien discourse). Discourse lives, as it were, on the boundary between its own context and another, alien, context. – M. M. Bakhtin

For as long as there have been movies, kids have been sneaking in without paying. Like many budding cinephiles, the young Henri Langlois developed his own modus operandi: according to his biographers, Langlois used to join and mingle with the crowds emerging from the exit, but instead of walking *out* of the movie house with them, he walked backward through the crowd, back *into* the cinema, where he could stay for the next showing without having purchased a ticket. Years later, having cofounded the Cinémathèque française in 1936, he made good use of his experience as a penniless moviegoer. So all-consuming was Langlois's passion for the cinema that his film collection was his first concern when his artillery unit was captured by the Germans in 1940. As his brother Georges recalls the story, what happened next could itself have been a scene from a movie: Henri let himself be rounded up and herded toward captivity. Amidst the disorderly marchers, however, he pretended to move with the crowd but all the while walked backward, until he could jump into a ditch and then hasten home through the woods to begin the job of hiding his precious collection of films.[1]

An avid movie buff even as a youth and an admirer of Langlois, François Truffaut adopted the Langlois maneuver as a kind of signature. In *Argent de poche* (1976; *Small Change*), for example, a troubled and abused boy, Julien Leclou, boosts his self-esteem and wins the admiration of his buddies by showing them how to sneak into the cinema through the exits. And like Langlois, Truffaut understood the broader application of this childish savoir-faire. In *Le Dernier Métro* (1981; *The Last Metro*), a Resistance fighter, played by actor Gérard Depardieu, reports how he escaped from Nazi capture by facing in one direction while walking the opposite way, thus giving each Gestapo officer the impression that he had already been interrogated by the previous one.

This book is about the alleged eclipse of the social in the Nouveau Roman (New Novel) and in cinema of the Nouvelle Vague (New Wave). I want to freeze-frame the Langlois escape scene for use as a composite image both of the back-door, possibly even inadvertent "engagement" of New Novelists and New Wave filmmakers with history and of the critical postures I believe are needed to bring this dimension of their works to light. Trying to think historically about the works examined here gives one a critical kink in the neck. It will be necessary to face in two directions: forward in order to take into account their aggressive foregrounding of autonomous and productive textuality and backward for an understanding of their often obsessive concern with memory, with a personal or historical past, with the insistent though shadowy presence of the world. Consistent with this Janus vision, a corpus of novels and films can be studied in light of the double meaning inherent in the formulation "fiction in crisis": both the crisis of representation that characterizes French postwar experimental fiction and the historical, political, and social crises during which such explorations take place. It will be possible to show the ways in which the works considered here, while facing in the direction of research on form, are shaped, even and especially in their formal dimensions, by the political events and ideas of the era. Like Henri Langlois, they often seem preoccupied exclusively with aesthetic problems, and yet they inevitably back into history even as they attempt to evade it.

It is my thesis that the artists studied here engage in a kind of historiography that has not yet been read as such. The chapters that follow receive the texts neither as historical fictions in any established sense (this would be difficult to do, given their opacity) nor as exclusively oriented toward problems of aesthetic innovation.[2] I look at a selection of the most enduring texts (both written and filmed) produced by New Wave filmmakers and New Novelists, giving attention both to historical themes (or the lack of them, which may itself be historically significant) and to the innovative strategies of representation that have had an important impact on postwar fiction both in France and internationally. I also consider what the novels and films actually do say about any historical referent they may evoke. I examine their literal dimension—their discourse and formal construction—to see what it may have to say about the historical context in which the work was produced. Most urgently, I look at connections between the two.

The works examined here rarely make unambiguous statements or take polemical stands with regard to the historical and political pressures that haunt them. They may or may not have a partisan purpose, serve a cause, or be politically *engagés,* but they are always and inevitably "engaged," like gears, with other contemporary discourses. They enact the conflicts, the double (multiple) binds of postwar history and representation. For these reasons, it may be desirable to keep in mind the term Linda Hutcheon coined to categorize novelists like Salman Rushdie and Manuel Puig, who are writing what she calls "historiographic metafictions": they are "obsessed with the question of how we can come to know the past today."[3] Hutcheon's formulation, substituting as it does the epistemological (the how) for the traditional ontological question (the what) and ending with its juxtaposition of past and present, the intertwined moments of *énoncé* and *énonciation,* serves nicely to encapsulate the task undertaken here.

Defenders and detractors alike have consistently missed the metahistoriographic dimensions of these works. After the earliest New Novels and New Wave films appeared, the critic's most immediate task was to explain, to render accessible, even to justify this new kind of fiction. Sympathetic readers of the New Novel (such as Roland Barthes, Gérard Genette, and Jean Ricardou in France and Stephen Heath, John Sturrock, and Leon Roudiez abroad) chose, quite rightly and often brilliantly, to analyze how the novelists disrupted inherited narrative norms and reading habits by deploying textual strategies that subverted the referentiality of language (or rather, made its inherent unreferentiality apparent). Ironically, these critics were so effective that many New Novels previously considered inaccessible or merely arcane have now become part of the modernist canon. The New Wave passed more smoothly into public acceptance, perhaps because cinema was already part of popular culture and more readily accessible to a wider audience and undoubtedly also because the filmmakers could depend for favorable publicity on the *Cahiers du cinéma,* the influential film journal where Truffaut, along with Jean-Luc Godard and others, started as a critic before turning to filmmaking.

From the beginning, there were also those who criticized New Novels and New Wave films for promoting a vision that was asocial, antihistorical, excessively formalist, and solipsistic and generally for adopting a head-in-the-sand posture toward the world. Some, like Pierre de Boisdeffre and Jean-Bertrand Barrère, attributed trivial content to frivolity or perversity on the part of the artists. Less polemical and more convincing critics (Jean Bloch-Michel and Lucien Goldmann, for example) reversed the terms, faulting the novels and films for reflecting the depersonalization and alienation of postwar capitalism. Only Jacques Leenhardt's study of Robbe-Grillet's *La Jalousie* gives any of the works a close reading in light of specific historical or sociological considerations.[4]

At times there has been a comic *dialogue de sourds* [dialogue of the deaf] between those who proclaim that the texts are completely dissociated from their context and those who sense some connections, that is, between approaches that view the texts as what Jean Ricardou called "the story of an adventure" and those that find only "the adventure of a story." Thus, Roy Armes can assert that the emerging Nouvelle Vague and the political upheavals of 1958 were "not closely linked. . . . Key contemporary themes—the war in Algeria, the need for social change in metropolitan France—are as absent from French cinema after 1958 as they were before." Later he states, again without elaboration, that Godard's work "conceals profound analysis of contemporary France beneath its inconsequential surface."5 And thus the 1985 Nobel committee bestowed its highest literary honor on New Novelist Claude Simon, citing his broad and humanistic vision of the twentieth century. Simon very amiably responded by using his acceptance speech as a platform from which to proclaim the productive (rather than reproductive) power of the signifier.

But not its disconnection. The way in which Simon formulated his message reveals the debate to be grounded in a misunderstanding informed more by polemic than by an attempt to account accurately for the nature of the texts themselves. Simon explains that language represents only itself, like mathematical formulae, which "constitute a world unto and for themselves alone; they play exclusively among themselves, expressing nothing but their own wonderful nature, which is precisely what makes them expressive: they reflect within themselves the strange relations among things." So far, Simon seems to play into the hands of the fiction-as-solipsism critics. But he continues: "It is in pursuit of this play that one could perhaps conceive of an *engagement* of writing, which, each time it changes by so much as a particle the relation that language sustains between men and things, contributes in its modest measure to changing the world."6

Simon is right to the extent that the New Novel, the New Wave, and other experimental fiction have altered the expectations of an educated public. But here he blends two kinds of connections between text and context: He puts forward an activist impulse to change the world that, in my view, remains as problematic as it is admirable and whose effectiveness is probably impossible to document. He also outlines a (meta)historiographic or essentially descriptive function—an attempt to fashion a discourse—that is demonstrable and deserves closer and more serious consideration.7 Although I address some of the issues raised by the first connection (notably in chapter 4, about May 1968), it is the second connection that is my foremost concern here.

But who are these novelists and filmmakers, and why should they be studied in tandem? The terms *Nouveau Roman* and *Nouvelle Vague* are themselves rather vague, and the two have rarely been considered in juxtaposition, and then only fleetingly. This critical lacuna is especially curious in light of the multifarious interconnections between literature and film that have characterized French cinema from its beginnings. (For starters, one might think of Jean Cocteau, Marcel Pagnol, the Marcel Carné–Jacques Prévert team, the film noir genre, and the omnipresence of literary adaptations, including the ones the New Wave directors derided as well as those they made themselves.) Separately, the New Novel and the New Wave have been understood as historical periods, as groups of artists, and as movements with particular aesthetic programs or recognizable styles. Each of these definitions is helpful, but only in part. Viewing either phenomenon as a particular moment in literary history can help us to situate it and evaluate its impact but at the same time overlooks the divergences among the artists and leaves muddy the questions of when individuals stopped making New Novels or New Wave films and how to classify what they have been doing since (and, in the case of the novelists, what they had been writing before). Viewing them as groups, on the other hand, helps identify common purposes and styles but tends to result in circularity, since definition depends entirely on whom you include, and vice versa. Numerous valuable studies have been undertaken as well of individual novelists or filmmakers and of specific works.

What both the personnel and the periodizing approaches to definition leave out are precisely the factors that are central to this study: a shared approach to certain problems of representation and a relation to history. These factors can best be brought into focus by examining cinema and novel together. I prefer to think of the Nouveau Roman and the Nouvelle Vague as a loosely assembled collection of artists and to use the term *movement* both to suggest their activist aspirations and to underscore the changes as well as the continuities discernible in their works from the 1950s through the 1980s. Viewed together, the New Wave filmmakers and the New Novelists can be seen as developing along converging paths that reveal common stages of evolution, stages reflected in the outline of this book.

In the early 1950s there emerged a call for a new esthetic both in cinema and in the novel. In the February 1950 issue of *Les Temps modernes,* Nathalie Sarraute published her essay "L'Ere du soupçon" ("The Age of Suspicion"), in which she announced the death of the character as a viable novelistic prop. The essay has the tone of a manifesto. Sarraute's title identifies a heightening of sophistication on the part of novelists and readers alike. No longer satisfied with suspension of disbelief or the realism of Balzac, they (at least the ones she praises) have learned the lessons of Joyce and Proust and have become willing to enter into a self-conscious and suspicious relationship with fictional texts. Sarraute concludes with a derisive jab at readers who persist in seeking the "light entertainment" that good novels have always refused to provide. Such readers, she sarcastically suggests, "can satisfy at the cinema, without effort and without needless loss of time, [their] taste for 'live' characters and stories."[8]

While several future New Novelists—Sarraute, Robert Pinget, Alain Robbe-Grillet, Michel Butor, Claude Simon, Marguerite Duras—were already publishing avant-garde novels, the filmmakers of the future New Wave were still working as critics for the *Cahiers du cinéma* (Truffaut, Godard, Claude Chabrol, Jacques Rivette, Eric Rohmer) or as apprentice directors (Alain Resnais).[9] In the January 1954 issue of the *Cahiers du cinéma*, François Truffaut picked up the gauntlet that Sarraute had implicitly flung with the publication of an essay entitled "Une Certaine Tendance du cinéma français" (On a certain tendency in the French cinema). The tendency in question was psychological realism, and Truffaut was venting his frustration with a "cinema of quality," whose plodding and inert literary adaptations underestimated the capacity of the cinematic apparatus to create a language—an *écriture*—of its own.[10] In condemning literary adaptations, Truffaut was not demanding that cinema separate itself from literature; on the contrary, he was calling for a new esthetic, a specifically cinematic experimentation (and suspicion) of the kind that was already becoming apparent in literature.

The second half of the decade saw the New Novel and the New Wave cohere, as much as they ever would, into recognizable movements. Although Jean-Paul Sartre had hailed Sarraute's *Portrait d'un inconnu* (1956; *Portrait of a Man Unknown*) when it appeared in 1948, placing it in the vanguard of a new "anti-novel,"[11] nearly a decade passed before the terms *Nouveau Roman* and *Nouvelle Vague* appeared for the first time. Françoise Giroud coined the latter term, not with reference to the cinema, but rather as a label for the comprehensive portrait that emerged from her survey, published in *L'Express* during the last months of 1957, of a postwar generation of youths born between the wars. That generation included the majority of the New Novelists and all of the New Wave filmmakers. Giroud was able to profile the young generation's opinions (about politics, about France, about World War II), their worries (about their future, about happiness), and their general world-view. The traits she found most often, in varying guises, echo those Nathalie Sarraute identified in the modern novel and could be summarized as an attitude of alienation and suspicion. The youths of the "nouvelle vague" saw themselves as solitary, possessed of an "anguish . . . in the face of mystifications" and a "great desire . . . to stop being duped"; they were unwilling to die for *la patrie* or to leap into any prefabricated collective identity.[12] Giroud's study clearly outlines a vogue of the "new" that corresponds to the emerging sensibility in fiction.

An extraordinary wave of creativity burst forth between 1958 and 1962 to claim the waiting rubrics. In 1957 the government (through its Centre national du cinéma) had moved to revitalize the cinema industry by liberalizing the guidelines for government subsidies to filmmakers. Deemphasizing past box-office success as a criterion for support brought in young artists, whose themes and stars in turn attracted a growing youth market. The following years saw the debut of some 160 new filmmakers,[13] and many new directors came to prominence with their first feature films: Claude Chabrol (*Le Beau Serge*), Jean-Luc Godard (*A bout de souffle*), Louis Malle (*Les Amants*), Alain Resnais (*Hiroshima mon amour*), Jacques Rivette (*Paris nous appartient*), and François Truffaut (*Les Quatre Cents Coups*). The same period saw the publication of a host of first novels: Claude Mauriac's *Toutes les femmes sont fatales,* Claude Ollier's *La Mise en scène,* Jean-Pierre Faye's *Entre les rues,* Philippe Sollers's *Une Curieuse Solitude.*[14] Among already published novelists, Robbe-Grillet consolidated his reputation with *La Jalousie* (1957) and *Dans le labyrinthe* (1959), and Claude Simon's *L'Herbe* (1958) and *La Route des Flandres* (1960) and Marguerite Duras's *Moderato cantabile* (1958) marked significant shifts in sensibility for those writers, beginning the period of their best-known novels. Those same years also brought public acclaim in the form of literary prizes and film festival awards.[15] This was the apogee of the New Wave in both novel and film, and even the most restrictive definitions of both movements retain this period.[16]

The chapters in part 1 of this volume look at works from this heyday. Coinciding with this flowering of fiction was the consolidation of structuralism as a force influencing culture (Roland Barthes's *Mythologies* appeared in 1957, for example, and Claude Lévi-Strauss's *Anthropologie structurale* was published in 1958). There was also, of course, the return to politics of Charles de Gaulle and the advent of the Fifth Republic, itself precipitated by the ongoing Algerian crisis. Many of the artists included here, some of whom had been active in the French Resistance against the German Occupation, mobilized to oppose the "French presence" in Algeria. Most of the New Novelists and New Wave filmmakers studied here joined Jean-Paul Sartre and Simone de Beauvoir, Michel Leiris, André Breton and Tristan Tzara, and many other recognized cultural leaders in signing the "Manifesto of the 121," a 1960 letter of protest in defense of military conscriptees who refused to serve in Algeria.[17]

That moment of protest, together with the official sanctions against it, provided an important occasion for looking backward at World War II. For many artists and intellectuals of the New Wave and the New Novel, their sympathy with movements for national liberation and decolonization was undoubtedly linked not only to an already firm oppositional posture with respect to Gaullism but also to their own experiences abroad, notably a period of their early life spent in the colonies—Robbe-Grillet in the Antilles, Simon in Madagascar, Duras in Indochina. Nathalie Sarraute was herself an emigrée from Russia, and Alain Resnais had served in the French military in Germany just after the war. Their experiences between two cultures and between two languages no doubt contributed to their heightened awareness of the materiality of language (and thus its poetic potential) as well as to their sensitivity to the politics of discourse, naming, and otherness. Although these historical contexts are peculiarly displaced and marginalized, in many ways they remain an insistent shaping force nonetheless.

Another significant stage began near the end of the 1960s. Many of the New Novel and New Wave artists were actively involved in the events of May 1968. In Paris, Godard, Duras, and Malle joined many others in the Union des ecrivains, working as journalists and participants, recording as well as shaping the events.[18] Then during the early 1970s Duras played a carefully distanced but significant role in the development of French feminism. After the upheavals of May, a new kind of "new" was in the air, and there was a foment of activity. The most actively experimental (and the most militant) New Wave filmmaker in this phase was Jean-Luc Godard, who had uncannily prefigured the 1968 events in *La Chinoise,* made the year before. Along with Truffaut, Godard was a prime mover in the tumultuous closing of the Cannes Film Festival that spring. This premonitory salvo to the May uprisings was brought about in defense of Henri Langlois, who had been deposed as head of the Cinémathèque by Minister of Culture André Malraux. The incident highlighted the fact that culture had become a state-regulated institution. Godard subsequently organized a film collective with the goal of creating a new kind of cinema—a new relation between cinema and power—by reshaping its processes of production.

The New Novel had its own post-1968 identity crisis. Was it possible that the avant-garde had become the establishment? A colloquium entitled Nouveau Roman: Hier, Aujourd'hui was held in the summer of 1971 at the château de Cerisy-la-Salle in Normandy to ponder this and related questions, and the infelicitous appellation New New Novel made a brief appearance. In the aftershock of 1968 and under the overbearing influence of Jean Ricardou and pressure from the *Tel quel* contingent, the focus shifted toward theory.[19] Among some New Novelists (notably Claude Simon, who moved into a new phase with *La Bataille de Pharsale* in 1969), there was a shift toward pure linguistic experimentation based on mathematical, algebraic, or game structures. Duras's *Détruire, dit-elle* (1969; *Destroy, She Said*) differs significantly from her previous novels, and her preoccupation with the borderlines of madness and silence finds new expression as she moves more intensely into the cinema. Part 2 examines some fictions from the aftermath of 1968. While the "the events" may or may not actually be represented in these works, I trace the ways in which the upheavals, if they did not prove a lasting political or social revolution, did constitute a significant moment of rupture in the cultural domain.

Many New Wave and New Novel artists are still working in the 1990s, and they are still striving to define and create the "new." Part 3 considers the apparent return to, or of, autobiography and history among these novelists and filmmakers who subscribed so resolutely to aesthetic doctrines and techniques that problematize referentiality and enhance textual autonomy. During the 1980s, Duras, Robbe-Grillet, and Sarraute wrote memoirs. Truffaut and Malle made fiction films based on childhood memories of the Occupation. This seems the most radical break of all, a swing from formal experimentation (or the thematizing of aesthetic problems) and systematic suspicion toward a desire to write personally and to create an illusion of referentially. I investigate what might have provoked these changes in orientation. They occurred, after all, in the context of a more generalized nostalgia and in a period marked by the end of Gaullism and the election of François Mitterrand to the presidency in 1981. Finally, there was the much-publicized extradition from Bolivia of Nazi war criminal Klaus Barbie and his trial in Lyon in the spring of 1987. I also ask what continuities might link the recent autobiographies with earlier, apparently more purely formal works by the same artists.

This latest shift suggests that it will be important to keep in mind not only the artists' activities between 1950 and the 1980s but also the role many of them played during World War II. Claude Simon was a volunteer on the republican side in the Spanish civil war, and then as a cavalry officer in 1940 he witnessed the defeat and rout of the French army by the Germans. Resnais was a member of the occupying forces in Germany after the war. Jean Cayrol was a prisoner of the Nazis. Simon and Duras were active in Resistance activities at home. Duras was for a long while a member of the Communist Party, and others were members or fellow travelers during the Occupation and just after the war, when, under the halo of the Resistance, the Party enjoyed its most widespread electoral popularity.[20] It will be necessary to come back again and again, with the artists themselves, to the profoundly (and literally) postwar character of the era under study here. As my final chapters suggest, the "afterlife" of that war remains a frame within which stories (and interpretations), even highly formalistic ones, must be continually reshaped and readjusted. Emerging in the context of what

Henry Rousso has dubbed the "Vichy Syndrome,"[21] these belated memories of World War II provide a new lens through which to read backward through earlier texts by the same artists and offer an opportunity to examine once again the historical significance of the asocial, even antisocial, posture of many of the works.

I have intermingled the Nouveau Roman and the Nouvelle Vague in this brief history in the belief that their parallel development is not just coincidental. Rather, it provides evidence that the two are best considered together, even at the risk of compounding the "vagueness" inherent in each. For while their individual styles and themes remain distinctive, they share an *écriture* that can be described as alternately, or interconnectedly, filmic and novelistic. On the one hand, the New Wave's adoption of a literary frame of reference for cinematic reform—its emphasis on the camera as pen, on the development of individual auteurist directorial forms of expression—reflected a desire to create a cinema that would be not derivative of literature but rather its equal. It was an attempt to give the filmmaker the creative range and freedom of the novelist. Thus, Godard's films are peppered with literary allusions and quotations, and many of Truffaut's most successful films are adaptations along the lines he recommended in his 1954 essay. And thus Resnais could say that with *Hiroshima mon amour,* "I wanted to bring into being the equivalent of a new form of reading, so that the spectator would have as much freedom of imagination as the reader of a novel." Resnais said he wanted to create a "novelistic cinéma," and one critic called him the "first novelist of the screen."[22]

If the filmmakers have attempted to bring into being what Agnès Varda calls a "cinécriture," the vision of the novelists is distinctly cinematic. Simon frequently uses movie metaphors, and his descriptions are often implicitly filmlike. He and Robbe-Grillet have both developed techniques of moving from one scene to the next—Ricardou calls them "transits"—based on cinematic editing: their novels contain fades, extreme closeups, wipes, rapid cuts and conspicuous montage, and cinematically articulated flashbacks. Duras repeats elements of a core story across novels and films. So visually oriented were the early New Novels, with their hallucinatory and minute descriptions of the physical world, that Roland Barthes and others characterized them as belonging to an "école du regard" emphasizing "chosisme."[23] In their more theoretical works, several of the novelists invoke filming techniques when explaining their writing procedures.[24]

It is not surprising, then, that there has been considerable crossover between novel writing and the visual arts. Claude Simon got his start as a painter, and Duras and Robbe-Grillet have both produced a considerable corpus of films.

Numerous collaborative projects brought filmmakers—notably Resnais, and Duras herself plays a role in Godard's 1979 *Sauve qui peut (la vie)*—and novelists together, contributing to the creation of an aesthetic that is both filmic and textual, not adaptation but rather co-creation. Resnais is the most remarkable of these, with his films made in collaboration with Duras, Robbe-Grillet, Jean Cayrol, Raymond Queneau, and others. The result is a network of intertextuality that crosses over from novels to films and back. This is an erudite group of artists who love culture and revel in cultural play. It should not be surprising, therefore, to find nomenclatures converging, as in a 1965 colloquium held in Paris under the title "Literary and Cinematic Works of the New Novel,"[25] or to read about the "novelists of the new wave."[26]

In addition to a shared *écriture,* the artists studied here share a general sympathy with the political Left.[27] That orientation has been expressed variously as participation in the Resistance or guilt about collaboration, opposition to Gaullist policies, sympathy with the student and workers' uprisings in 1968, anti-Americanism (especially during the American war in Vietnam), critiques of capitalism and consumerism, writing for politically identified journals, signing petitions, and so on. It has been as concrete as Duras's membership in the Communist Party or Godard's espousal of Maoism and as indeterminate as Resnais's benevolent internationalism. It is especially visible in the persistent but rather shallow rhetoric linking Balzacian realism or a "cinema of quality" (alternately dubbed a *cinéma de papa*) with everything that is outmoded, stale, bourgeois, and reactionary. In light of many of these artists' real political commitments, though, it would be unfair to attribute the sort of diatribe one often finds in their theoretical essays entirely to Oedipal petulance.

But this identification is not only multifarious and often sketchy; it is also ambivalent. There is as much resistance to realism of the socialist as of the Balzacian strain, and the Cold War context is as defining as that of World War II. Whether or not they were actively affiliated with the French Communist Party, all of the artists considered here (even Truffaut and Robbe-Grillet, who remained the least overtly political) were influenced by its evolution and its policies. Between the Liberation and the heyday of the New Novel and the New Wave, the appeal of the so-called Parti des Fusillés had slipped steadily. Gaullist erasure of its role in the Resistance (even to changing street names) diminished its prestige and inhibited its growth. Soviet domestic and foreign policies (in Hungary and Yugoslavia especially), the French Communist Party's unyielding Stalinist orthodoxy, and Khrushchev's 1956 denunciation of Stalin provoked repeated crises of conscience on the Left.

At least until the mid-1950s the French Communist Party insisted that communist artists adhere to the requirements of socialist realism as interpreted after the war by A. A. Zhdanov, Stalin's agent for cultural affairs. Enumeration of the features of this realism is instructive: a good communist writer was expected to write fiction that was clear and widely accessible; it should steer a neat path amid the confusions of real life, aim for immediate and transparent political efficacy and utility, and portray the Truth.[28] This view of literature is reflected in Sartre's definition, in "What Is Literature?" (1947), of prose as transparent and utilitarian, a definition that was the cornerstone of the philosophy of committed writing and the dominant model of leftist artistic practice in the postwar years.[29] Given that for the communist Left culture and politics have traditionally been inseparable, formalism itself can be seen as a type of resistance. I think the New Novel and the New Wave can be seen in the context of an allegiance to the political values of the Left, modified by the project of moving away from transitive aesthetic practice. Their dilemma was as follows: Was it possible to practice revolutionary art while subscribing neither to existentialism nor to a political party? Could art be both "engaged" and formally innovative? Could one reject realism without giving up politics? And, of course, recent memories of the denunciations and counterdenunciations endemic to the Occupation and collaboration and post-Liberation periods also held up clear incentives to monitor the overt political content of one's art. To their research on form can thus be applied Serge Guilbaut's insights into American painting. Guilbaut argues that American abstract expressionism "provided a way for avant-garde artists to preserve their sense of social 'commitment' . . . while eschewing the art of propaganda and illustration. It was in a sense a political apoliticism."[30]

In short, the works studied here betray the strains of being radically "caught between." They are caught between socialist and Balzacian realism and between commitment to ideas and the forging of an aesthetic avant-garde. They struggle between the pressure to move forward and an impulse to look backward. Striving toward the "new," they are haunted by the past. They are held captive between the world war and the Cold War. They attempt to avoid choosing between "expressing" (a taboo word) their views and taking into account new theories of subjectivity and knowledge. And, of course, like all artists, they are suspended between the signified and the materiality of the signifier, that is, between history and language (in the novel), or between the past of history and the presence of the filmic image. If there is playfulness here, the works (and the characters) also wrestle with problems of agency that can at times brush with nihilism or despair.

These tensions result in a condition of restless immobility. The works, especially those examined in parts 1 and 2, turn in place. They enact a state of hyperactivity without progress. There is clearly more than stasis here, and more than a perverse desire to obstruct the reader or viewer's access to meaning or pleasure. Of course an extreme, narcissistic attention to the work's internal construction and formal dynamics also constitutes, as many critics have pointed out, a retreat. But a retreat from what? If these artists fail in their efforts to be committed, it is because of their inability to write or film their way out of an impasse. Perhaps this condition of aporia within the works accounts for many of the artists' tendencies to spin off from their difficult and often opaque fictions in order to write theoretical essays, explanatory prefaces, *prières d'insérer*, to review their own books, to make new films about the process of filming the previous ones, to give interviews, attend conferences, accept visiting professorships at (often American) universities. They jump at every opportunity to explain themselves. But this too is part of their metahistorical dimension. Henri Langlois in a freeze-frame.

Juxtaposing their political contexts with their various formal characteristics as outlined above leads me to propose that the works can best be understood as evolving attempts to formulate a counterdiscourse. Individual works and artists construct their discourses along divergent paths, to be sure, but all are motivated by an inherently ideological unorthodoxy in the sense that Barthes has given to the term: against the *doxa* or dominant systems of representation, whether these be aesthetic or political (or both at once). Theirs is a negative impulse, a desire to undermine and dismantle, to defamiliarize received discourses and narratives. Thus, if the New Wave was so far from being a monolithic bloc that Truffaut claimed the only way it could be defined was by age, Pierre Sorlin adds that although the artists had no common program, "the New Wave was mostly an idea, a sign. Once the young film-makers, who had begun by merely inveighing against their predecessors, were gathered under the same flag by newspapers, they felt obliged to question their own practice and—at least the most interesting of them, Chabrol, Godard, Truffaut—permanently to modify their approach to the cinema."[31]

And Jérôme Lindon, Resistance veteran and head of the Editions de Minuit since 1948, explained in an interview that *New Novel* was a term invented by critics to describe a group of writers whose "principal quality was to be profoundly original and different each from the others. . . . If they have anything in common, it is to be found more in their refusal of certain attitudes about literature than in any true program."[32] Thus, if there is any unity or continuity, it is to be found in the self-conscious and paradoxical search for the new, reaffirming the project of modernism described by Baudelaire as a striving for "du nouveau." The New Novelists and the New Wave filmmakers continue that project in their desire to be oppositional, confrontational, sometimes unpleasant, always stubbornly *contestataire*.

The concept of counterdiscourse, or what Mas'ud Zavarzadeh calls "oppositional intelligibilities,"[33] may thus help us enlarge the notion of newness to embrace both the hyperformalism of the sixties and the autobiographies of the eighties. Listen to Robbe-Grillet, as he formulates the problem from the vantage point of 1984. Reminiscing about his former role as champion of the absent author and the auto-referential text, he declares:

> I myself have done much to promote these reassuring idiocies, and have now decided to refute them because I feel they've had their day: within the space of a few years they have lost any shocking, corrosive, and therefore revolutionary force and have been assimilated as received ideas, fueling the spineless militance of the fashionable journals, yet with their place already prepared in the glorious family vaults of the literature textbooks. Ideology, always masked, changes its face with ease.[34]

Richard Terdiman confirms the point when he defines counterdiscourse in the nineteenth-century novel as "discursive systems by which writers and artists sought to project an alternative, liberating *newness* against the absorptive capacity of . . . established discourses." Counterdiscourse is not new here or then; or rather, it is new whenever it appears. In this sense, *new* means oppositional. Viewing the New Wave and the New Novel in this way may thus also help us to account even for the unreadability of the apparently referential memoirs of recent years. Terdiman explains: "Situated as other, counter-discourses have the capacity to *situate,* to relativize the authority and stability of a dominant system of utterances which cannot even countenance their existence. They read that which cannot read them at all."[35]

Understanding the novels and films as instances of counterdiscourse or alternative representational practices suggests in its turn alternative reading strategies. I selected the works studied here because they are among the most successful and most often invoked products of artists associated with the New Wave and the New Novel since those terms emerged. Some works, such as Louis Malle's *Au revoir les enfants* (1987) and Truffaut's *Le Dernier Métro* (1981), were immediate box-office successes. The value of others, such as Malle's *Lacombe Lucien* (1974) and Resnais and Duras's *Hiroshima mon amour* (1959), was hotly contested. A few, such as *L'Année dernière à Marienbad* (1961) and Duras's *L'Amant* (1984), have attained cult status. Many of the novels and films have won prizes, and all have been the object of countless reviews and essays. Any selection from among such a diverse group of works is of necessity idiosyncratic and incomplete. The organization of the chapters below is not designed, however, to give a panoramic overview; rather, it is to trace the varying modalities in which novels and films intersect with historical contexts. This, in turn, will permit us to cross borderlines between aesthetic and political concerns and to hear echoes reverberating between fiction and history. In the words of M. M. Bakhtin with which this introduction begins, "The internal politics of style (how the elements are put together) is determined by its external politics (its relationship to alien discourse). Discourse lives, as it were, on the boundary between its own context and another, alien, context."[36]

Reading these boundaries, then, will depend upon three interconnected critical approaches.

Reading for metafiction and metahistory. The novels and films are often about fictional and historical discourse rather than about history. Because their dominant characteristic is that they are self-consciously novelistic or filmic, what these texts enact is always more revealing than what they talk about. Their thrust is epistemological: they never stop asking *how* we know. They demystify received discourses and reveal their objectivity as imaginary, destroying their reality effect, their "effet de réel."[37] Thus, it will be necessary to read hyperliterally to see how these works are indeed mimetic: what they mirror is social positions and relations, conflicts, attitudes. Whether or not there is referential material incorporated into the text, it is through their discursive and structural mimeticism that the works are the most profoundly historical.

Taking structuration as a point of access. New Novel and New Wave texts have alternately been lauded and deplored for their characteristic structural devices: repetition, circularity, return, refusal (or inability) to achieve closure, spiraling in on themselves, gaps, holes, blank spaces, aporias of all kinds, jumps and cuts, proliferating *mises en abyme* and figures of infinite regress. Such features inevitably resonate, however, with the world beyond the works themselves. Because meaning since Ferdinand de Saussure's 1916 *Course in General Linguistics* has been understood as the product of structures and relationships, I will look for *in*scription as well as *de*scription of history. Taken as points of departure rather than ends of analysis, all these tense and conflicted forms are, I believe, the places where historicity and formalism converge.

Studying semantic fields. I will be attentive to the presence of historical discourse in the absence of or alongside historical narration. Two examples will provide the best explanation. In the postwar period, trains and showers as images have been permanently contaminated by the use to which they were put during World War II. In *Stardust Memories* (1980) Woody Allen has only to show two trains moving in opposite directions, one populated with elegantly dressed and laughing partygoers, the other with frightened, dazed, bedraggled, and isolated figures clad in black, to evoke the horrors of the concentration camps. A similarly uncanny shadow effect is suggested in the famous shower scene of Alfred Hitchcock's *Psycho* (1960). A brutal murder that takes place in a shower and features closeups of a hand scraping desperately at the walls, I would argue, is in and of itself a historically overdetermined image. We have become sensitized by other such references, for example, in Alain Resnais's *Nuit et brouillard* (1955; *Night and Fog*), where a voiceover narration accompanies pictures of the scratched walls and ceilings of the "showers" at Auschwitz. Hitchcock's Norman Bates wiping blood off the bathroom tiles after he murders Marion Crane can thus serve as another emblem of the erasure of historical contexts in postwar representation. Such images, uncanny icons of a postmodern age and sensibility, have the status of a discourse that is haunted by history. That discourse is the subject of this book.

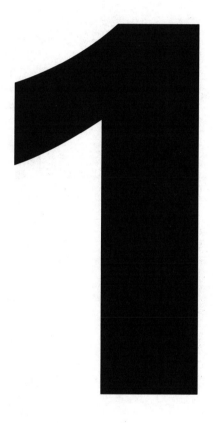

1. Myths of Textual Autonomy: From Psychoanalysis to Historiography in *Hiroshima mon amour*

What we call reality is a certain connexion between these immediate sensations and the memories which envelop us simultaneously with them—a connexion that is suppressed in a simple cinematic vision, which just because it professes to confine itself to the truth in fact departs widely from it. – Marcel Proust

The 1961 inaugural issue of the review *Communications* reported the results of a survey of eighteen so-called New Wave films made between 1957 and 1960, comparing them with a slightly more numerous selection of traditional films produced during the same period. The team of sociologists who conducted the survey contrasted the two groups of films on the basis of a variety of criteria: major themes and situations, types of endings, the nature of spectator sympathy with heroes, and so on. Appearing very early in the history of a new kind of experimental cinema and remaining one of the few sociological analyses of its content, the survey is a precious document of the widespread fascination mixed with malaise provoked by an emerging sensibility in fiction.

According to the survey, the main cause of this malaise was the absence of any clear perspective, on the part of either the characters or the stories, toward social and historical reality. The new filmmakers, it was suggested, did not advocate any specific non- or anticonformist behavior, but seemed instead simply to take "malign pleasure in blurring the trail [*brouiller les pistes*], either by erasing the habitual clues or by juxtaposing contradictory signposts." Along with a general "inability" to tell coherent stories, two major features of New Wave films recur in almost every section of the report: the heroes are *isolated* from society, living a life "amputated from any background collectivity," and the stories are set in a world that is unremittingly *contemporary* ("preference for events of the moment," "complete autonomy of the present"). These two absences—of collectivity and of history—were indicative of what the survey called a generalized "loss of meaning."[1]

Hiroshima mon amour, included in the survey, was considered only mildly exceptional, in spite of its historical themes. The 1959 film by Marguerite Duras and Alain Resnais is not "about" World War II, nor is its action set during the war.[2] The basic story is simple enough: a French movie actress (played by Emmanuelle Riva) on location in Hiroshima has a brief love affair with a Japanese architect (Eiji Okada). Their encounter prompts her to remember her wartime lover, a German soldier, who was killed during the Liberation. The French woman and the Japanese man (they are given no other names) meet in a socially and temporally isolated present. Neither their choices nor their actions will have an impact on public events or even on the future course of their lives after she leaves Japan. Similarly, the story of her first love in Nevers, with its implied historical setting, seems to have had no consequences. She even claims to have forgotten it until now. Thus, one reviewer's remark about Jean-Luc Godard's *A bout de souffle* (1960; Breathless), also included in the survey, seems to apply as well to both love affairs in *Hiroshima mon amour:* "These two characters live in a sort of exile. [. . .] their adventure takes place in the margins."[3] It would appear, then, that history plays some role in *Hiroshima mon amour* but not a familiar one.

The contrast between *Hiroshima mon amour* and conventional historical adventure stories is signaled within the film itself. Near the end, the French woman wanders into a café. It is before dawn on her last day in Japan, and all that is left to do, as the Japanese man has said, is to "kill the time left before your departure" (83). The café is called the Casablanca. This allusion to a great film of an earlier era at first provokes a smile of recognition. Michael Curtiz's *Casablanca* (1942) was, after all, set during the same war remembered by the protagonists of *Hiroshima.* Appearing at the end of the 1959 film, however, the citation points to the gulf that separates the two. Humphrey Bogart and Ingrid Bergman play heroes in the style of the Golden Legend: their exemplary behavior consists in renouncing personal happiness for the sake of a higher cause, thereby affecting the outcome of events. If Rick and his fellow Resistance sympathizers are fictional, the events for which they sacrifice their lives or loves are posed as unproblematic background, the medium that permits them to unfold their essential heroism. In contrast, the "loss of meaning" inscribed in the dead time of *Hiroshima mon amour* figures the loss of classical Hollywood stories like *Casablanca* and the confident historical discourse that subtends them.[4] Such stories have mediated our understanding and even our experience of history. Duras and Resnais's conviction that it is no longer possible or even desirable to tell such stories was confirmed in another mood by Woody Allen, who both cites and comments on *Casablanca* as he shows that you cannot, in the words he borrows for his title, "play it again, Sam." While the *Communications* survey failed abysmally to account for the asocial behavior and ahistorical attitudes portrayed in the new films, and while one gathers that its purpose was less to characterize than to condemn, the survey is useful as a description not of the films themselves but of the narrative norms that the new fiction was consciously attempting to disrupt, norms embodied in films like *Casablanca*.

The survey's design did not permit it to evaluate *Hiroshima*'s major point of access, which is also its dimension of greatest difficulty: its form. If, as one review reported about its first showing, "the shock was intense," this shock was due to the film's formal complexities, which the reviewer went on to outline:

> I think it is safe to say that no one was able, at the exit, to summarize the film in a few clear ideas. There was a short subject within a feature film, a parody of a pacifist, antiatomic sequence within an overwhelmingly anti-war work, an interweaving of multiple themes—individual and collective—within a space-time wherein converged past, present and future, symbols, contradictions. The real density of consciousness: our life, our memory.[5]

The repeated preposition *within* points to some of the film's overlapping abyssal constructions, which it will be necessary to examine in detail. The key word here, however, is *contradictions*. If the film does systematically try to "[blur] the trail," it does so not out of perverse pleasure but with the serious intent to contest every discourse that it proposes, particularly those by which an understanding of the past is constructed. No sooner is a possible vision of the past suggested than it is subverted by another, or by the thickness of intervening layers and a mediating present. Although the reality of Hiroshima's destruction is never denied and the events of Nevers are not erased, the possibility of narrating is repeatedly undermined. Each of the film's several stories is filled with repetitions and gaps where elements from the other stories intrude. The need to forget the traumatic events of Nevers is contested by the necessity of remembering the destruction of Hiroshima. Desire to unburden oneself of the story is frustrated by the impossibility of conveying its intensity.

It is thus not surprising that the film's organizing rhetorical strategy is irony, carried out through foregrounding and subversion of contraries. This strategy is visible in palinodes ("You destroy me. You're so good for me"; "I lie. And I tell the truth"), oxymorons ("banality . . . that . . . terrifies"), antitheses ("madness" and "reason"), and reversals ("HE: You saw nothing in Hiroshima. Nothing. SHE: I saw *everything* . . . *Everything*"). The oxymoronic juxtaposition in the film's title is elucidated by Duras's statement that one of her major goals was "to have done with the description of horror by horror, for that has been done by the Japanese themselves, but make this horror rise again from its ashes by [inscribing] it in a love [story]" (9). These ironies derive their structure from a triangular and dynamic interweaving of three times, which are given to us as three places: Hiroshima then (August 1945, the bombing and its aftermath), Nevers then (August 1944, the Liberation and the French woman's personal drama), and Hiroshima now (August 1957, the French woman's encounter with the Japanese man). Any attempt to reduce any of these to meaning or closure is prevented by the presence of the other two.

If we seek the film's content in its forms, as Alain Robbe-Grillet enjoins us to do for *L'Année dernière à Marienbad* (1961; Last Year at Marienbad),[6] it should be possible, by examining the structuration and permutations of these three moments, to determine what *Hiroshima mon amour* can tell us about the role of history in the film and even, perhaps, about what kinds of historical discourses it is possible to imagine from a postwar vantage point. *Hiroshima mon amour* is aware of the problematic nature of sign systems, of time, and of memory. It knows, for example, that the desire to represent horror through a love story must be counterbalanced by an awareness of the danger of forgetting the horror entirely. Its primary areas of investigation are the very issues that the *Communications* survey lamented were not taken as unproblematic background. The film's experimentation with character and flashback, its hyperliterary texture, and the figures of contradiction mentioned above are indicative of the film's pervasive self-consciousness, which can be understood in light of Hayden White's designation of irony as the mode corresponding to "a stage of consciousness in which the problematical nature of language itself has become recognized."[7] It is precisely those ironies and that self-consciousness that mandate that one look for historical and social perspectives in the film's quest for alternative modes of representation.

HISTORY IS NOT IN THE PAST

If any general statements can be made about all the works studied here, one must be that the past is always viewed through the eyes, the languages, and the rhetoric of the present. No longer is the past part of a coherent cosmogony that leads (chrono)logically to the present. Gone is the conception of history, shared by the novel and historiography in the nineteenth century, that depended, according to Roland Barthes, on use of a past historic tense that captured and packaged the past as a convenient commodity for consumption.[8] The rigorous priority of present over past signals a major shift in perspective that, far from being a defect of contemporary works, is the very prerequisite of their discipline, and it is what makes them modern. To be sure, many older stories are narrated from the perspective of their ending. What distinguishes contemporary works is that they are told not only *from* the present but self-consciously *through* the act of narration, which thus becomes their origin. "To apprehend the present as the generative act of time in its concrete reality is . . . without a doubt, the tendency of our epoch," writes Georges Poulet.[9] Paul de Man further sees this perspective in terms of its possible motives, as an "obsession with a *tabula rasa,* with new beginnings," that makes modernity and history antithetical.[10]

It is between its repetitions and the strict priority of the present that *Hiroshima mon amour* can be approached. The film's interior duplications disrupt the progression of the foreground story—fragmenting it, filling it with holes and discontinuities—in the very way that memory and history impinge upon the present. Chronological linearity is thus translated into concentric spatial configurations, so that the present frames, gives birth to, and coexists with the past, yielding a complex mixture of sensation and memory that Proust, writing before the development of sophisticated flashback techniques, thought impossible in the cinema.[11] How the French woman knows and why and especially where she remembers are as important as what she remembers. The film's thrust is less historical than epistemological, and thus to read it well is to understand it at the level of its metahistory. To a certain extent, *Hiroshima* embodies that alienation from the past that is said to characterize much contemporary fiction. More importantly, it also tells the story of that alienation, so it should be viewed not as an exposition of the contents of memory but as a drama of remembering and forgetting.

Subordination of historical past to a present tense of remembering and narrating has an important corollary: it brings the creative activity into view. The visibility of the discursive present in turn shows historical content to be of the same substance as fabulation. This self-reflecting focus is dramatized *en abyme* in *Hiroshima* by means of at least two interior films: one, a reconstruction of the bombing, permits emphasis of the spectator's active creativity while showing the danger of forgetting; the other, in which the French woman is an actress, shows the participant's ironic distance from events and the impossibility of remembering effectively.

Resnais's intentions as a filmmaker have much in common with the writing strategies of the New Novelists. He has habitually invited the collaboration of novelists, in fact, and worked with Jean Cayrol on *Nuit et brouillard* (1955) and *Muriel* (1963) and with Raymond Queneau on *Le Chant du styrène* (1958). Two years after making *Hiroshima* with Duras, he used Robbe-Grillet's scenario for *L'Année dernière à Marienbad.* Writing in the wake of Saussure and in the aura of Lacan, these novelists know that reality and consciousness are always displaced by the play of signifiers. The postulate that art can only describe itself, tell about the conditions of its own existence, and mourn its limits reveals not so much a choice these writers have made as their awareness that such is the nature of representation. Reality cannot be reflected, but only projected, as an illusion. This is one significance of the gaps in Robbe-Grillet's novels, of the silences in Duras's dialogues, and of the fact that Resnais systematically banishes artificially coherent narration of an anecdote.

Resnais shares with his collaborators an awareness that the work of art is radically separate from the real and the self-imposed task of working not only within but against the limits of their medium. For Resnais this has meant striving toward a literary cinema; he has said that he tries to make films in which the experience of watching images resembles the act of reading.[12] Duras feels that Resnais "works like a novelist," in that "what is shown is surpassed by what is not shown. Why? Because by only showing one aspect among hundreds of aspects of a single thing, Resnais wanted to be conscious of his 'failure' in being able to show no more than one one-hundredth."[13] I take this to mean that Resnais seeks to use film in the way certain novelists use language: to signify art as a self-conscious absence, even as loss of the world.

This is why I am inclined to call what Resnais shares with New Novelists and other postmodern writers an Orphic vision. Like Orpheus, the French woman in Hiroshima travels into a lost past in an attempt to bring back her dead German lover, and along with him, her youthful innocence. She resurrects him in the person of the Japanese man, who tries to follow her and to incarnate her absent past. But the miracle cannot last, and she must give him back. "I offer you to oblivion," she says. All she can do is invent words in his place, cheat her sense of loss by repeating it: "You will become a song," she decides. The fragmentation of her story reflects a "dismemberment of Orpheus,"[14] to which she responds with her efforts to re-member. The loss of the past through forgetting is a dangerous loss because it invites repetition. It is also a necessary loss because it is a prerequisite to survival and invention. Orpheus can only sing after he has lost Eurydice, or as Maurice Blanchot puts it, "Writing begins with the glance of Orpheus."[15]

Although the comparison of images to linguistic signs can remain a fruitful working hypothesis, an Orphic vision is more difficult to realize in the cinema than in writing because film is by nature more realistic: it not only tells but shows. Roland Barthes has explained how photography permits an impression of unmediated transmission of messages. Unlike a verbal utterance, a snapshot is uncoded; it is a literal record of the scene it signifies, not its arbitrary transformation or translation into something else. As such, a photograph can be invoked as a sort of proof that something existed; it is a monument to what Barthes calls a "having-been-there [*avoir-été-là*]." Photographs are thus a perfect medium for preserving the past. Cinematic images, on the other hand, while they share in the uncoded objectivity of photography, are not simply animated snapshots. Rather than incarnating the past, film gives an illusion or simulacrum of reality in the present: it is a "*being-there* of the thing [*être-là de la chose*]."[16]

Christian Metz refers to Barthes when he argues that cinema is not a language [*langue*] because it is not a system of signs. The image is a spectacle in which both signifier and signified are equally visible, and so the image "*is* sufficiently what it shows so as not to have to *signify*."[17] Put another way, images, unlike words, are not obliged to point to something that they are not, to take the place of something absent. In another essay, Metz again takes his cue from Barthes as he develops a further feature characteristic of the filmic image. It is movement, he says, that creates the impression of reality in cinema. Furthermore, "the spectator always perceives movement as of the present time [*actuel*]."[18] It would seem, then, that the representation of the past on film is exceedingly difficult, if not impossible. Only the spectators' learned acceptance of cinematic conventions such as the flashback allows them to believe that a scene shown on film is intended to represent the past.

In outlining their arguments, I have deliberately accentuated a central and undesignated semantic shift in both Metz's and Barthes's formulations. The image has no code because it does not depend on signs; unlike language, it does not designate what is absent by means of a signifier that is present, that is to say, here. The cinematic image is further distinguished by its contemporaneity. It happens in the present, that is to say, now. *Present,* it turns out, means both here and now; it is either spatial or temporal. Consequently, it can be contrasted with what is absent or what is past.

This polyvalence is crucial to Resnais's cinematic vision. He is able to "work like a novelist" by loosening the necessity of images and their sequence in order to play them like a language. If New Wave films seem cut off from the past, this is at least in part a consequence of the filmmakers' awareness of the limits of their medium; the present may be the only time portrayed because it is the only time film *can* portray. Resnais's famous disarticulated montages introduce discontinuities into the sequence of images that correspond to the silences in Duras's text. A montage full of gaps and a narrative full of dead time show a history that occurs in both another place and another time. In *Hiroshima mon amour* the question of the past and the limits of the media (both verbal and filmic) coincide. An interweaving of three places suggests what is forgotten by means of what is absent: the past, displaced with respect to what is shown, can only be represented as disarticulated and mediated. Time is a displacement of place, and nothing precedes the film, just as there is nothing hidden behind the text. There is only the play of presence and absence. Thus, when the French woman's German lover is there, he is there in the present, and when he is not there, he is both past (passed) and gone. This absence is felt as a loss, and forgetting is a void (a "horror of indifference") and a death. It is burying someone definitively in a *trou de mémoire*.

Framing the past within the languages and images of the present is not the exclusive province of cinema or even of fiction in general. To the contrary, the New Novelists and New Wave filmmakers merit study because they work within and contribute to a network of questions shared by other disciplines, in particular for our purposes here historiography and psychoanalysis. Each of these proposes a model for reading the past. Especially since the advent of structuralism, however, the innocence of both these models has been called into question, and historians and psychoanalysts have been compelled to examine the role of their own subjectivity and historicity in the discourses they produce. In each field there are those who insist that the past is only knowable through the perspectives and rhetorical grids of the present. Some practitioners of historiography, psychoanalysis, and fiction (written and filmed) speak to and through each other in a common language. If the same vocabulary returns uncannily from one field to another, this is because the disciplines overlap, influence each other reciprocally, even act directly to transform the objects of each other's study. The result is a complex discursive space resembling, perhaps, a labyrinth to which one image, a multifarious reel or spool [*bobine*], might give us access.

The reel is the material unit of film, emblem of its movement, its discontinuities, its reversibility, and its repeatability. When the Lumière brothers showed the first movies in Lyon and then Paris in 1895, they inaugurated a new way of seeing that has influenced verbal modes of expression ever since. Claude Simon often describes peculiarities of perception or memory in terms of blurred or jerky successions of film images, and while he insists on the material differences between films and novels, he admits that cinema has had an effect on his writing. "For me, as for everyone," he says, "the cinema has enriched our vision of things (angles and distance of shots, panning shots, stills, dolly shots, closeups). And naturally, that new way of seeing shows up in what I write."[19] It is thus not surprising that authors like Kurt Vonnegut and filmmakers like Truffaut have used the device of a reel played backward to convey a wish to return to the past.

Historians too have been influenced by cinematic vision. "Every society thinks itself 'historically' with its own particular instruments," writes Michel de

Certeau,[20] and his statement points to a reciprocal relationship between film and historical knowledge. Pierre Nora points out that until the advent of television, history was located exclusively in the past, and historians only studied the past. Nowadays, the possibility of viewing news "as it happens" has created an unprecedented sense of the historicity of the present: the mass media give us a present tense that is already historical. Nora believes that modern mass media, especially television, have transformed the category of historical thought that has come to be called the "event." A further consequence, particularly applicable to *Hiroshima mon amour,* is the increased complexity of the distinction between public and private, as "the event is projected into private life and served up as spectacle." Nora also suggests that the repeatability of the filmed image causes events to shed their context and grow monstrous, as one watches the Kennedy assassination over and over again.[21] One can add that the historicity and repetition of the televised present gives events an overdetermined and inevitable cast. It is thus certainly symptomatic rather than coincidental that critics attribute the narcissism and refusal of history, the fatalism and passivity they find in New Novels and New Wave films, to the very forces Nora describes, especially the increasing dominance of impersonal and ahistorical mass culture.

While the visual or spectacular media (de)form our notions of what is thinkable in historical terms, they also tend to transform the event itself. Nora suggests that in addition to breaking down distinctions between past and present and between public and private, the television camera can confer historical status on a *fait divers,* or the reverse: it can shrink momentous occurrences into trivia. It accomplishes this by reducing events to their spectacle, by staging a convergence of the event and its expression. Nora's observations find their counterpart in Marcel Ophuls's troubled awareness that the presence of a camera can change the course of events or even provoke a riot, for example, because the public knows that an unrecorded event is not an event at all.[22]

A more generalized common preoccupation ties many contemporary historians to the fiction in question here. Growing awareness of the linguistic forms and discursive frame of historiography has led to a self-consciousness among historians that corresponds to self-reflecting tendencies found in postwar fiction. With the reintroduction of the historian into history, the two meanings of the French word *histoire* converge. Hayden White describes how historical discourse always points in two somewhat contradictory directions: toward the events it purports to describe (one could say toward *histoire* as "history") and toward itself as the embodiment of a rhetorical mode (the "story" the historian tells framed in the present time of telling, or what I have been calling historiography).[23] These two functions reappear in the linguistic distinction between *énoncé* and *énonciation* and apply to literature as a relationship between *récit* and *histoire* (Gérard Genette) or *discours* and *histoire* (Benveniste), or *fable* and *sujet* (Tzvetan Todorov and the Russian Formalists) and between Jean Ricardou's literal dimension (or narration) and referential dimension (or fiction) of a text.

Traditional views of historiography hold that study of the past elucidates the present. On the other hand, Jean Chesneaux, among others, believes exactly the reverse: "It is necessary—and this further upsets our habits—to comprehend the fact that historical reflection is regressive, that it normally proceeds from the present, moving against the current of time's flow." This occurs because "it is the present that asks the questions and serves the summons."[24] And Marc Bloch, cofounder of the influential *Annales* school of historiography, wrote in 1944 that the historian must "understand the past by means of the present." To explain his conviction, he prefigures Chesneaux and adopts the same image used later by Vonnegut, Truffaut, and others: the historian must take the known world of his own epoch as his point of departure, Bloch argues, so that to reconstruct the past, you have to "unwind the spool in reverse [*dérouler la bobine à rebours*]."[25]

Bloch's reel image suggests a film threading backward in time through the present toward the past. His argument and its appearance in the context of a historian's personal reflections demonstrate a cognitive shift from the content to the practice of historical writing. If traditionally it was collective or individual heroes (Bloch qualifies in this category too) who determined the forward movement of events, it is now historians themselves who "make history." As a recent collection of essays entitled *Faire de l'histoire* makes clear, contemporary historiography is taking on the task of redefining itself in light of "historians' growing acknowledgment of the relativity of their science." This relativity is based on examination of the media that convey history (verbal, filmic, etc.) as well as the ideological and institutional framework in which it is produced, and it generates an awareness that history is inseparable from historiography: the activity in the present of a historian writing, the identical gesture that defines the novelist and is itself thematized in so many New Novels. The volume's introductory essay affirms that a disciplinary redefinition must take into account both ends of the reel, both poles of the historian's "oscillation" between "lived and constructed history, suffered and fabricated." This oscillation could be described as that of the linguistic sign itself between its concept, or signified, and its material expression. The problems language poses to historiography are summed up in one poignant sentence: "Perhaps history awaits its Saussure."[26] For historians conscious of their medium, as well as for writers and filmmakers, the past is what is absent.

The historian who must unwind the reel in reverse plays a game that has undoubtedly already called to mind a third spool: the famous bobbin of *Beyond the Pleasure Principle*. I will examine Freud's description of the child's game of *fort* and *da* later on; for now, I want to draw attention to Lacan's interpretation of the game as the child's initiation into the symbolic order. As he throws the bobbin out of sight and then reels it back, the syllables that accompany this alternation are, Lacan argues, "a first manifestation of language. In this phonemic opposition, the child transcends, raises to a symbolic level, the phenomenon of absence."[27] What the child transcends is the parent's absence. He does this by replaying (forward and backward) the experience of loss with a representation, a spool. The symbol emerges finally as the fusion of presence and absence in the verbal sign.

A similar configuration arises in the analytic situation, where the analyst coaxes into verbal presence what was both absent and past. For the analyst, the patient's forgotten or repressed experiences are simply memories in search of their signifier.[28] Lacan insists that underlying all Freud's work is the tenet that the unconscious cannot be analyzed in its absence but must be read in some form of presence (jokes, dreams, the analytic conversations). It is this observation that brings him to declare that for the individual, "history is not the past. History is the past only insofar as it is historicized in the present because it has been lived in the past." Each individual case history is then less a process of remembering than an attempt to "rewrite history."[29]

For Michel de Certeau, who was both a historian and a member of the École freudienne, the historical past is to the present as the unconscious is to conscious awareness and linguistic representation. History is the absent Other of the present. As if in response to Lacan's dictum that "the unconscious is the discourse of the Other,"[30] de Certeau proposes that historiography is the "*performance of the other* on the stage of the present."[31] And where Lacan sees the appearance of the unconscious as a product of the "scene" of analysis, de Certeau sees the activity of re-presenting history as a function of what he calls its "place," that is, the social, institutional, and, therefore, ideological situation of historians and their profession in a given society.

Because since its inception the cinema too has attempted to represent the past, film theorists also have logically turned to psychoanalysis and historiography in their work. As Philip Rosen points out, although cinema emerged during a moment of crisis in the novel and in historiography, for the most part classical cinema nonetheless adopted the totalizing narratives of an already discredited historical positivism. Examining films like *The Birth of a Nation* (1915) and *The Roaring Twenties* (1939) and referring to Lukács's descriptions of the traditional historical novel, Rosen spells out what characterizes classical cinema's historical discourse: its narratives offer secure knowledge through totalizing systems of explanation (e.g., the use of voice-over narration as a voice of neutral and impersonal history); its individual characters are not isolated but presented as typical; and it unselfconsciously obscures the means by which its world is constructed.[32] These strategies produce an illusion of epistemological security that historians continue to grapple with and modernist writers and filmmakers and later the New Novel and the New Wave intentionally destabilize.

Because the New Wave filmmakers, like the New Novelists, so often chose to focus on the representation of mental processes, they incorporated into their films an awareness that the nature of their medium or apparatus itself shapes how the past can be shown.[33] Let us take as one example the use, so very common in early New Wave films, of flashback. Maureen Turim explains how developments in the use of cinematic flashback have shaped how history can be understood and even experienced. Especially useful for our purposes is her insight into the "framing" of the past. Despite early Soviet cinema's attempts to represent collective viewpoints, flashbacks have usually required the circumscribed perspective of one consciousness, and this in turn has meant an inevitably subjective point of view. As Turim puts it, "Flashback subjectivates history." In turn, the character's position is such that the flashback frames the subject in history. The person who remembers is thus isolated as a subject both in and of history. Identifying a disruptive type of modernist flashback that emerged in the late fifties, Turim argues that the new emphasis on disjunction and decontextualization in flashbacks of the postwar period brought an even more intense subjectivization and dehistoricization of the past and memory. She points out that in *Hiroshima mon amour* the French woman's story in Nevers, known through flashback, is rendered more personal, more individual, and thus more ahistorical than the history of Hiroshima, which is not presented through flashback.[34] This difference no doubt accounts, if only partially, for the impression among reviewers and scholars (such as those cited earlier) that the characters' adventures and memories are "amputated" or marginal.

If, as Rosen asserts, historiographic explanations are forms of consciousness, it becomes clear what is at stake in cinematic representations of history: a change in discourse reflects a change in consciousness. Thomas Elsaesser, for one, has studied how German films play out in their structures of representation the collective traumas, the denials, the mourning process, and the evolution of national identity and national myths in postwar Germany.[35] Taking a more activist approach, Anton Kaes believes that consciousness can be changed by changing discourse. Examining cinematic representations of the Holocaust, Kaes emphasizes modernism's capacity to give us new ways of thinking about history, and he issues a call for a "postmodern historiography on film" that would systematically transform the ways history is represented. Using as a model Hans-Jürgen Syberberg's controversial 1978 film, *Hitler—A Film from Germany,* Kaes proposes that this transformation entail a "rejection of narrativity." ("Does not narrative always excuse?" he asks.) The transformation would also involve a "specularization of history" capable of capturing on film the ways history itself is manipulated as spectacle; it would produce a "proliferation of perspectives" by refusing to resolve contradictions; and it would be an "affirmation of nostalgia," putting meaning into question and showing a past that is fragmented, unrepresentable, or irretrievably lost.[36] The similarities between Kaes's proposed activist strategy and the fictional forms of the New Wave and the New Novel are striking. In their quest for representations of personal memory and the collective past, the artists studied here can be understood as doing nothing less than creating a new (postmodern) historiography in the novel and on film, and with it a new form of what Rosen calls a "historiographic imaginary."

Perhaps because representation of the past always involves the imaginary, psychoanalysis, particularly Lacanian psychoanalysis, has been as important to film theorists as it has to historians. Perhaps even more so, since psychoanalysis so often involves dramas of looking—dreams, primal scenes, or screens. Even the psychoanalytic session is a form of spectacle that, like the cinema, provides a *mise en scène* of the past. Psychoanalytic film theorists like Jean-Louis Baudry and Christian Metz have asked why viewers are fascinated with the cinema in the first place, exploring similarities between films and dreams and between film watching and regression to infantile states.[37] Baudry, Metz, and others have drawn on what Lacan described as the "mirror stage" of ego development in order to elaborate a theory of the spectator's involvement in cinema. In Lacan's account, the young child first gains an idea of its own separate and coherent (i.e., ideal) ego when it catches sight of its image in the mirror. In fascination, the child begins to identify with that image, but the identity that derives from that representation remains imaginary.[38] According to psychoanalytic film theorists, the film screen functions like a mirror in which the spectator can identify, and identify with, a more ideal image, because more whole, of him- or herself.[39] Induced by camera work and editing to identify with the perceiving eye of the camera (primary identification) and with larger-than-life characters on the screen (secondary identification), the spectator does not, for all that, passively consume the cinematic image. If film historians like Turim show us how history is framed by and unknowable without the subject ("flashback subjectivates history"), there is nevertheless no fully constituted subject that watches the filmic image. Rather, filmic images, like other forms of culture, play a role in constituting the subject. In short, what is at stake with any new form of historiographic representation is nothing less than reconfiguration of the subject in and of history.

The purpose of this brief excursion has been to map a conceptual and semantic field of force located at the intersections of several fields of knowledge where *Hiroshima mon amour* takes (its) place. In light of the three bobbins described above and certain preoccupations shared by contemporary theories of historiography, psychoanalysis, and cinema, the presence of history in Resnais and Duras's film can be examined as an articulation of personal story and public history, of the unconscious and the visible, and of history and fiction. History intrudes on the present for the French woman from two directions: the bombing of Hiroshima and the liberation of Nevers. As they appear in the film, these events seem so disproportionate and heterogeneous that no relation between the two seems possible at first. Most critics have considered Hiroshima to be merely the setting for a personal crisis. Others have seen the Hiroshima and Nevers stories as parallel or related metaphorically.[40] I think, however, that we are now equipped to explore the film's infinitely more complex vision of the French woman's place in history and her relation to subjectivity, knowledge, and the collectivity.

The Nevers axis (Nevers-then remembered in Hiroshima-now) is a personal experience in a precise historical setting that poses a problem: what can be the place of history in the life of the individual? The Hiroshima axis (Hiroshima-then remembered in Hiroshima-now) asks the reverse question: what can be the attitude of the individual with respect to the mass catastrophes of history? The Nevers axis points in the direction of forgetting as the healthiest response to a traumatic past, while Hiroshima—the name and the event have become virtually synonymous—demands ritual commemoration. Each story is ironic with respect to the other, intruding to strike a chord of *dubitatio* that contests the assumptions and context in which the other is presented. To further complicate matters, each of the two appears as contained within the other in some way. To discover the implications of these intersections, it will be necessary to examine each story in turn.

HIROSHIMA

"Impossible to speak about Hiroshima," writes Duras in her preface to the scenario (10). *Hiroshima mon amour* approaches the history of Hiroshima obliquely. Duras and Resnais envisioned the film as a love story, but a love story from which a certain "atomic anguish would not be absent." This curious formula required protagonists who would not participate directly in the event—the bombing—itself but instead would play the marginal role of "witnesses, which is what we are most often when we are faced with catastrophes or major problems: spectators."[41]

The French woman's specular distance from events is embodied in the film's many mediating *mises en abyme*. The first of these is, appropriately, a filmed reconstruction of the bombing and its aftermath. "I saw *everything*," she declares as she relates her visit to the Hiroshima memorial museum (15). The reconstruction creates an intense emotional response, and the illusion is so convincing that the tourists weep. "You saw nothing," replies her Japanese companion (15), aware that the film and the event are separate realities. As an actress, however, the woman can move from experience to imagination and from perception to identification, and she betrays this slip by juxtaposing sensation ("I was hot at Peace Square. Ten thousand degrees at Peace Square"]) and intellect ("I know it. How can you not know it?"). Literally, her words refer truthfully to having seen everything at the museum, "for want of something else" (17). Like most of us, she has seen not the event but a filmed representation of it.

And we watch her watching it. Further, if I am a spectator watching a spectator, one might wonder, who is to say that the inner spectator is not in turn watching another spectator? And sure enough, at the museum the French woman scrutinizes the other visitors with as much attention as she views the exhibit, if not more. Her reactions are mediated by theirs, and since she is a good actress, her feelings are both real and mimetic ("the tourists cry. [. . .] I've always wept" [18]). In her confession that she weeps for Hiroshima, she is literally beside herself, displaced in relation to the tears of others. Historical knowledge is thereby shown in the context of its transmission. The abyssal configuration can thus create an illusion of immediate perception of an experience in which all spectators are by definition already distanced from the scene.

Believing that "looking closely at things is something that has to be learned," the French actress is learning to experience the past through the present and through other people. Her identification with the inner film and, perhaps, her need to know that her companion is "completely Japanese" (25) and therefore somehow closer to the event than she serve as a model for French moviegoers, who experienced the war (or its memories), but elsewhere, and short of these scenes of instant mass annihilation. Watching *Hiroshima mon amour,* we too see the bombing through (or on) the protective screen of the present; segments of the museum movie—its images of horrible mutilation—are intercut with a love scene in which the perfect bodies of the lovers (*intact* is the word used) are evidence of their distance from the bombing.

The concentric configurations of Hiroshima implicate the viewer in the disaster far more effectively than a linear genealogy of knowledge would do. Like the bombing itself, the film breaks down the comforting distinction between participant and witness. The figure of protagonist-as-spectator provides a structured distance from the event through time and through a possibly infinite regress of specular identifications. But the reverse figure of the spectator-as-protagonist brings the outer viewers into complicity with the film. We can identify with the French actress; that is, we can put ourselves in her place while remaining in our own. We alternately watch her watching and, by means of a subjective camera, share her gaze. The spectator in and of *Hiroshima* thus enacts Christian Metz's description of primary identification: "The spectator, in short, identifies with himself, with himself as pure act of perception (as awakening, as warning): as the necessary condition that renders the perceived world possible."[42]

To have seen, however indirectly, and remembered an event of extreme and uncontrolled violence, one has to have "survived to tell the tale." All tales, in fact, are told by survivors, and so perhaps all tales are refracted to some degree through what psychologist and historian Robert Jay Lifton, in a study of Hiroshima's aftereffects, calls "survivor guilt." During the course of his research, and in order to account for the reactions he observed and even those he himself felt, Lifton had to broaden what he meant by the term *survivor*. As he realized that the psychological damage of the bomb spread beyond the group of physically injured, he adopted the Japanese term *hibakusha,* which means, literally, "explosion-affected person." This larger group included those who, although left physically "intact," were permanently damaged psychically by what they had witnessed. Their symptoms included a sense of failed responsibility and a protective numbing of memory. What is startling is that ultimately Lifton found himself included in a concentric ripple effect resembling the dynamic spectator-participant mediating structures of *Hiroshima mon amour.* As he documented and classified, through interviews, the kinds of reactions he encountered, he became aware of his own role as a "spectator of spectators," and he observed in himself a similar progressive immunity to the horror of the stories he heard. He points to his own case as "an unforgettable demonstration of the 'psychic closing off' . . . characteristic of all aspects of atomic exposure, even of this kind of 'exposure to the exposed.'"[43] Lifton's project, on the one hand, and his own contamination by the effects of the bomb, on the other, correspond to the two opposing forces in *Hiroshima mon amour:* the necessity of remembering and the need to forget. These themes of survival elucidate the French woman's obsessive return to "residual images . . . of ultimate horror" (Lifton's terms) and the *carpe diem* quality of her encounter with the Japanese man.[44]

An experience of violence escaped where others died always makes one prey to the temptation of denial. Such is the logic of the second interior film, where the French woman heals her historical lapsus not only by being an actor, rather than a spectator, in the events but by playing the role of a nurse. Here, alongside a reconstruction of the event, the interior film represents war by means of its reassuring opposite: it is a documentary on peace ("What else do you expect them to make in Hiroshima except a picture about Peace?" [34]). The bad faith of this kind of retrospective pretending, this commodification of trauma and of history, is signaled by the evident falsity of the inner film and by its status as parody of the kind of cultural commemoration Resnais and Duras refused to make. We see only fake blood, wax wounds melting in the sun, staged antiwar demonstrations. The theme of that film as it appears in the marchers' pickets—"Never Another Hiroshima"—is an appeal to resist the need to forget or repress, but this intention is subverted by the theatricality and reversals of its presentation as framed within the larger film.

The filming is in progress at Peace Square, and the French actress is staying at the New Hiroshima Hotel; the necessity of remembering is counteracted by the inevitability of forgetting, as the very mechanisms that permit survival erase memory. Since Freud, we have known that memories of what one would prefer to forget are inevitably filtered through a distorting rhetoric or censor. Material that makes its way through the censor is often displaced onto surprising representations, whether these be screen memories or the manifest images of dreams. It is affect, Freud claimed, that opens the image to interpretation.[45]

Freud's insight can help us uncover what links the Nevers material to the history of Hiroshima in the film. To suggest a parallel or metaphorical connection would be absurd. Rather, it is the affective experience of spectatorship and survival of Hiroshima that triggers the memory and guilt of Nevers in what was homologous in that experience: a specular encounter with death and the fact of having survived. The desire to forget or repress that experience (the French woman dreams about Nevers but never thinks about it) and the fact that she has never been back to the scene of its occurrence bring back the memory in another place. The film expands the notions of place from their initial meaning as literal geographical locales to a wider metaphorical conception of *topos*, at once spatial, rhetorical, and political. The French actress is a displaced person whose personal memory resurfaces in the form of a commonplace, a *lieu commun*, which is the collective memory of Hiroshima. Her memory also wanders from one language to another: the desire not to repeat Hiroshima ("Jamais plus Hiroshima"—"Never Another Hiroshima") somehow depends on its obverse, a repetition of Nevers ("Nevers another"). Now that reversal [*l'envers*] and the nature of its necessity must be investigated.

The French woman experiences her memory of Nevers in the same way she reacted to the filmed bombing of Hiroshima: by reliving it. Her story, like those of other Durasian heroines, is animated by the alcohol she drinks while telling it. Nevers emerging from her glass of beer as she and the Japanese man sit at a table in the Café du Fleuve signals a change in the texture and tempo of the present: "They don't notice the time passing. A miracle has occurred. What miracle? The resurrection of Nevers" (53). The Proustian comparison is inevitable: in the same way, Proust calls the resurgence of Combray from his teacup "the miracle of an analogy" that permits him to transcend chronology. He describes this miraculous reappearance as a sudden awareness of "the image, a visual memory" of his past,[46] as if memory were a movie that suddenly started to (re)turn.

Such is exactly and literally the nature of Nevers as it appears within an "analogous" experience in Hiroshima. Unlike Proust's memories, however, the story of Nevers is in fact an image, or more precisely, a film-within-a-film. The French woman does not simply remember, because film is incapable of remembering: it, and therefore she, can only re-present the past, that is, restore its immediate presence. Thus, technically, the story of Nevers is not a memory in the form of a film; it is a flashback, that is, a film in the form of a memory. If it can be understood as a replay of a forgotten or repressed past (forgotten and repressed have the same status with relation to the image), this is because Resnais finds that the unconscious is structured not so much like a language as like a "spectacle."[47]

Accordingly, the Nevers episode is staged not as a latent content but as another companion spectacle to the present story taking place in Hiroshima. In fact, the French woman relives her trauma twice during the course of the film: when she reveals it to her Japanese lover as a memory and at the same time as she reenacts it in her relationship with him. The articulation of the two stories, one within the other, is of crucial importance. As she simultaneously relates and relives the past, her narration forms part of and is also circumscribed by its reenactment. The abyssal configuration subverts the idea of linear chronology, and with it the mythology of a "first time"; chronological priority dissolves in spatial contiguity. "He was my first love," she exclaims (65). It will shortly become obvious how problematic her statement is.

Both the Nevers and the Hiroshima love stories are radically illegitimate by the standards of the surrounding society. About her wartime loss the French woman cries, "My dead love is an enemy of France" (62); her current affair transgresses marital, national, and racial boundaries. Both experiences are accompanied by fantasies of escape that turn into a nightmare of loss and exclusion. The scenario describes the Japanese man and the French woman as they

1. *Hiroshima mon amour.* The French actress (Emanuelle Riva) relives her wartime loss with her Japanese lover (Eiji Okada).

must leave the café at closing time with a remark that applies as well to the Nevers love story: "The well-ordered world has thrown them out, for their adventure has no place in it" (70). The French woman explicitly links the two experiences when she exclaims that in Hiroshima she has rediscovered "the taste of an impossible love" (73). The film does not condemn either love affair, but uses them to question both the place of the individual in society and the reverse, the impact of social norms in the individual's life.

As a consequence of the simultaneous presence of the two love stories, the memory begins to look like a neurosis. The similarities of the two stories and the intense, involuntary quality of the woman's (re)experience suggest the existence here, as with other Durasian heroines, of a compulsion to repeat.[48] The café episode, that scene of a repetition-within-a-repetition, has the external signals of a psychoanalytic session: the woman's story is elicited by her Japanese lover, who encourages her most insistently to continue when she seems to have nothing more to add. Her retrospection is accompanied by regression to infantile gestures, as when she asks him to hold a glass for her to drink. A transference of affect from one story to the other emerges as the woman resurrects her lost German lover in her present companion ("You are dead" [54]). Her Japanese companion is willing to enact the transference as well, as he plays the role of the dead man.

Freud describes the compulsion in terms of a distinction between repetition and recollection. The patient's illness, he explains in a 1914 essay, consists in involuntarily repeating a repressed and forgotten experience. The traumatic event is thus reproduced, "not in his memory, but in his behavior, he repeats it without of course knowing that he is repeating it." In other words, the patient reenacts because he cannot remember; he cannot narrate and therefore repeats it, an unwilling actor in the spectacle of his own unconscious representation. The goal of therapy is to release the patient from involuntary and hysterical repetition (behavior) by transforming the memory into conscious recall (speech), a process that takes the form of a "translation": "This condition of present illness is shifted bit by bit within the range and field of operation of the treatment, and while the patient lives it through as something real and actual, we have to accomplish the therapeutic task, which consists chiefly in translating it back again into terms of the past." The goal of remembering is thus, therapeutically but paradoxically, to open the way toward forgetting.

Freud's conception of the analytic task is based on his observation that the past cannot be addressed in its absence. Analysis consists, therefore, in "conjuring into existence a piece of real life" by means of a transfer of the past into the present situation ("the transference is itself only a bit of repetition").[49] In other words, it is not that repressed memories are visible, at least not directly, but rather that they are translated into behavior, or as Resnais would put it, into spectacle. The psychoanalytic process is thus constrained by the same limitations that constrain cinematic representation. The patient, says Freud (and the same can be said for film), "is obliged to repeat the repressed material as a contemporary experience instead of, as the physician would prefer to see, remembering it as something belonging to the past."[50] The scene of analysis thus has the same components as the café scene in Hiroshima: a fragmented tale pieced together and told as it is called forth within and by its reenactment in the present.

Among the more striking parallels between the Hiroshima and Nevers love stories is the similarity in their rhythm. Both—and the film as a whole that contains them as well—move through a phase of maximum lyrical idyll and erotic intensity that then degenerates into an interminable, agonized waiting for an inevitable end. Because it is postapocalyptic, this dead time is non-narrative: seen through flashback, it is a painful and timeless decrescendo (reenacted in the framing narrative) that plays with subjective time and the impossibility of locating either a fixed origin of the trauma or any future tense. After her German soldier has been shot, the French woman lies with him on the ground all day and night and into the next day. "Oh! How long it took him to die!" she cries (65). After his death, she falls into a stubborn and desperate mourning during which she was, she says, "mad with hate [*folle de méchanceté*]," a madness whose duration, she says, was "eternity." Fixated to the image of her loss, she is stuck in time. Unheeding of an "after" as she is of a "before," isolated in her room and then in a cellar, she can avoid remembering.

Eventually time begins to move again. The moment of her reemergence from "eternity" is signaled by a marble that rolls into her cellar prison, a marvelous visual pun of someone who has "lost her marbles" and then gets them back again. This return to "sanity" is a return to the pain of remembering. Her regained memory includes a before and a during:

> One day, it's true, I hear them [the churchbells]. I
> remember having heard them *before—before—when* we were in love,
> *when* we were happy.
> I'm beginning to see.
> I remember having already seen *before—before—when* we were in
> love, *when* we were happy.
> I remember.

But it refuses an after:

> I see my life. Your death.
> My life that goes on. Your death that goes on.

This is because "after," life and death are identical:

> The moment of his death actually escaped me, because . . . because even at that very moment, and even *afterward,* yes, even afterward, I can say that *I couldn't feel the slightest difference* between this dead body and mine. All I could find between this body and mine were obvious similarities. (63–65, emphasis added)

What follows his death, then, as she recreates it, is the absence of an "after," that is, her own symbolic social and physical death. Her "dishonor" is sealed in the ritual shaving of her head by the outraged citizens of Nevers. This social death is followed by her burial in the house, first in her room, then in the cellar, where she is finally silent and without feeling ("I'm numb [*Je ne sens rien*]" [61]—insensitive, insensible, and finally a loss of sense). Her madness imitates death in its timelessness and morbidity. Her family even reports that she has died.

There is a period of madness in the Hiroshima adventure as well: the moments during which she relives Nevers. The episode in the café, where the River Ota replaces the Loire as an image of time's normal flow, is marked by the "miracle" of repetition. What is miraculous about the Nevers memory is that it provides a way of "killing time" in order to forget an imminent separation, and this is what it shares with the Nevers madness. All repetition, as Proust knew, and Kierkegaard before him, has the potential to make us happy by arresting the passage of time in favor of a mythical temporal dimension where past and present coincide. The French woman's repetition of her Nevers story, framed by its reenactment, uses the repetition of a loss to ward off the finality of another, ongoing loss, as Zeno's arrow never reaches its destination. In this way, repetition recreates the timeless eternity of forgetfulness that occurred in the Nevers cellar. The French woman is reliving a fantasy of loss that resembles the repetition compulsions of other Durasian heroines, such as Anne-Marie Stretter of *India Song* and Lol V. Stein in *The Ravishing of Lol V. Stein*. In her remarkable reading of Lol's story, Elisabeth Lyon relies on Laplanche and Pontalis's observation that it is the work of fantasy to "cover the moment of *separation* between *before* and *after*" in order to describe Lol's compulsion to relive the traumatic scene (of her loss of her fiancé to another woman) as a "desire to see loss" and as "Lol's desire to see herself not being there."[51] Similarly, for the French woman in Hiroshima, remembering is itself a form of absence or madness, a trance of hypnotic repetition, arrested finally by her companion's slap, which, like the marble, brings her back to chronology.

But the Japanese man is her lover, not her therapist, and so reenactment of her loss with him, although it permits resurgence of the Nevers story, does not constitute closure or cure. She may now allow herself to forget Nevers ("I bequeath you to oblivion" [80]), but only at the price of creating in its place a new loss, the loss of her love in Hiroshima, and the possibility of an endless chain of repetitions. Whereas the Freudian paradigm suggests the possibility of closure that never materializes here, this film's *mises en abyme* suggest the possibility of an endless, repetitive series. It is in Hiroshima, after all, that repetition is felt as a mortal danger, not only to individuals but to the entire human race.

Freud recognized that some repetitions serve a pleasure principle, while others seem to be motivated by a contrary and destructive impulse or death drive. What possible benefit could induce the French woman to stage this repetition of loss? This, of course, is the question Freud asks as he ponders the *fort/da* game of little Hans. Discarding and then retrieving his bobbin, the child reenacted the painful experience of his mother's frequent departures and the joy of her return. In addition to the pleasure of repetition for its own sake, Freud proposes two interpretations of the child's game, both of which are applicable to *Hiroshima mon amour*. By voluntarily and symbolically staging what could not have been a pleasant event, he speculates, the boy substituted his own active will for a passive feeling of abandonment; furthermore, by defiantly throwing away a substitute object, the child is able to satisfy a fantasy of revenge that he would have to deny in reality.[52] The French woman in Hiroshima stages Freud's hypotheses: faced with her own inevitable departure, she chooses to reject her Japanese companion, refusing to see him again even while time permits. She thus gains control over her fate while correcting the memory of her abandonment by her first lover in the loss she compulsively repeats.

The revenge hypothesis is more complex. How, in the context of Hiroshima especially, can the Japanese man play the role of a substitute (transference) victim? The nature of the French woman's repetitions and the reappearance of her madness suggest that she is punishing not the Japanese man but herself. The major focus of her repetition is not the lovers' idyll but the loss of love, the punishment and loss of self. As I have suggested, the most salient episode of her reenactment is her own symbolic death. It might instead be more accurate to say that she wishes she had died. She feels the scissors on her head as a comfort, and her madness is less an involuntary affliction than a willed hatred [*méchanceté*]. What she repeats with the Japanese man is her own symbolic suicide, which turns out to be a suicide manqué, like the first. About Nevers she says, "I was hungry. Hungry for infidelity, for adultery, for lies, hungry to die." But she did not die. "I would have preferred that you had died at Nevers," says the Japanese man, angry at her refusal to stay with him. "So would I," she replies. "But I didn't die at Nevers" (77–78). In restoring an earlier stage of her life ("Oh, how young I was, once!") and in rehearsing or repeating her own death (a "death . . . by identification," as Lyon suggests about Anne-Marie Stretter), she enacts a death instinct.

If a compulsion to repeat articulates the reappearance of Nevers in Hiroshima, one cannot avoid asking about the bombing; surely this important historical content is not included in the film simply as backdrop. The French woman's belief that she has unluckily survived her own death, her postapocalyptic condition of "death in life," to borrow Lifton's phrase, is what she reexperiences as a survivor of the bombing in Hiroshima, where the awareness of imminent ending connected with an "atomic anguish" can envision no "after." As his numerous essays on war and its neuroses make clear, Freud was interested in the effects of war, and his conclusions about compulsive repetition intersect with Lifton's analyses when he observes that the likelihood of posttraumatic neurosis is greater in the absence of any serious physical injury.[53] It is an inverse relationship of this kind that links Hiroshima to Nevers and permits the French woman's itinerary from personal subjectivity to a sense of collective history. To pursue an exploration of the overall functioning of the film's intersecting stories, a somewhat odd question must now be asked: Who remembers? Who repeats? Who exactly is the subject of trauma and of history?

"RIEN N'AURA EN LIEU . . . QUE LE LIEU [Nothing Will Have Taken Place . . . But the Place]"

The bombing of Hiroshima is a collective memory. It is a historical occurrence whose reality can be verified in other texts both written and unwritten, such as the reconstructed cities and bodies of survivors. But the film assumes nothing outside itself except spectators; it creates its own memory from within. Hiroshima is recognizable as a *topos,* a place in the text, situated in a network of imbricated spectator positions beginning in the film and extending, by implication, beyond it. By means of its structures, the film constitutes a community of spectators, including the French woman, confronted as she is confronted with Hiroshima as an "image of ultimate horror."

The bombing of Hiroshima is not presented in terms of its political causes or consequences or even in terms of the bomb itself, whose most recognizable image, the mushroom cloud, was deleted from the scenario. Instead, the catastrophe is represented in terms of its mass human cost. The war in France, on the other hand, is portrayed by means of subjectivizing flashbacks and other techniques that emphasize the effect of one death on one person. It would appear, then, that while the Hiroshima losses and memory are held in common, the French war is portrayed as a personal trauma. As she confides it to her companion, the French woman believes in the inalterable uniqueness of her story. Many critics have been troubled by their observation that her memory is not situated in any community. Close examination of the film reveals, however, that this is not the case. Both catastrophes are conveyed as collages of images accompanied by discontinuous commentary. Like Hiroshima, Nevers also emerges almost as a tale without a teller. As a typical story that anyone could tell, it too reveals itself to be a transpersonal or collective memory.

The French woman begins her story with inaugural statements typical of an autobiographical narrative, recounted from a position of authority she considers privileged:

HE: I can't picture Nevers.

(*Shots of Nevers. The Loire.*)

SHE: Nevers. Forty thousand inhabitants. Built like a capital—(but). A child can walk around it. (*She moves away from him.*) I was born in Nevers (*she drinks*), I grew up in Nevers. I learned how to read in Nevers. And it was there that I became twenty. (53)

From the start, however, the "autobiographical pact" that should assure her authority and the credibility of her story is undermined.[54] First, these events, like the views of Nevers that accompany their telling, are not confided as remembered, but simply as known. Usually the statement of one's birth is assumed, unproblematically, to be reported fact, and evidence here suggests that other statements are reported as well. More specifically, they are known through *reading*. Before the French woman's birth, there was Nevers as it can be recited from a tourist guide or a schoolbook in which a child learns to read. The text's only other reference to reading subsumes the bombing of Hiroshima within the Nevers story; having left Nevers under cover of darkness, the young French woman had arrived in Paris in time to see "the name of Hiroshima [. . .] in all the newspapers" (67). Before the museum film, then, she is acquainted with both Nevers and Hiroshima through the written word. Preceding the above dialogue, the Japanese man asks whether *Nevers* means anything in French. His question brings the name into view as a word that *might* mean something, as in fact it almost does in English. The English *never* casts a negation on what the French woman recounts and suggests the possibility that she remembers a Nevers-neverland of her lost past. The inclusion of her initiation to reading as one of her life stages points to her statements as a product of reading and thence to an autobiography and history known indirectly, patched together by a logic of intertextuality and *bricolage*.[55] The French woman's success as a professional actress depends not on memory but on memorization and repetition of other people's texts. Theatrical repetition suggests both rehearsal and performance in a situation where there is only the text and no original. Each repetition refers only to other representations of the same script.

It is in this light, then, as an already intertextually constructed autobiography, that the French woman's reconstruction of her trauma must be evaluated, for it is here that a transpersonal collective makes its existence known. When she falters, her companion adds details to her "memory" that he could not possibly have known, and the scenario notes that it is "as if they were aware of these things together" (59). An important intertext here, unknown to both, is Duras's *Moderato cantabile,* on the basis of which Resnais invited Duras to write the script for *Hiroshima mon amour.* In that 1958 novel, a man and a woman, united by their chance encounter in a café at the scene of a passionate murder, reconstruct the story of that crime and relive it symbolically. Anne Desbaresdes, aided by her chance companion Chauvin, produces her own social disgrace and then a theatrical death (created through words and gestures) in imitation of the scene she witnessed. It is clear that they create a story that never took place, another death by identification. Their reconstruction is in fact a construction. The reenactment *is* the story, invented around an enigmatic scene and propelled primarily by Anne's intense need to enact it. Anne and Chauvin do in this case know the story together because it is *their* story. In the same way, the Nevers story is subordinated to and produced by its telling. Memory serves the needs of the framing situation in both cases, and historiography is shaped by the present as its most insistent intertext.

In an essay entitled "Le Mythe du premier souvenir" (The myth of the first memory), Bruno Vercier tests his hypothesis that autobiographical narratives follow predictable rhetorical sequences. In what he calls the "narrative of childhood," the first memory enjoys a special, "sacred" status simply because the subject experiences it as an origin of consciousness. Vercier's comparison of autobiographies by Pierre Loti and Michel Leiris shows to what extent these first memories, considered unique, are in fact stereotypical and codified. Vercier considers the first memory to be a sort of screen memory, even going so far as to claim that regardless of its content, the most primitive memory in an autobiography represents "the true birth of the individual."[56]

While not actual birth memories, several of the first memories Vercier cites are accounts of a fall. "The carriage tips, the child falls" (Georges Sand); "I was two years old, and a maid let me fall from her arms" (Abel Hemant). Other examples could be added, and still more first memories are accounts of separations or other traumas. Even Proust begins with the night Marcel's mother did *not* appear at his door at the appointed time to kiss him good night. For the present context, it is worth adding that many early memories reported in autobiographies (by Rousseau and Sartre, for example) are related to first experiences of reading.

In this light, the French woman's trauma in Nevers can better be understood, not as a first love, but as a first memory. The love affair itself is a prehistoric fantasy, presented according to the conventions of a romantic fairy tale. The images themselves, as if patched together into a story from a pastoral or gothic novel, include a first glance, secret rendezvous among the ruins of an old castle and in a peasant hut, and so on. Vercier could have added this stage of the French woman's narrative to his list of examples illustrating "a search for that plenitude that the child once knew" and an effort to "recapture that moment of perfection."[57] Perfection, that is, before the fall, before the trauma, before knowledge of evil, before reading.

It is the death of her lover that marks her transition from idyll into history, her fall from timelessness into chronology. Her madness is a last attempt to grasp that vanishing "eternity" before being catapulted into duration. Her trauma has the characteristics of a fall: into the cellar, into madness, and especially from grace, a public disgrace. Now she considers herself a fallen woman ("of doubtful morals"). Her curious claim to have been "mad with hate [*méchanceté*]" is illuminated by the root verb *choir,* to fall, suggesting her resistance to the fall into knowledge and secular time.

Further details indicate that the French woman is marginal to her own story and receives it indirectly from others. Her episode of madness makes it credible that she has forgotten what happened, and so it is repeatedly made clear that she tells her story as it was told to her:

Yes, it takes a long time.
They told me [*on m'a dit*] it had taken a very long time. (62)

I'm becoming reasonable. They say [*on dit*]: "She's becoming reasonable." (66)

The story she tells is actually composed through and through of instances of "on dit" (or *dictons,* that is, proverbs or sayings). Her memory is common knowledge, and Nevers is a *lieu commun* that has no need of her to be told. "I don't understand who is in my place," says Lol V. Stein.[58] Lol is not the author of her own tale, which has no origin except in myth. Similarly, the French woman of *Hiroshima mon amour* is not the subject of her story: she is its spectator, its object, its place.

I call the two protagonists "the French woman" and "the Japanese man," in spite of the formulation's clumsiness, to highlight their peculiar status as characters. They have no other names in the scenario. Almost noncharacters, they can best be understood in terms of the novel form that Resnais would like to approximate, where the disappearance of individualized and discrete characters can more effectively be realized. If it were possible to film a pronoun, this would be an appropriate form for the roles played by the man and woman of *Hiroshima mon amour.* As simply *je* and *tu,* their identities shift and are defined only by their discursive contexts.[59] As her story is revealed to be a layered intertextual archive of collective memory, the French woman fades away as a speaking and remembering subject. If we view her, for a moment, in terms of her narrative function rather than in terms of the actress's presence on the screen, we can see that the French woman is told by her stories more than she tells them, and her subjectivity is the product rather than the source of the spectacles she sees. Traversed by images, she becomes a vanishing point or optical illusion (a projection) that materializes at the place where they converge. By the end of the film that place has been located in history and geography: "Your name is Nevers. Ne-vers in France." Nevers is not the origin of a story, then, but the story itself.

In his *Repetition: An Essay in Experimental Psychology,* Kierkegaard recounts his efforts to recreate the pleasures of an especially enjoyable trip to Berlin. As each attempt fell short of the mark, he realized the impossibility of repeating a "first time." Paradoxically, all that can be repeated is the distance from a mythical original experience. That is, the only thing that can be repeated is the inevitable failure to repeat.[60] By the end of *Hiroshima mon amour,* the French woman has demonstrated that same failure, a fundamental feature of her Orphic vision. As she (re)constructs her memory, she despairs at having betrayed the story by telling it. The repetitions within the film, appearing as ripples around an empty center, produce an insurmountable distance from the past in which, in Ihab Hassan's words, "images beget further images without benefit of an original."[61] Since all that can be repeated is this distance, it is never possible to tell of the origin of the loss, but only of the loss of the origin. Whence the irony of the Japanese man's exultant "discovery" that he is the first to know his companion's story, unaware that he is part of a concentric arena of spectators that enlarges each time the film is shown. Furthermore, he hears the story for the first time again at each showing! He also believes that since she has returned to her youth, she is so young that "you still don't belong to anyone in particular. I like that" (51). Here and elsewhere—such as in Resnais's *Muriel,* where another protagonist tries to recapture a first love, while the scenario specifies that even then she was already "marked" by an earlier tragic loss of love—cultural obsessions with and figurations of virginity betray a nostalgic belief in the possibility of a "first time."

The value of the French woman's story lies, however, not in its originality but precisely in its similarity to other stories. The blurring of her character foregrounds the story itself as anonymous or transpersonal, as "common knowledge." For if, in the survey I mentioned at the outset, New Wave characters were thought to exist in a condition of exile and marginality—of alienation—I believe that in *Hiroshima mon amour* the very insubstantiality of the characters, particularly the French woman, points to their status as figures of the film's epistemological quest to move beyond portrayal of individual trauma in order to imagine a collective or historical subject. As the French woman loses her personal story, there appears in her place a sense of history.

A SENSE OF LOSS—A LOSS OF SENSE

At the center of the Nevers story are three images of loss, three signifiers of absence: the young French woman's dead lover, her shorn head, and her madness. Each of these can be described as what the *Communications* survey called a "loss of meaning." The first is a loss of intimate connection; second, the public shaving ritually severs a social code; finally, madness is a loss of sense. Afterwards, she finds herself excluded from society; she disappears into isolation, and finally leaves town.

The Nevers idyll is a silent movie whose soundtrack comes from the framing story in Hiroshima. We could even say that it is a preverbal or purely imaginary story. The French woman's exclusion from the social contract and her retreat from the Symbolic order can be verified and summarized by her loss of speech. As Edward Saïd points out, "Language is one of the actions that succeeds the lost origin: language begins after the Fall. Human discourse . . . lives with the memory of origins long since violently cut off from it."[62] As the French woman clutches her German lover's corpse, she holds an empty signifier, inert matter whose meaning is lost. After the body is taken away, she becomes mute, severing the important connection between speech and memory. "I only have one memory left, your name," she says (57). Eventually, the proper noun is lost, and the only sounds she makes are screams and animal noises.

SHE: I think of you, but I don't talk about it any more.
HE: Mad.(61)

Here, madness consists most immediately in the repression not of memory but of speech, of the means to share memory and thus constitute a community. Her capacity to speak, and with it her means to participate in a community, return only in Hiroshima.

In order to understand how the eruption of Hiroshima into her field of vision causes a return of speech and memory, it is necessary to look more closely at the second loss, the shaving of her hair. This peculiar ritual punishment is clearly to be understood in a collective context; especially in light of her retreat into autism (that is, her rejection of interpersonal communication, of the Symbolic order, and, by extension, of history), the shaving of her head signals an exile from community. The shorn woman [la tondue] has become an almost obligatory image in films where love and war are opposed (for example, David Lean's Ryan's Daughter [1970], Marcel Ophuls's Le Chagrin et la pitié [1971; The Sorrow and the Pity], and Claude Lelouch's Les Uns et les autres [1982; Bolero]). The force of this image no doubt derives in part from its value as a symbolic sexual punishment for a sexual transgression. More important is the fact that the notion of "horizontal collaboration" with the enemy poses a question of boundaries: between personal and public, between endogamy and exogamy. The shorn woman has become an image of fascination perhaps because it points to the problem of the individual's relation to history. The line between individual and collective often appears in fiction as a confrontation between individuals from enemy camps ("enemy brothers"). This is an existential confrontation, frequently portrayed as a failure to turn the other into Other in order to kill him. A specular identification with the Other as an image of the self has always had strong appeal as an antiwar theme. At that zero point of national or racial differences, oppositions break down and there is a danger of reversal of position, of indifferentiation. This risk underlies many of *Hiroshima*'s rhetorical figures of antithesis and reversal, as embodied in the cry "My dead love is an enemy of France" and even in the film's title.

Commenting on the film's opening scenes in her preface to the scenario, Duras discusses the juxtaposition of *Hiroshima* and *mon amour:*

This beginning, this official parade of already-known horrors from Hiroshima, recalled in a hotel bed, this sacrilegious recollection, is voluntary. One can talk about Hiroshima anywhere, even in a hotel bed, during a chance, an adulterous love affair. The bodies of both protagonists, who are really in love with each other, will remind us of this. What is really sacrilegious, if anything is, is Hiroshima itself. There's no point in being hypocritical and avoiding the issue [ce n'est pas la peine de déplacer la question]. (9)

But of course the head-shaving ritual in Nevers, as well as the love and madness in Hiroshima, *do* avoid the issue. The film's rhetoric is designed to displace the question and then to call attention to its own displacements.

The historical situation in which the French woman's head is shorn corresponds to what René Girard has called a "sacrificial crisis," and the woman herself to his description of the *pharmakos* or "surrogate victim."[63] Girard explains that the sacrificial crisis poses a danger of uncontrollable repetition of reciprocal revenge. One violent act—real, remembered, or imagined—can provoke an endless series of alternating acts of vengeance that will eventually destroy the community. The crisis is provoked, he says, by a breakdown of distinctions. Categories of thought and oppositions between groups break down, so that it is no longer possible to distinguish enemy from ally, inside from outside. The enemy—violence itself—is within, and the risk is one of undifferentiation. (The French woman stresses her "fear of indifference.") Such situations invite identification of a substitute victim or scapegoat on which unanimous hostility can be exorcised, thus arresting or preventing a potentially endless chain of violence.

The Liberation provoked just such a crisis of distinctions. With the departure of the Germans (in the film, the representative death of one German), there was no longer a clear sense of who the enemy might be or from where violence might come. The distinction between *collaborators* and *resisters* was no longer a usable one. Especially among the majority, which was neither, this tension risked erupting in an outbreak of a chain of recriminations. Focusing its anger on a surrogate victim, the community could reach new unanimity and cohesion. The substitute victim must come from within the society, Girard explains, but also be marginal to it, so that no champion will come forth to avenge the victim and perpetuate the violence.

The French woman in *Hiroshima mon amour* serves as such a substitute victim: she is a member of the community but at the same time marginal to it because of her sex and her age;[64] she is also innocent of any real military or political crimes and deflects attention from them in the town. It is clear she has no champion: even her parents concede the inevitability of their daughter's humiliation. She is thus a substitute for all the members of the community, and her expulsion protects it from its own violence. Through her future career as an actress, we know that she consents passively to her role and that she has an aptitude for taking on the suffering of others. Even her position in the society—she is the pharmacist's daughter—designates her in advance to fulfill the role of *pharmakos*. The nature of the *pharmakos*, meaning both "poison" and "remedy," further emphasizes the film's rhetoric;[65] the young woman's sexual "crime" and then the displacement of scandal and punishment ("sacrilege," says Duras) from war to love signals a breakdown of oppositions and launches the sorts of reversals and repetitions that structure the film.

If the young woman's role as scapegoat culminated in her own symbolic death, which she repeats in Hiroshima, we have to ask whether she plays the role of a substitute victim in the framing story as well. In Hiroshima, a return of speech (to tell the tale of Nevers) is occasioned by her position as survivor or spectator as I have outlined it. Hiroshima evokes the anxiety and guilt that were lacking the first time. It supplies as well a sense of participation in history that was lacking in Nevers. In the context of a second love and of her discovery of the bomb, she realizes, to refer again to Duras's remark, that the question has been displaced. The problem for the survivor, as Bruno Bettelheim puts it best, is to learn to live with the belief that "someone died in my place."[66] In Nevers, the French woman could have said with Lol V. Stein, "I don't know who is in my place." She was absent from herself, mad. She could also have said, "I don't know in whose place I am," as she accepted the role of surrogate victim with no consciousness of her place in a community. In the framing story, she repeats her exclusion, this time substituting (like little Hans) her own voluntary control for her passivity. In Hiroshima, then, she finally occupies her own place, ironically (but not surprisingly, as I will show), when she is away from home.

If the French woman repeats her own exclusion in order to prevent a chain reaction or repetition of atomic violence, it is clear that the society from which she ritually excludes herself is not Japanese. To think so would be not only to misread Girard's schema but also to adopt an orientalizing posture of the same type that made the bombing thinkable in the first place. If the film's first spectators had perceived it as an expiation of some sort of racial guilt, the film might not have produced the scandal it did when it premiered in France. As Girard specifies, the sacrificial victim can absorb the community's violence only if it both belongs to and is marginal to that society. The French woman is not marginal to Japanese society because she is not part of it at all. A scene where her Japanese companion converses in Japanese (without subtitles) with an old woman makes clear that the French woman is a complete outsider to the Japanese (speech) community. This is not the context in which she plays the role of scapegoat.

In her preface and filming directions, Duras repeatedly points out that the bomb itself demands that we think in terms of an international community. The film is not a Franco-Japanese production, she insists; it is "anti-Franco-Japanese" (109). But I would suggest that the French woman is a surrogate for another sort of community—the one constituted by the film itself, that is to say, the community of spectators. Being a spectator herself, she is part of that community, but she is also marginal to it in that she is a *projection,* or a character in a clearly delimited frame separated from the real. For the same reasons, she can receive and convey collective sentiment without unleashing a danger of reprisal. The imbricated *mises en abyme* create a direct and structured continuity between the inner and outer spectator and survival roles.

Spectators of the film, especially among a French public, are survivors of both Hiroshima and Nevers. The issues surrounding the role of individuals in World War II in France are still sensitive and have yet to be resolved or even addressed publicly or officially at all until very recently. (I will return to these issues in later chapters.) Some official archives will not be opened to historians for many years to come. In light of continuing anxieties, repetition of *Hiroshima mon amour* itself takes on a function of public ritual.

THE CIRCLE GAME

As the film itself shows, and the theories of historiography surrounding it confirm, neither individual nor collective history is available except as it is framed in the present tense of an act of telling, repeating, or reading. It follows, therefore, that in order to situate the film in its proper frame of reference, it is necessary to bring that perspective to the film itself as a whole. As it happens, the history *of* the film repeats the history *in* the film. The production and reception of *Hiroshima mon amour* reveals an uncanny reenactment of the story it tells, and inversely, the film's story describes the scene of its own production. Inside and outside are given another twist.

The first shaping factor was economic: one of the earliest of the New Wave films, *Hiroshima* could not guarantee in advance even the restricted public appeal that experimental cinema could command only a few years later. At the mercy of distributors and the star system, restricted by economic pressures extending beyond their own personal investments or losses, filmmakers risk more than novelists when they tamper with the narrative habits of their potential public. That *Hiroshima* challenged these norms is demonstrated by its inclusion in the survey I mentioned at the outset. Its success in spite of the obstacles it faced was in large part responsible for the more favorable economic conditions under which later New Wave films could be made.

Behind the film was Argos, a company founded in 1949 with the goal of supporting the efforts of filmmakers working outside conservative public taste in both the formal and ideological dimensions of their art. Argos had commissioned Resnais to make an earlier film on the deportations and was well satisfied when he produced *Nuit et brouillard*. In the meantime, a satellite of Argos had become associated with Pathé Overseas, founded to encourage joint ventures between French and East Asian film industries. From this conjuncture of forces arose the idea of a Franco-Japanese documentary on the consequences of nuclear weaponry.

Resnais, for his part, had been eager to create a poetic film that he conceived in abstract terms as "the idea of two stories, each contained within the other, and both of which would be recounted in the present."[67] He had read *Moderato cantabile* and wanted to design something along those lines. When he accepted the offer from Argos, he abandoned his idea and went to work on the documentary, working with first one scenarist, then another.[68] With the decision to seek financial support in Japan, Resnais's project began to crystallize. Abandoning the documentary approach on the grounds that the subject was too vast and that, in any case, documentaries on the atomic bomb already existed, Resnais returned to the possibility of a fiction film, and his collaboration with Duras was initiated. When financing was offered by the Japanese distributor-producer Nagata, the contract required further modifications in the story: it would have to take place in Japan and include Japanese actors. From this set of circumstances emerged the curious formula of a love story colored by the presence of an "atomic anguish" and a tale that resembled *Moderato cantabile* in a Japanese setting.

The details of the Franco-Japanese project are many and fascinating, but the point is this: the story of the film itself evolved to adapt to the place and conditions of its production. The story of the French woman and her memories of Nevers, enclosed in flashback from within a Japanese setting, reflects the fact that the film could not be made exclusively with French financing. It should not escape notice (but it has) that what was the case for the French woman also holds true for the film: it was only in Japan that the story of Nevers could be told. Only framed by the Japanese film industry could the individual or absent stories of the French war and the conceptual categories in which it had been understood be exposed and contested.

Another anecdote confirms this hypothesis. When the 1959 selection committee at Cannes selected *Hiroshima mon amour* as one of three French entries for the year, the film festival commission, perhaps at the instigation of the ministry of culture, intervened to remove it from the list. The grounds given were that the film could damage foreign relations, particularly with the United States. Resnais must have had a sense of déjà vu, as this incident repeated the 1955 brouhaha over *Nuit et brouillard,* likewise rejected from the festival, in that case for fear of offending the Germans. But this time, there was hue and cry, and a special showing was held at the American Embassy in Paris. No, it was not offensive, Resnais was told, because, after all, everyone knew who bombed Hiroshima. It seems that it was not the Americans that the film would offend, but the French. According to Edgar Morin, Resnais was told that his film was incompatible with the ideals of the Fifth Republic.[69]

A note in the same issue of *Communications* in which the survey appeared evoked the spirit of the times with respect to reopening the dossier of collaboration and resistance. Reporting the beginning of the Eichmann trial in April 1960, a news gazette remarked that the trial failed to capture public attention or to become a media "event." Speculating on why this might be so, the writers point to one of the basic oppositions called into question by *Hiroshima mon amour:* "April, 1961: Opening of the Eichmann trial. From the point of view of the mass media, the event doesn't 'take'; there is probably a profound collective censorship at work: people feel like living, not remembering." Considering once again the present as the relevant frame of reference, I want to suggest that the French "question" of Algeria, current in 1957–60, made it undesirable to remember the past. France's wartime position as an occupied territory, and thus the implied ironies and reversals of the Algerian situation, made it particularly imperative that the French government (through its ministry of culture) maintain a clear separation between the two. While *Hiroshima* was being filmed, and when it was excluded from Cannes, France was on the brink of civil war, and French international prestige was at its lowest ebb since World War II. In this climate of crisis, the minister of culture (none other than André Malraux, who had memories of his own) must have been especially dismayed to see the collective mythology and accepted categories in which that war was officially remembered brought into question. *Hiroshima mon amour* thus played at Cannes the role of another surrogate victim, excluded from public view in order to maintain the safe distinctions between past and present history.

Hiroshima mon amour's challenge to categories of past and present, inside and ouside, can be understood, as I have proposed, as a function of the film's formal construction. Showing the context in which a story is told uncovers the ways in which history is a product of its telling in the present. The appearance *en abyme* (or in flashback) of historical material has two significant effects. First, abyssal repetition opens the possibility of an infinite number of mediating screens between the moment of recall and the event recalled; it elevates the text itself to a status of sole verifiable reality. In the case of a spectator watching a spectator, a reader reading a reader, or a historian reading a historian, repeatedly regressive interior duplications bring into doubt the existence of an ultimate origin, or *arche*, in the past. This effect of *mise en abyme*, what Bruce Morrissette calls its "postmodern transformation" and which I want to describe as its centripetal motion, is responsible for the (erroneous) conclusion that many contemporary works are exclusively autoreferential, self-contained and self-generating.

There is a centrifugal force in *mise en abyme* as well, however, what Morrissette calls its modernist version,[70] which calls up psychological or referential meaning within the work by forcing characters to become aware of what the author wants the reader or viewer to know. This second effect casts doubt not on the work's inner (or historical) origin but on its outer frame, or *telos:* if each spectator within the work is watched by a spectator in a larger frame, who is to say that the outer spectator is not part of the work as well? Gérard Genette calls this effect *metalepsis*, about which he says: "The most troubling effect of metalepsis is surely the unacceptable but insistent implication that the extradiegetic is perhaps always already diegetic, and that the narrator and narratees, that is, you and I, perhaps still belong to some story."[71]

Both the centrifugal and the centripetal effects of abyssal constructions suggest the possibility of endless metonymic repetition, within the work or outside it. The two are not separate, however, or even separable, but rather each is the correlate of the other. If the origin of narration is revealed as unattainably beyond the work and even beyond language, the visibility of the present instance of enunciation problematizes the time frame in which the film is made and viewed and the text read or heard. In other words, the logic of imbrication brings into view not only interior regression but exterior duplication as well, and with it the possibility that the entire film is a kind of *mise en abyme* of the surrounding (but, for reasons we have begun to explore, unspeakable) reality. The rigorous textual autonomy of a work can only be guaranteed by maintaining a separation between history *in* the film and the history *of* the film, and between its informative and performative dimensions. Such separations are arbitrary at best, however, and ultimately prove purely hypothetical or even impossible.

In the case of *Hiroshima mon amour*, it was in the interests of the French ministry of culture to maintain just such a separation. In addition, the structuralist climate in which the film was released no doubt encouraged critics to view texts' own histories as alien and thus to police the separation of text from context. To wonder how its conditions of production might shape a film's internal functioning, structuration, and even its thematic material would raise apparently taboo questions. To illustrate the arbitrary barriers maintained between internal textual functioning and the texts' history (both the history evoked thematically in the works and the history of their production as this might shape the text), we have only to compare two projects by Edgar Morin. We have already examined the UNESCO survey that he supervised. In an essay about the conditions in which the New Wave appeared, Morin was able to provide a concise and perceptive overview of the historical context in which the New Wave films were created.[72] He then appended his essay as an introduction to the survey report, in which contextual evidence was never taken into account in the analyses of the films' content!

Most theories of *mise en abyme* emphasize the centripetal movement of the device, its internal mirroring mechanisms, its aporia, and its erasure of origins. Even if its centrifugal effects are noted, as they were by Genette and Lucien Dällenbach,[73] these are interpreted as bringing the reader or viewer into the fiction but never as implying that a work can actually be turned inside out and examined in the light of the "text" of its own history. Only by realizing that the two movements are inseparable, however—that complete textual autonomy is a myth—can we begin to appreciate the interpenetration of history and text.

2. Problems of Plotting: *La Route des Flandres*

One must imagine Sisyphus happy. – Albert Camus

Claude Simon's *La Route des Flandres* (1960; *The Flan-*
ders Road), for which he won the Prix de l'Express and which many consider his
best novel, is another tale told by a survivor.[1] The narrator, Georges, partici-
pated in the defeat and rout of the French army in Flanders in May 1940, and he
attempts to reconstruct that traumatic experience some six years later. Like the
French woman of *Hiroshima mon amour,* he is fixated on an "image of ultimate
horror," a scene that he witnessed: his cousin and commanding officer, Captain
de Reixach, was shot down by machine-gun fire during the disorderly retreat.
Like the French woman, Georges tries to reconstruct that half-remembered,
half-repressed scene. The result is a narrative pervaded by a sense of destruction,
death, and collapse at all levels. The reality of the event, however, along with its
possible meanings, is inaccessible to him, and while he brings it into the present
by telling it again and again, it becomes progressively more enigmatic, complex,
and ramified, blending with other events and with thoughts and sensations
from the present. Again like the French woman in *Hiroshima,* Georges finds his
rambling memory triggered by a sexual encounter in the present, although the
links between the framing situation and the memories are structured differently,
as I will show. This encounter too ends in separation; the novel inscribes a military and national debacle in the present story of a romantic failure. As in *Hiro-*
shima mon amour, the past in its reality is absent and can only be evoked by fragments within another tale, itself full of enigmas and discontinuities. Unlike the
French woman, however, Georges and his readers do not even have before them
the filmic images that could create an illusion of presence, an *être-là.* While film
can materialize and then erase the past in a re-presentation, language maintains a
varying but insurmountable distance from the past as absence. Georges is an Orpheus who never manages to bring back the past at all, even to lose it again; he
can only wander in a tangle of words.

55

If in *Hiroshima mon amour* historiography arises from the interplay of memory and image, the epistemological quest of *La Route des Flandres* turns on the intertwining of memory with language. The inherent material features of a linguistic medium (its power to produce metaphors, connotations, and rhymelike connections based on sonorities) and established literary codes (generic conventions and the expectation of closure as they shape plot) create a magnetic field that repels recollection. In Simon's writing, the forward metonymic pull of language is incessantly at war with its (metaphoric) capacity to embody recollection.[2] From this struggle emerges a vision (if not a version) of the past in which it is impossible to disentangle language from history. As Simon put it, "Water is composed of oxygen and hydrogen, of course, but who can distinguish between the two when the water runs from the tap?"[3]

This entanglement is played out as a tension between simultaneous mental images and the unavoidable progression of narration and plot and as an opposition between history and its representations. In whatever direction its themes or temporal dimensions point, the novel is constrained to move forward, away from memory and history. This, among other reasons, is why it is impossible to reconstruct the past outside the mediation of language. Thirteen years before *La Route des Flandres,* Simon was already exploring his realization that what we call memory is as much a process of invention as it is one of recall; asking himself why he concerned himself with memory at all, in that case, he replied that he wrote "in order to try to recollect what happened during the moment I was writing."[4] If the process of writing produces its own memories, history becomes very problematic indeed.

Among his other difficulties, Georges suffers from his own contradictory status as a character. The reader must continually ask who is speaking, as the story passes from a historical third-person "il" to an intersubjective "je" and back, between interiority and exteriority. Maurice Merleau-Ponty credits Simon, along with Michel Butor, with inventing an "intermediate person," neither first nor third person, who narrates from nowhere and everywhere at once.[5] Text and character converge, so that a multifarious surface gains ascendancy over any individual speaking voice. Georges, in whose mind (in whose narration) everything takes place, is himself no more than a place where images and memories intersect. His voice is so dispersed and refracted that in the end it hardly matters which of the characters does the telling, as is suggested in a dialogue from a prison camp: "and Blum (or Georges): 'Are you through?', and Georges (or Blum): 'I could go on', and Blum (or Georges): 'So go on'" (140). Along with other New Novelists, Simon believes that character is a convention of reading: the self, the subject, is defined by the images that constantly traverse it. "You might just as well try to hold water in your hands. Go ahead and try," writes Simon in *La Corde raide*. "Try and find yourself. 'I is another [*je est un autre*].' Not true: 'I is others."[6] Ludovic Janvier, writing in praise of Simon, and Jean-Bertrand Barrère, for the opposition, agree that in Simon's novels history is something that passive survivor-rememberers undergo, rather than "make."[7] Not simply the hapless survivor of the events he recounts, Georges is also the product rather than the origin of his story.

In addition to calling Georges a character, therefore, it is helpful to think of him as dramatizing at least two other functions. First, *Georges* can be considered the name of the tenuous and unreliable narration itself, as it struggles to weave a coherent discourse from discontinuous strands of memory. Michel Butor calls novels a form of research or quest, adding that the modern world requires new cognitive tools that will upset old habits of perception and foster new forms of consciousness.[8] And Simon points out that in Ancient Greek "the word *istoria* does not mean 'history' in the sense we understand it today, but research, inquiry."[9] In keeping with these views, we can say that *La Route des Flandres* is not "about" the public events of the Flanders defeat in any ordinary sense. Even most of the historical signposts are missing or merely suggested through detail or allusion. Rather, it is about the (re)search to remember, to master, and especially to formulate that experience in words. Georges (or the narration) finds that he is unable to become a discourse on history, but only a tentative meta-discourse. Rather than formulating anything coherent, the narration (or Georges) repeats, turns back, and is unable (or refuses, for reasons to be investigated) to conclude.

Second, Georges is a reader—of his own experiences and their interconnections with historical events and processes and of books, as Blum repeatedly points out. The extent to which the past can be understood in the present is constantly diminished by the capacity of words to produce their own events. As readers of Georges's readings, we are subject to the same contradictory pull between a (hi)story that can be reconstructed and attention that must be paid to the distancing and creatively proliferating textual work. Thus we are in a position relative to the novel that Georges occupies with respect to the past, and his desire to interpret that past is analogous to the critical attempt to interpret the novel. Any attempt to forge a coherent whole on his part or the reader's is undermined by its own contradictions and mediations. His task and ours can be described by borrowing the epigraph from Simon's novel *Histoire* (1967): "It submerges us. We organize it. It falls to pieces. We organize it again and fall to pieces ourselves." Where *Hiroshima mon amour* figured forth a scene of spectators *en abyme*, *La Route des Flandres* can be seen as a novel about interpretations or readings of the past (and interpretations of interpretations). Again, an abyssal configuration suggests the possibility of endless repetition and infinite mediation.

In trying to construct a reading of history's enigmas, Georges is repeatedly frustrated, and his identity fragmented. His anguished question, "How can you tell [*comment savoir*]?" reverberates throughout the novel, revealing to what degree the events themselves are displaced by the drama of interpretation. In the framing story, in which he tries to reconstruct the past, Georges never gets out of bed. He is a fairly absurd hero, condemned to repeat his stories ad infinitum in a doomed attempt to understand. He is also an absurd hero in some of the senses meant by Camus: he lucidly undertakes a task he knows to be futile. The reader of Georges's reading, that strange metacharacter, is also condemned to repeat, either because the text itself tells its story over and over or because it is often necessary to flip back a few pages to locate the beginning of a sentence or of a parenthetical digression itself dilated by digressions. As each reading contests the one before, interpretation becomes a rock to be rolled uphill. This is why I have chosen Camus as epigraph and intertext here and Sisyphus as a patron of readers in and of the novel.

DOING TIME, MAKING TIME

Victory authorizes all sorts of representations, the novel maintains. As an example from Revolutionary times, an allegorical painting reminiscent of Delacroix's *Liberty Leading the People* (1830) describes a woman wearing white robes and a Phrygian bonnet and holding a sword as she confers on successive generations "the right to make speeches [*le droit de discourir*]" in picture, song, and tale (159). A discourse of defeat is more difficult to formulate, however, especially years after the events, when memories are relived. Governments, or an "established sense" ("un sens institué," as Jean Ricardou calls it),[10] tend to suppress stories of defeat, humiliation, and disillusionment or transform them into comforting and justifying mythologies. Even when it is described, defeat is portrayed as a momentary dip in a plot line that will turn out better later on and upon which it is possible to reflect in habitual ways. When Stendhal's Fabrice del Dongo suffers defeat at Waterloo, he is embarrassed at his unheroic showing and mourns at the thought that his ideals of glory have been smashed "like those of the heroes of the *Jerusalem Delivered*."[11] Yet his sense of self and the literary categories of character and plot remain undisturbed and coherent, protected by the affectionately condescending care of an omniscient narrator. Fabrice's is still a hero's destiny; history is still going on out there even if Fabrice missed the boat this time around.

By contrast, *La Route des Flandres* construes the debacle of 1940 as responsible not only for the fall of France but also for the defeat of language and the disintegration of representation: Georges and his fellow soldiers find themselves "in full retreat or rather rout or rather disaster in the middle of this collapse of everything as if not an army but the world itself the whole world and not only in its physical reality but even *in the representation the mind can make of it*" (16, emphasis added). Collapsing along with belief in the objectivity of history and the possibility of heroism, then, are the traditional means to formulate the loss.[12] In Georges's view, the memory of war leads to reinterpretation of everything that went before. Exploration in and of a language that is inherently fragmentary is a highly unreliable (but the only authentic) way of knowing the past. The novel's working title was "Fragmentary description of a disaster."[13] In the final title, the word *route,* derived from the Latin *via rupta,* or "broken way," points both to the debacle itself (a rout [*déroute*]) and to the fractured narrative path to its reconstruction.

Furthermore, in contrast to the Stendhalian "mirror one carries along the road," Simon sees the novel as a "stationary mirror" (and, we might add in light of the above, a cracked one). Whereas events occur in some order, or at least some temporal sequence, memory contains everything all at once, in images. Writing inevitably imposes a new sequence, much as archaeologists unearth ambiguous shards and glue them together, filling in the gaps of a forgotten monument with grey putty. Simon rejects this manner of reconstruction, preferring to preserve or even emphasize discontinuity, ambiguity, and loss.[14]

In his infrequent statements about literature, Simon refers repeatedly to the plastic arts and spatial images to help him describe the activity of writing. A painter before he became a novelist, Simon sees the novel as pictorial and the writer's task, like that of an artisan, to "fabricate a text, or rather, a textual object."[15] He has even described writing as if it were a purely spatial or geometric problem of the type "consider a triangle; what are its properties?"[16] The problem of writing is that of describing a visually imagined scene. Although language and time evolve successively, he says, "for me, it's not at all a question of translating time or duration, but of *rendering what is simultaneous.* In painting, the painter must reduce to two dimensions a world that has three. In literature too the problem is to transpose from one dimension to another: to translate into duration and time images that coexist in memory" (emphasis in the original).[17] Before Georges begins to remember the war, then, his creator has had his own struggle with time. Simon claims to have written *La Route des Flandres,* not from an outline, but using instead as a visual guide a skein of colored threads, which helped him to keep track of his intricate and dispersed composition of characters and themes. In this sense, the novel is less a temporal narrative than a spatial, pictorial ensemble. Describing the novel as a tableau (Simon) and remembering the war (Georges) are thus analogous activities. Georges is not a writer; in fact, he rejects writing and words as he repudiates his father, portrayed in Lacanian fashion as a personification of Language. Nevertheless, Georges's refrain— "Comment savoir?"—evokes the same dilemmas as Simon's "Comment écrire?"

Georges's consideration of the past is concentrated in his search to know whether de Reixach walked his horse deliberately into an enemy ambush. He suspects that, if so, this virtual suicide may have been motivated by his wife's infidelities. Initially, his only evidence for this suicide hypothesis is the remembered scene itself. Especially insistent is the image of de Reixach's final, fatal gesture before falling from his horse: his sole response to machine guns was to charge anachronistically with an aristocratic ancestral sword. In his desire to know the truth about de Reixach, Georges seeks out his widow, Corinne, and seduces her. Her presence both unlocks and complicates his memories. The narration unfolds, mostly as interior monologue, while Georges lies half-awake in bed beside Corinne, unraveling bits of memories, fantasies, evidence, and sensations from the past and present. Each time his memory returns to the scene, more detail emerges and more layers of personal and public history adhere to his story. Eventually the novel encompasses a period of almost a century and a half, ending in the late summer of 1946 (the present tense of Georges's narration) and stretching back to the last decade of the eighteenth century, when a common ancestor, a de Reixach and a member of the Revolutionary Convention, voted the death penalty for Louis XVI.[18] If novels are a form of research or a means of knowing, Georges's quest is a double one, articulated around his desire to "know" in both the sexual and the epistemological sense.

Tension between the "stationary mirror" and the temporality of writing appears in the novel in the form of two qualities of temporal experience. One of these is stopped time, described as gluey and viscous, a sort of "greyish [formaldehyde]" (92), or again as frozen solid, like ancient worlds and extinct species imbedded in ice (27). This is the synchronous imagery of myth: "We weren't in the autumn mud we weren't anywhere a thousand years or two thousand years earlier or later in the middle of madness murder the Atrides, riding across time" (93). It is also the arrested time of traumas to which the mind returns as to a vivid nightmare, as in this description of a trainload of prisoners: "swarming slowly creeping over each other like reptiles in the suffocating odour of excrement and sweat, trying to remember how long we had been in that train a day and a night or a night and a day and a night but that doesn't have any meaning time doesn't exist" (19). Portraits and mental images have a similar atemporal immobility: "collections of legendary sires immobilized for eternity in the tarnished gold frames . . . haloed" (47). And it is in this ahistorical dimension that women exist for Georges, who sees not individual women but all women fused into an Ideal Woman, simultaneously mother, virgin, and whore, "not a woman but the very idea, the symbol of all women" (34). Ultimately Woman represents for Georges a fantasy of return to a prehistoric womb and beyond to a primal and undifferentiated magma. But if these images of synchrony seem sometimes to offer an escape from the universal collapse and decay, such protection is only momentary, as ice melts revealing stinking rotting mammoths, and the woman turns out to have a will of her own. Or again, timelessness represents not escape from time's flow but entrapment in its traumas and their consequences. Georges cannot, any more than the French woman in Hiroshima can, retreat for long into an ahistorical, mad "eternity." Instead, he frantically repeats his question, "What time is it?" as if seeking reassurance that chronology, and with it the possibility of a future escape, might exist somewhere.

Interwoven among the images of frozen time, writing, and recounting, Georges's memory traces a contrasting path in historical time, or what the novel calls clock time [*le temps des horloges*]. This is the dimension in which decisions are made and events happen and are remembered. What Mircea Eliade calls "profane" and Sartre "existential" time, this dimension could be represented by a horizontal line. Although its logic is chronological (or metonymic), it is inherently disorganized and characterized by entropy and accumulation, always prey to the temptation of retreat into the atemporality of myth. If this is the time in which people can verify that they are alive (Georges asking, "What time can it be?"), it is also the temporal dimension in which they must imagine their own death at the end of the line. Georges (with Simon's other narrators from *Le Tricheur* through *Les Géorgiques*) sees chronology as bringing disintegration, decay, and the erosion of any meanings he could construct. Everything is incessantly worn down by "the incoherent, casual, impersonal and destructive work of time" (231).

In "The Myth of Sisyphus" Camus also visualizes life as a chronological line as he confronts questions of suicide and meaning: "After all, it's a matter of dying. Yet a day comes when a man notices or says that he is thirty. Thus he asserts his youth. But simultaneously he situates himself in relation to time. He takes his place in it. He admits that he stands at a certain point on a curve that he acknowledges having to travel to its end. He belongs to time, and by the horror that seizes him, he recognizes his worst enemy."[19] Along this diachronic axis, Georges's desires to remember, to recount, and to "know" take the form of linear quests to escape mortality, and events and memories evoked can be geometrically "plotted." The past is seen from the night Georges spends with Corinne in late summer 1946. From that point, his retrospection takes him back to 1940, his capture, his years as a prisoner of war, and to the time of the Convention and the ancestor, become a general under Napoleon. The movement of memory, especially involuntary or sensory memory, away from death toward the allure of a mythical temporality has led many critics to compare Simon to Proust.[20]

But the plot line of *La Route des Flandres* is more complicated than time moving forward and memory moving back, because for Georges death lurks at both ends of the line. Thinking forward means encountering his own inevitable decline and death, but looking back means the war, and especially de Reixach's death or suicide, preceded by that of the analogous ancestor. From 1946, the novel moves in flashbacks and flashforwards. Time and memory move in both directions: Georges remembers, but he also remembers himself remembering, and he remembers himself looking forward. Moreover, he looks forward from the present toward the future. His stories emanate from not one but two nodes: the present, where he is making time with Corinne, is interwoven with the past, where he was doing time in a prisoner-of-war camp. In both cases, narration is desire—for sex, for survival, even for salvation.

In the German camp, Georges and his two companions exchange valuables for a sack of dirty flour. Like three grizzly Scheherazades, they also exchange fantasies and scabrous stories, drawing from the past, the future, and the imagined. Their interpretations of de Reixach's death and of Corinne's behavior and personality are a narrative escape route along a syntagmatic axis. To appease their hungers, they invent Corinne as an edible delight: she is candy, milk, even a communion wafer. Georges sees her as dressed in cherry red, and it is his mouth that imagines her most vividly. Past and present stories implicate each other reciprocally. In prison, Georges reinterprets de Reixach's death in light of the ancestor's, and vice versa. In the present, his failure with Corinne seems determined by the stories he told and imagined about her in the past, and since he retells those stories in the present, her physical presence determines them as well. Georges survives because he tells and retells stories, reshaping them according to his needs. In fact, it is his stories that constitute his survival. They weave back and forth, avoiding narrative and mortal linearity, and in the process produce the novel's "plot," in both the narrative and geometric senses of the term, and the history it contains. To continue, it will now be necessary to examine some of the shapes that plot takes.

If *Georges* is the name of the narration, as I have argued, then wherever it goes, he goes also; its repetitions are his. When he turns back and retraces ground already covered, the reader must do the same. Moreover, as Georges's memories turn and return in the flow of his words, historical events and epochs are brought into the tangle of his stories, so that transformations the novel effects on the shape of narration will have implications for what can be imagined as the plots of history. I suggest toward the end of this chapter that Simon's meandering historical novel points the way toward new ways of confronting history as it happens. This is possible because of Simon's implicit conviction, which he shares with other New Novelists and with critics, that there exists a reciprocal determination between the stories a civilization tells itself and the history it produces.

In prison, and especially with Corinne, Georges remembers endless time and space covered on horseback—fleeing in panic during the cavalry retreat, wandering lost in the Flanders forest, or simply riding from town to town in search of food and shelter. The rhythm of riding informs that of the sentences, and its vocabulary provides many of the puns that articulate the story. (For example, as de Reixach's jockey, Iglésia "had ridden [*montait*] for him, and not only his horses they said" [39].) In addition, large segments of the novel are devoted to a horse race. Shortly, I will discuss one particular horse in detail, but for now I want to take a look at the paths traveled by horses and their riders. The itineraries followed by Georges and the narration are what permit reconciliation of the chronological temporality of writing and reading with the spatial images of a painterly imagination. They also constitute the novel's innovative redefinitions of the concept "plot." Key words are *cheminement* [trudging, plodding], *carrefours* [crossroads], and *chevauchement* [horseback riding, but also overlapping of categories, as occurs in puns and in the use of fictional scenes that also allegorize problems in theory].[21]

Descriptions of the text as a traveler appear in Simon's statements after the period of *La Route des Flandres,* as he increasingly aligned himself with the theoretical views of other New Novelists. In particular, his images resemble Ricardou's description of the novel as "the adventure of writing" rather than "the writing of an adventure." The retroactive aptness of the image to describe *La Route des Flandres* suggests the affinities that drew Simon to the other New Novelists and led him to evolve in the directions he has since the early 1960s. Images of the text or traveler and its relevance to Georges are most apparent in Simon's preface to his *Orion aveugle* (1970; *Blind Orion*). Taking as his point of departure the name of the series in which the book appeared, Les Sentiers de la création, he declares that he knows no other paths of creation than "those cleared open step after step, that is to say word after word, by the plodding along [*cheminement*] of writing itself."[22] The novel thus becomes an imaginary landscape to be explored by a process of narration, by a narrator, and by a reader. That *cheminement* is not a linear quest, however: its only goal is "the exhaustion of the voyager exploring an inexhaustible landscape." Along the way, the traveler comes upon semantically and phonetically loaded words that Simon calls "crossroads [*carrefours*] where several routes intersect." These words send the narration off on multiple, overlapping excursions and unexpected digressions. The traveler faces choices, and the path bifurcates and returns, all of which makes for an involuted and looping itinerary.

Simon's description of blind Orion's narrative path, continually proliferating at the *mots-carrefours,* is so strikingly applicable to the path followed by the protagonists of *La Route des Flandres* that it is worth a closer look. That path, we read,

is quite different from the path [*chemin*] usually followed by the novelist . . . who, setting out from a "beginning" arrives at an "end." Mine turns and returns on itself, as might a traveler lost in a forest, retracing his steps, trying again, misled (or guided?) by the resemblance of certain spots that are in fact different and that he thinks he recognizes, the different aspects of a single spot, his course cutting across itself, passing again through points already traversed, like this

and at the "end" one might even find oneself back at the "beginning."

It is difficult to believe that this passage describes not Georges but Orion. Elsewhere, Simon makes the link explicit between his image of narration as a wanderer and the lost soldiers of *La Route des Flandres.* That novel, he says, follows "the horsemen in their wandering (or the narrator wandering in a forest of images)."[23]

Another figure, devised specifically for *La Route des Flandres,* is described so as to resemble a segment of the above tangle. Three loops in the form of a cloverleaf (Simon calls it a "trefoil") form the path that brings Georges and his cavalry companions back to a spot in the road where they find a dead horse in progressive stages of decomposition. This horse, to which I too will return shortly, remains imprinted in Georges's mind. It becomes an obsession, and it colors his descriptions of other things. Since Georges's own spiritual itinerary and the novel's tripartite organization follow the same outline, the cloverleaf motif must be considered a major structuring pattern. Finally, in a theoretical essay, Jean Ricardou uses a trilobate figure (which he too calls a "trefoil") as a graphic image of a text as it is structured by reading. Using a series of dots, Ricardou plots repetitions of words (or phrases, images, or large segments of text) along a wavy line representing the flow of narration. When these dots are superimposed—as they are in the consciousness of a reader—the resulting figure resembles a series of knotted loops.[24] Repetition, then, is the raw material of fiction both in the novel and in Georges's memory, and the cloverleaf path of the soldiers' wanderings becomes a model for other repetitions in the novel.

Almost nothing in *La Route des Flandres* happens only once. The debacle of 1940 repeats the fall of Napoleon's army, and de Reixach's possible suicide is a refiguration of his ancestor's death.[25] Corinne is the ideal fantasized woman, but so is a peasant woman glimpsed momentarily by the light of a lantern. That peasant woman figures in a tale of jealous animosity that mirrors the novel's other amorous triangles. If Corinne might have been unfaithful to de Reixach by having an affair with Iglésia,[26] Georges then plays Iglésia's role in Corinne's second marriage. And while Georges repudiates his father, Pierre, he finds a substitute father figure in de Reixach, a configuration that casts an incestuous coloring on his liaison with Corinne and recalls the incest theme in the peasant's story. Part of the novel's thickness is to be found in this endless dance of substitutions in a proliferation of often very sinister doubling effects.

The most insistent of all such duplications is Georges himself, who is both past and present, character and story, "je" and "il." The first time we become aware of his double pronominal status is just after the first description of the dead horse (23). Until then the only narrator had been a "je." Otto Rank helps to explain this switch when he maintains that duplication can be a way of denying death and loss. Commenting on Rank's study of doubles, Harry Tucker observes that the theme of the double seems itself to return to popularity during or just after major upheavals such as wars. Although Tucker concludes that no causal relationship has been established, he finds, quite sensibly, that "wars and other extensive disturbances of society are among those occasions which cause man to ask himself fundamental questions about his identity—an identity which he finds existing on various levels or even in fragmentation." *La Route des Flandres* lends credence to these and other speculations.[27] Although death is everywhere, finality is nowhere: de Reixach dies at least three times, and other scenes and characters multiply at least as frantically following the tangled plot line sketched above. Simon claims that Corinne and the dead horse are two fixed points to which the narration (and Georges) must consistently return.[28] I think these points must be seen, at least initially, as more abstract narrative principles. Georges's desire for Corinne is his desire to tell (her) his story; she is the motivating intention that makes his narration travel from its first word to its last. Georges's fantasy of Corinne propels him forward just as surely as his need to know the past pulls him backward in time. The riderless dead horse is an image of disintegration and the end (if not closure) at which life and narration must ultimately arrive. The doubling back of plot and the pairing of scenes, characters, images, and words are the loops that fill the space between desire and its extinction.

There is, of course, repetition in every fictional text, and the project of a non-linear plot is not a new idea. Rarely are these concerns elevated to the obsessive and theoretical status they attain in certain New Novels, however, and rarely are repetition and bifurcation used as richly and productively as in *La Route des Flandres* to determine the shape of a narrative. Serge Doubrovsky has remarked on the "obsessional unity" of Simon's writing, which he says is often characterized by a "compulsion to return."[29] Peter Brooks proposes that our understanding of beginnings, middles, and ends in fiction can be refined by considering Freud's formulation of the repetition compulsion as a dynamic model of plot. Freud's model, writes Brooks, and he could just as well be describing *La Route des Flandres,* "effectively structures ends (death, quiescence, non-narratability) against beginnings (Eros, stimulation into tension, the desire of narrative) in a manner that necessitates the middle as detour, as struggle toward the end under the compulsion of imposed delay, as arabesque in the dilatory space of the text."[30] *La Route des Flandres* takes these narratological givens hyper-literally: desire takes the form of sexual desire, and the end is death, a return to an earlier state, which Freud finds beyond repetition. Pleasure takes the form of Georges's return to the womb via Corinne, but his pleasure mimics the dead horse's return to the earth, its forelegs folded in a fetal position (24). What is inhabitual about the plot of *La Route des Flandres,* and what makes Freud's, Brooks's, and Rank's remarks particularly apt, is that the end of the novel is not an end at all; on the other hand, death is to be found everywhere in the middle.

DÉJÀ VU

The importance and centrality of the dead horse are indisputable. Its links to other themes are less clear. While its reappearance provides a motif of repetition and structure, for Georges it becomes an object of simultaneous obsessive fascination and horror. Here is the second discovery of the horse:

They (Iglésia and he) stayed where they were, stupefied, sitting on their skeletal mounts in the middle of the road, while he thought with a kind of stupor, a despair, a calm disgust (like the convict letting go the rope that has allowed him to climb up the last wall, crouching, standing up, preparing himself to jump, and then discovering that he had just fallen at the very feet of his guard who is waiting for him): "But I've already seen this somewhere. I know this. But when? And where was it?" (78)

Thus ends the first part of the novel. The parenthetical comparison to a prisoner recaptured conveys the asphyxiating panic of the experience while suggesting already its deadly reduplication. Georges will see this scene again at least twice.

Now compare the above description with this one:

Once, as I was walking through the deserted streets of a provincial town in Italy which was strange to me, on a hot summer afternoon, I found myself in a quarter the character of which could not long remain in doubt. Nothing but painted women were to be seen at the windows of the small houses, and I hastened to leave the narrow street at the next turning. But after having wandered about for a while without being directed, I suddenly found myself back in the same street, where my presence was now beginning to excite attention. I hurried away once more, but only to arrive yet a third time by devious paths in the same place.

This narrator follows the same sort of looped itinerary as the one Simon's soldiers follow. There is nothing inherently frightening about his experience, any more than the sight of a dead horse on a battlefield would seem to warrant Georges's exaggerated horror. But this narrator too describes his feeling of panic at this continued involuntary return to the very spot he was trying to leave behind. Repetition seems to be determined by a fate or compulsion these narrators cannot control. The panic derives, not from the situation itself, but from a "sense of helplessness sometimes experienced in dreams."

The narrator in the second quotation is Freud, and the anecdote supplies an example of the uncanny, that dreamlike realm of the simultaneously strange and familiar.[31] Freud's example imitates the trefoil configuration of the soldiers' wanderings and the narrative structure of *La Route des Flandres,* and indeed, Freud's discussion of the uncanny describes not only the reappearance of the horse but many of the novel's other features as well. Unlike the French woman of *Hiroshima,* Georges is self-conscious about the repetitions in his behavior and in his story, feels that they are compulsive or involuntary, and finds them sinister. Perhaps it is his awareness of the uncanny nature of events that makes him find history overwhelming (something he undergoes rather than controls) and respond to it passively. Or, as Freud puts it, "It is only this factor of involuntary repetition which surrounds with an uncanny atmosphere what would otherwise be innocent enough, and forces upon us the idea of something fateful and inescapable where otherwise we should have spoken of 'chance' only." What seems to be a fortuitous encounter is the work of the unconscious, bringing back what was repressed or forgotten, and so Simon's tangled cloverleaf loops mark the itinerary of the wanderer brought back to the scene of trauma. These returns are thus anything but random or arbitrary, and what seems strange is strange only because it is strangely familiar.[32]

Freud defines the uncanny as "that class of the terrifying that leads back to something long known to us, once very familiar," and then more pointedly asserts that "the uncanny proceeds from something familiar which has been repressed." Before discovering why Georges is compelled to reencounter a scene that so horrifies and disgusts him, it will be necessary to determine just what it is that he is repeating. There are horses everywhere in *La Route des Flandres* and in Simon's other novels. The attention that this single dead horse commands seems disproportionate given the surrounding massacre of men and beasts. It would not be surprising to find that horses are the focus of a displaced concern or that this one dead horse tells the story of Georges's contradictory impulses to remember and to forget.

First, through the rhythm of their gait and a convenient homophony, horses are associated with negation, as in the following passage:

the horse apparently starting of its own accord and still at a walk [*au pas*] naturally without haste yet not slowly either [*non plus*] and not [*pas non plus*] even casually: simply at a walk [*au pas*]. I suppose he wouldn't [*n'aurait pas*] have started trotting for all the money in the world, that he wouldn't [*n'aurait pas*] have driven his spurs into the horse wouldn't [*n'aurait pas*] have moved faster if a gun had gone off in his ear and that's exactly what happened there are expressions that are convenient: at a walk, then [*au pas donc*] (15).

Here, *pas* is a *mot-carrefour* where horses and negation intersect. A return to the crossroads where one horse lies rotting is thus simultaneously a return to (but not yet of) a repressed theme, as Freud points out that *unheimlich* [uncanny, unhomelike] crosses the path of its opposite, *heimlich,* with the prefix *un-* appearing as the "token of repression."

What obsesses Georges is the cadaver's state of decomposition, which seems to progress at an unnatural rate, "by a kind of transmutation or accelerated transubstantiation" (81). The earth reabsorbs her own issue by digestion or more insistently by a curious sort of reverse birth, with the horse returning toward a preanimate form folded in a fetal position (25). Here the uncanny rejoins the repetition compulsion of *Beyond the Pleasure Principle*. It is in this context too that the horse's return to a muddy "matrix" can be compared to Georges's fantasy in his affair with Corinne of a return to the womb. Sex with her seems to him "the milk of oblivion" (193), which makes time stop ("only for a second, drunk thinking it was for ever") or move backward, like "all the rivers beginning to flow in the opposite direction rising towards their sources" (196). Alternating between Corinne's body and memories of hiding terrified in a grassy ditch, the description itself is a lyrical and tumultuous outpouring of words and images that transports Georges back to what Freud too fantasized as a fairy-tale return to a forgotten origin, "the former *heim* [home] of all human beings, to the place where everyone dwelt once upon a time and in the beginning."

In its return to the earth, the horse passes through stages in which it is neither horse nor earth, neither animate nor inanimate, another situation likely to evoke terror, according to Freud. Georges describes the horse vividly, as "something unexpected, unreal, hybrid," as "what you could recognize as having been a horse" (23). *La Route des Flandres* teems with hybrids and monsters. Characters are half-human, half-animal: Iglésia has a face like a lobster claw; a portrait shows a great-grandmother with a carnival mask that causes her to resemble a monstrous bird; an enemy soldier with murderous intent disguises himself as a maid, and so on. By far the majority of the half-human composites refer to horses: Corinne is called a "woman-chestnut [*alezane-femme*]." In an image borrowed from an old letter describing a centaur, the ancestor is first called a "sire [*géniteur*]," then a "stallion," and later simply a "man horse [*homme-cheval*]." The sexual act is described as a violent coupling of incompatible classes or species, for which the idea of *chevauchement* conveys the monstrosity. These are examples of the collapse and overlap of categories that demonstrate the defeat of everything, including language.

All these metaphorical and literal *chevauchements* bring the reader continually back to the ride through the Flanders woods and to what is the most insistent *homme-cheval* of all: the "equestrian statue" composed of de Reixach and his horse, walking toward sudden death before the narrator's eyes. So united are the two components that it is "as if he and his horse had been cast together out of one and the same material, a grey metal" (13). This and other passages suggest that Georges's obsession with the dead horse must be seen as a return to de Reixach's death, as if the horse itself, like some mutilated synecdoche, stood for the whole "equestrian statue." Focus slides from horse to man without warning. In the midst of describing the horse's "accelerated transubstantiation," for example, Georges asks, "How can you say how long a man is dead" (81). At points such as this one, he breaks off abruptly or moves on to another subject, such as Corinne.

The return *of* the obsessive image is related to Georges's failure to return *to* the scene: "saying: 'See what?', and I: 'If he's dead. After all even like that at point-blank range the sniper might have missed him, might only have wounded him or only killed his horse since the horse fell when we saw him take out his sabre and . . .', then I stopped" (39). Betraying the dictates of his conscious will, he suppresses the story, but subsequently he returns involuntarily to the spot where only the horse remains. The erased scene, however, the one he did not go back to see, becomes the subject both of his incessant, uncanny return and of his floating question, "Comment savoir?" Not having seen, he imagines. Having survived, he is obsessed with the idea of his own death.

If Corinne is a mother principle in Georges's imagination, in overdetermined ways de Reixach plays the role of a father. The novel's first scene shows him receiving a letter from Georges's mother, Sabine, informing him—as fathers always have to be informed—that he is related to her son.[33] Georges rejects his own parents only to put others in their place. Through a series of substitutions, Corinne replaces Sabine (aided, perhaps, by the similarity of the names) and Georges replaces de Reixach in Corinne's bed. It is no wonder that he is haunted by the possibility that de Reixach might not be dead after all. Fallen at the crossroads, de Reixach is at the center of the novel's Oedipal configurations: the *x* at the center of his name reappears in all the narration's intersecting paths; a displaced incest theme turns up in a story of peasant jealousies; and any hybrid monster might be a sphinx.[34]

In a parallel network of allusions, however, de Reixach also plays the son. His mysterious disappearance from the scene of his own death brings into focus another figure killed at or on a cross(roads). In this version, de Reixach's death turns on a pun: it is a double "passion, with this difference that the site the centre the altar wasn't a naked hill but that smooth and tender and hairy and secret crease in the flesh. . . . Yes: crucified, agonizing on the altar the mouth the cave of" (14). And if, as the stimulus to involuntary memory, Corinne is Georges's *petite madeleine,* for de Reixach she is Magdalene, as the above passage continues: "But after all wasn't there a whore at the other crucifixion too, presuming that whores are indispensable in such things, women in tears wringing their hands and penitent whores, supposing that he had ever asked her to repent."[35]

Although there is more evidence in the text that points to both these stories, and it would be possible to linger at length over either one, their presence in *La Route des Flandres* is not in itself an end of analysis. While the multiple mythical subtexts give the novel an extraordinary density, what interests us here in the stories of the martyred father and son is the narration of the guilty survivor of Laius's or Christ's death. Georges's failure to go back and look, his obsessive memory, and the confessional form of his narrative suggest that what he seeks is not memory at all, or at least not memory alone, but rather something resembling absolution. For while he seeks to remember, he also wants to forget; and although he asks, "Comment savoir?" his rediscovery of the past is uncanny and threatening. Thus can we understand his quest for Corinne, whom he describes as a communion wafer and as the "milk of oblivion." Simon uses Oedipal and Christian motifs self-consciously. The death of de Reixach, like the execution of the king (for which the ancestor was partly responsible), has the mythical function of an archetypal Curse or Original Sin. It is the Fall. And that Fall is inscribed in the fall of France in 1940.

Fall, betrayal, failed responsibility, collapse of everything, suicide—these are the themes of Simon's novel, and they are also the terms in which the debacle of May and June 1940 is described by historians. Although Simon's novel is in no sense a document or an account of the events, aspects of the military and spiritual defeat appear within the novel in countless fictional analogues. Examples range from major failures (anachronistic weaponry and strategy) to curious detail (rumors of German military spies disguised as nuns appear in the form of an allusion to a disguised and deadly "maid"). Historian Marc Bloch, like Claude Simon, served in the army in Belgium and Flanders in 1940, and both were eyewitness-participants at the defeat at the Meuse and the subsequent retreat. Bloch's thorough, thoughtful discussion of the disaster reveals many of the facets that find echoes in *La Route des Flandres:* abdication of responsibility on the part of intellectuals is embodied in Georges's father Pierre; outmoded communications in the field are responsible for the fact that Georges learns from a frantic peasant that the battle has been lost; a sense of betrayal is revealed in Georges's emphasis (and invention) of Corinne's infidelities and de Reixach's disillusionment; rigid conceptions of space and time that prevented effective response to panzer advance might have reproduced a cloverleaf retreat path combining frenetic movement with failure to advance or retreat; and so on.[36]

Bloch emphasizes the fatal failure on the part of the French military and political leadership to realize that a war in 1940 could not be fought with technical and conceptual equipment left over from World War I. He points out that most of the military leaders earned their ranks in the earlier war and were brought out of retirement in 1939. To Bloch's description corresponds de Reixach's advanced age and the ludicrous inappropriateness of his response to attack: his horse is helpless faced with columns of advancing tanks, and his sword is less than useless to fend off automatic weapons. His death is the death of a social and historical anachronism, as poignant and as emblematic as that of de Boeldieu in Jean Renoir's retrospective but also prescient film, *La Grande Illusion* (1937). Although the situations differ, de Reixach, like de Boeldieu, represents a class, even a nation, looking backward. The failure, Bloch makes clear, was not only military, and the suicide was collective.

Indeed, the most telling dimension of Bloch's account, and one of its most striking parallels with *La Route des Flandres,* is its presentation within the conventions of a confessional genre. "The generation to which I belong has a bad conscience," Bloch declares, and he calls the defeat a "stain" and a "sin." France was guilty at all levels of blindly repeating outmoded behavior from earlier eras, he insists, even when such behavior was suicidal. While the Germans were aware of the need to fight a new war, France helplessly reiterated the mentality of previous defeats. In this light, the title of Bloch's indictment—*Strange Defeat*—is itself strange. So convincing is the historian's explanation of France's weaknesses that the defeat takes on the inevitability of his logic. What is strange about this defeat is not the fact of the defeat itself but that it was not strange enough. We might say, in other words, that Bloch's title suggests the presence of compulsive and involuntary repetition in history.

De Reixach's anachronistic gesture has both a historical and a dreamlike quality, then, and its repetition at intervals throughout the novel creates for the reader the same sense of déjà vu that Bloch, a veteran of the First World War, describes. Georges's image of horror—his memory of de Reixach with his sword —is an appropriate one in terms of Bloch's analysis, as it expresses the futility and absurdity of the French predicament in 1940. The national "suicide" must have been on Camus's mind too while he was writing "The Myth of Sisyphus" in 1940. In that essay, Camus describes the human fate as the repetition of futile gestures, with the only possibility of heroism being lucidity. One of his examples of an absurd gesture is familiar: "If I see a man armed only with a sword attack a group of machine guns, I shall consider his act to be absurd."[37] Simon has in effect borrowed Camus's image of absurdity, an image that corresponds only too well to his own vision.

La Route des Flandres introduces another sense of déjà vu with the story of the ancestor, and there emerge some unexpected implications of repetition in history when we compare his story with de Reixach's and the Flanders defeat with Napoleon's "suicidal" war in Spain. Piecing together details about the ancestor, we can read the story of a liberal noble who gave up his privileges (and the particle preceding his name) on 4 August 1789. Fired with enthusiasm for Rousseau, this de Reixach's (or simply this *Reixach's*) career follows the vicissitudes of the Revolution: he votes at the Convention for the king's execution, rises to the rank of general, and leads Napoleon's imperial army into Spain. That invasion, however, more poignantly than most of Napoleon's other campaigns, showed to what extent the Revolution had changed color. Popular resistance was constant during the period of French presence in Spain; only the rich and the hereditary nobles had anything to gain by welcoming the French. Even Joseph Bonaparte, appointed king of Spain in 1808, was horrified when he discovered that the Spanish did not welcome him enthusiastically as his brother had promised. This war, generally called the Spanish War of Independence, ended only when the French army was defeated and driven out of Spain in 1813. By then it was clear that an imperialist conquest could no longer be disguised as a liberating mission. If the de Reixach ancestor waited until 1813 to lose his Revolutionary illusions, he must have been one of the last. In any case, he returns to his family home defeated and disillusioned and shoots himself.[38]

As the details unfold, the ancestor's and the descendant's stories seem to repeat each other. Both de Reixachs are commissioned to lead what turn out to be utterly futile missions. Both die, apparently by suicide, after suffering what Georges sees as a loss of illusions. In each story there is a marital betrayal that mirrors (or stands for) a betrayal by ideals and by superiors; and each suicide prefigures the suicide of a government. Georges even imagines that Captain de Reixach's death is a reenactment of the general's, "as if war, violence, murder had somehow resuscitated him in order to kill him a second time as if the pistol bullet fired a century and a half before had taken all these years to reach its second target to put the final period to a new disaster" (62).

This is Georges's story, however, and it simply does not work. The two deaths might resemble each other, but if we look at their contexts as described by historians more reliable than Georges, we can see that the two disasters are virtually mirror opposites. Although both de Reixachs might have been disillusioned, those disillusionments are different. And if it appears at first that the ancestor did kill himself, this becomes unclear as the novel progresses, and it may even be the result of Georges's inventions that bring the two stories into parallel alignment. The suicide might even stem from Georges's childhood referential illusion, as he contemplated the ancestor in a portrait whose surface had cracked and developed a smudged, ruddy hole in the forehead. Or perhaps the ancestor was shot by his young wife's lover at the end of a midnight ride that brought him home earlier than expected. Most important, while de Reixach dies defending his country from aggression, the ancestor dies as a result of perpetrating a similar invasion on behalf of a French empire.

The role of repetition is again instructive. Georges overlooks differences between his two stories because they are disguised in progressively thicker layers of repetition: disillusionment, betrayal, and suicide mask fundamental ironies contrasting the two historical circumstances. The Flanders defeat of 1940 was not a repetition but a reversal of Napoleon's 1813 retreat from Spain. In other ways, 1940 was also a mirror image of the overall outcome of the "Great War": Hitler's choice of Compiègne (where Germany had conceded defeat in 1918) as the place to conclude the armistice drove home the bitter ironies of that reversal. According to Bloch and others, that change of fortune was to be attributed to France's repetition of outmoded ways of doing things. The pairs 1940 and 1918, 1940 and 1813, evoked by the novel reveal an underlying rhetoric of reversal disguised as repetition (1813 and 1940) and repetition within reversal (1940 and 1914–18). That Simon sees history and especially revolution as ironic series of repetitions and reversals of direction is demonstrated by many of his novels and especially by *Le Palace* (1962), whose epigraph from the *Dictionnaire Larousse* brings us back to graphic images of plot: "Revolution: movement of a body traveling around a closed curve and passing in succession through the same points." While Georges may not be aware of it, the history he tells is "emplotted," to borrow Hayden White's term, in an ironic mode.[39]

One consequence of irony is that it brings the speaker into the story, and along with him, the present frame of his narration. Georges is repeatedly brought back to the present. His question, "What time is it?" threads through the novel as an indication of the present, which is the only time watches tell. And the visibility of the narrative frame again encourages us to look at the temporal frame of the work's production. Simon said he had wanted to write *La Route des Flandres* for twenty years.[40] He finally began the project during a period that was itself characterized by repetition and reversal of past national crises. As a trefoil has three leaves, the stories of the two de Reixachs invite comparison with the historical situation of 1958–60, the period when the novel was written and published. Reversals that come to light when those two stories are compared in their contexts mirror some of the ironies of postwar French history, and 1958 in particular.

For writers and journalists of the Left, former *Résistants* like Camus, Simon, and Sartre among them, the French war in Algeria produced not only disillusionment and a sense of futile effort and failed collective responsibility but also a peculiar sense of déjà vu. For Sartre that war was an eerie trip through the looking glass: commenting on the referendum and constitution that defined de Gaulle's return to power in 1958, he writes that since the execution of Louis XVI, "every good Frenchman is an orphan." Now, however, he says in another article for *Les Temps modernes,* by choosing Charles de Gaulle, the electorate has gotten what it wanted: "King Charles XI." And writing to condemn the use of torture in Algeria, Sartre observes that it is no longer possible to look in the mirror of 1940–44 and see the French as victims, because "victim and executioner no longer have but one face: ours."[41] The Fourth Republic's inability to resolve the Algerian "question" seemed an ominous forecast; that the emblem, if not the hero, of the Resistance should take the reins of a government apparently committed to continued presence in Algeria invited historical comparisons. Seeking parallels for events of 1958, historian Gordon Wright has recourse to reversal and irony, as he describes the situation in terms significant for *La Route des Flandres*:

De Gaulle was authorized to draft a new constitution for approval by popular referendum. If this was a revolution, it was an unusual sort—bloodless, like that of 1870. But if there is any historical parallel for the events of 1958, it may be found not in 1870 but in 1940. There was some irony in the fact that de Gaulle arrived in power in much the same fashion as Pétain—by the abject surrender of the members of parliament, a kind of suicide of the regime. In both cases, there was little popular opposition or even protest; the Fourth Republic, like the Third, died almost without mourners.[42]

Within the weave of Simon's novel, the Algerian war takes its place in a series of national crises that brought national unity and identity (self-representation) into doubt.

I am not arguing that *La Route des Flandres* is *about* Algeria, or de Gaulle, or the Constitution of the First or the Fifth Republic. Rather, I think these structural and discursive echoes indicate that the novel demands to be read in its own time frame. The fact that Georges tells his story within the context of another failure is significant here. His story emanates from his encounter with Corinne; that relationship ends in disaster because Georges is repeating attitudes toward her that seemed natural in prison (in 1940) but are at the very least inappropriate in his dealing with a real (not a fantasized) Corinne, who resents being treated as a "fille à soldats." Like de Reixach and the ancestor, Georges is so fixated on the past that he misses the present. We do not need to repeat his mistake. By emphasizing its own anachronisms and dislocated temporality, and by constantly recalling that Georges's memories are a function of (and in parallel or reversal to) the situation of their enunciation, the narration invites us to place the novel itself in its own history.

It is also significant that Georges's present predicament is a romantic one. Just as evidence (or invention) of tales about sexual betrayal masks the differences between de Reixach and the ancestor and makes their stories seem parallel, Georges's present interpersonal debacle is part of his generalized retreat from involvement in society. He tries, but fails, to understand history as a love story.

He gives up his studies and takes up farming, preferring its more reliable cycles to the uncanny and irregular loops of public events.

One lesson that can be drawn from Georges's juxtaposition of the two de Reixachs is that he too, like his mother Sabine, is motivated by a need to see his progenitors as heroic. Like de Reixach and the ancestor, he has lost many of his illusions as a result of his firsthand experience of defeat, but he has not abandoned the referential illusion of his own stories. His sense of the uncanny nature of events is induced by the stories he tells himself. But if he reads history as uncanny, we can read his stories as ironic.

DÉJÀ LU

"We historians are always reinterpreting the past," Joe went on. "But if history is a trauma, maybe the thing to do is redream it." – John Barth, from his novel *Letters*

In *The Eighteenth Brumaire of Louis Bonaparte,* itself a treatise on certain uncanny elements in French history, Marx makes his famous statement about repetition in history: "Hegel remarks somewhere that all facts and personnages of great importance in world history occur, as it were, twice. He forgot to add: the first time as tragedy, the second as farce."[43] In *La Route des Flandres,* there is no "first time" outside legend, rumor, and family oral history as it is passed down through Sabine's self-serving prattle. There is only the chronological order of the narration, which develops its own characteristic pattern of theme and variation. Therefore, for the purposes of reading Simon, Marx's statement will have to be amended to read that he forgot to add: the first time *recounted* as tragedy, the second time as farce.

As I have suggested, there is nothing uncanny about the historical episodes in the novel once the frame is enlarged to include the teller. What appeared to be fate turns out to be the intention of a storyteller, whether that teller is a general's granddaughter or a former cavalry soldier. Episodes recur again and again, modified and varied at each retelling. Each version contests the previous ones, emphasizing the gaps and absences in history. Historiography, however—that is, the making of history in language—is present at every level. Freud remarks that an uncanny effect is often produced by "effacing the distinction between imagination and reality."[44] If this is the case, then it can be inferred that the referential illusion is a kind of neurosis and the uncanny is a reading effect.

The novel shows a great deal of concern with the genres in which events are cast. As episodes are retold, each version reveals more strings and mirrors and other stage tricks. Furthermore, the implications of each story for the others become apparent. For example, we can see how the death of de Reixach is rewoven to incorporate bits of the ancestor's story, and vice versa. By following the fate of one story—the ancestor's—we can see the progressive rings of skepticism or suspicion that bring the act of telling into perspective and indicate by what mechanisms the novel arrives at an ironic, if inconclusive, reading of history.

The ancestor's story, told for the first time as tragedy, is fairly unembellished. Georges remembers "how that de Reixach had so to speak forfeited his noble status during the famous night of August fourth, how he had later held a seat in the Convention, voted for the king's death, then, probably because of his military learning, been assigned to the armies to get himself beaten at last by the Spanish and then, disavowing himself a second time, had blown his brains out with a pistol" (46). This is the story of Revolutionary enthusiasm, disillusionment, and suicide as it comes to Georges via family legend. The above account, straightforward as it is, is contested by its context, which describes the story's sources and motives. It is Sabine who preserves it, along with the de Reixach family house, papers, and portrait collection; it is Sabine, herself a de Reixach, who believes the story in its tragic form. Georges maintains a certain distance. For him Sabine's ramblings are an "insipid and obsessive chatter," designed to augment the glory of her ancestry—"the line, the race, the caste, the dynasty of the de Reixachs" (42). The hyperbolic crescendo of this series models in miniature the sequential retellings of her story. Especially important, then, is the fact that even though Georges knows the story serves sometimes to deprecate the nobility Sabine did not inherit, sometimes to augment the glory of her ancestry, it is always told as a story of some kind: "these scandalous, or ridiculous, or ignominious, or Cornelian stories" (46). Sabine's account seems coherent enough, and it fits its historical framework, but as Georges elaborates its context, we can see reflections of dictums [*dictons*] ("disait-on, c'est-a-dire disait Sabine"), *faits divers,* and Sabine's Cornelian readings. Although he ridicules Sabine's perspective, Georges inherits her talent for verbal *bricolage.* In order to understand it properly, we have to read his story the way he reads Sabine's.

Which is how Blum proceeds when he rewrites the story of the ancestor as farce. Whereas Georges saw the Revolutionary de Reixach as an "ancestor," Blum calls him a "stallion." Incorporating elements from Georges's musings about Corinne and de Reixach, Blum spins a tale of a defeated general returning home to his only remaining illusion, his little wife, his little pigeon (148), whom he finds in bed with the coachman. In the process of Blum's telling, wife and illusions merge in the figure of "one of those plaster Mariannes in a schoolroom" (141), so that the ancestor is cuckolded and made ridiculous not (only) by his wife but (also) by his illusions and by the Revolution itself, reincarnated as an unfaithful woman. The imagined sexual escapade satisfies their desire for stories, while the woman functions as a mask, as an explanation of what remains puzzling, even as a scapegoat for the disasters of history.

If Sabine's stories are refracted through a Cornelian lens, Blum's intertexts are comedies. He seizes upon Corinne's extreme youth and de Reixach's age to re-emplot the ancestor's demise as a version of Molière's *School for Wives,* rebaptizing his characters accordingly as Agnes and Arnolphe. Of all the novel's characters, Blum is the most conscious of his own storytelling prowess, of the pleasure of reading and textual production. It is he who mocks the ancestor's alleged reading of Rousseau, explaining solemnly that the affinity was motivated not by high ideals but by Rousseau's sexual perversions. According to him, the ancestor ingested the "twenty-three volumes of sentimental, idyllic and confused prose" containing "the prolix and Genevese lessons in harmony and *solfège,* in education, silliness, effusions and genius" (65). And when those illusions (in the form of the Revolution he saw as their fulfillment) were shattered, it was the volumes of Rousseau that furnished, as Blum sardonically puts it, a way to find what could be called a glorious death. That is, unless the family invented this myth afterward.

In spite of his own distance with respect to Sabine's stories, Georges resists Blum's retelling, revealing to what extent he has inherited from his mother the characteristics he mocks. He punctuates Blum's recital with corrections and protests: "No!" "No. you're mixing it all up," "Oh for God's sake," and "Oh, stop!" Unlike Georges, Blum is aware that he is telling stories just for the pleasure of invention and to pass the time in prison. When Georges protests that Blum is mixing up his "facts," Blum calmly replies, "That's right. But I think you can still imagine it" (145), and proceeds to deliver his deliberately composite comedy. It might even be Blum's self-conscious storytelling that fuels Georges's impossible quest to know and his confusion when, in spite of his efforts, history always turns into stories plotted in recognizable genres. Georges is aware that Blum is the projected figure of his own doubts; he echoes Marx and Hegel (and Blum) when he reflects that the story of the ancestor might very well be either high tragedy or a vaudeville act, since "vaudeville is always only an abortive tragedy and tragedy a farce without humour" (147). Blum's understanding of the plots of history is the most sophisticated and self-aware of those proposed by the novel, and it probably corresponds closely to Simon's own.

In Blum's view, history is always told by someone. Moreover, it is always told *for* someone. It is "confiscated, disinfected and finally edible, for the use of official school manuals and pedigreed families" (140). Blum's perspective is made possible by his distance not only from the de Reixach family preoccupations but also from their social class. He sees their stories and their world-view as a function of their class concerns. Like the others, Blum's interpretations are elucidated by their context (in the novel and in society). Shoveling coal in the prison camp, Blum describes his own poor Jewish ancestry, a family of tailors on a street of tailors too concerned with making a living to paint portraits of their ancestors or to consider suicide, or if they did, putting it off until later. From Blum's point of view, "suicide, the drama, the tragedy become a kind of elegant pastime" (210). His is a tradition that has many stories but whose history is silent. His voice intrudes to contest the dominant notions (in the novel and in society) of what constitutes history. Significantly, Georges makes no comments about Blum's own story, which is one of the most humorously wise passages of the novel (and also one of the only firsthand ones). On the other hand, Blum adopts and retells the tales and "pedigrees" of the aristocracy in ways that surpass Georges's capacity for self-irony. What the dying Blum leaves Georges to ponder after the war is the suspicion that his own stories have no function, that they do not even belong to him. Each time Georges's stories fall apart, so does Georges, since he and his stories are coterminous.

These retellings of the ancestor's story (and those of all the novel's other major episodes) show that it is the teller who makes the story tragic or comic or uncanny. The accomplishment of *La Route des Flandres* is to have created a discursive environment in which history becomes denaturalized and strange. That environment extends beyond the novel to include Camus, Marc Bloch, Sartre, Gordon Wright, and others. It is this self-conscious highlighting of its own strangeness that constitutes the novel's most effective historical dimension.

That language itself is uncanny is demonstrated in the novel's first sentence, where we are given a model of the kind of lively *chevauchement* of words that keeps the text moving. The sentence, spanning the entire page, begins with de Reixach holding a letter from Sabine and ends with his statement addressed to Georges, "Your mother's written me." Framed by the letter, the scene takes place early one winter morning in 1940, after a sudden drop in temperature. While de Reixach chats with Georges, horses pass by incessantly in the background, and Georges remembers that the night before the mud was so thick that horses and men sank ankle-deep. Near the end of the sentence he notices that the mud has frozen, leaving horseshoe imprints. Buried in the middle of these careful symmetries is Wack's odd statement about the change in temperature—"The dogs ate up the mud"—and Georges's reflection on Wack's remark: "I had never heard the expression, I could almost see the dogs, some kind of infernal, [mythical] creatures their mouths pink-rimmed their wolf fangs cold and white chewing up the black mud in the night's gloom, perhaps a recollection, the devouring dogs cleaning, clearing away" (11). These monstrous dogs announce the novel's transformations and hybrids, and the phrase "I could almost see" becomes Georges's refrain to describe the vividness of memory (and imagination). But why "perhaps a recollection"? The first "recollection" of the novel is an important clue to all the rest. How often do we hear an expression or a word that we have never really heard and suddenly find it strange? It is familiar and yet unfamiliar, because it is known but at the same time, in a sense, repressed.

Here on the first page, *La Route des Flandres* points out that language itself is uncanny and capable of giving birth to monsters when it reappears in the full force of its literal dimension. Not by accident is this parable of language's return surrounded by the arrival of the letter. Not surprising either is the presence in this first sentence of horses, prefiguring the obsessive and uncanny dead horse, for a *cheval de bataille* [war-horse, even a dead one] is no other than an obsession, an "argument, preferred subject, to which one returns" (*Le Petit Robert* dictionary). Like the escaped convict who finds himself back "at the very feet of his guard," the mud at the captain's feet is thus, in a way, *au pied de la lettre*, that is, literal, which is how we must take the language of the novel. The problem is that when a *cheval de bataille* is seen as an obsession by definition, the historical horse itself fades away, like Mallarmé's "disparition vibratoire selon le jeu de la parole [vibratory disappearance according to the play of words]."

In a 1982 public lecture Simon asserted the following:

In the same way that Valéry used to say that the world was threatened by two dangers, order and disorder, language could be said to be threatened by two dangers as well: on the one hand, that of being considered only as a vehicle of meaning and, on the other hand, that of being considered only as a structure, for it is always *simultaneously* both. It is really in these two potentialities and their perpetual interference that there appears to dwell this wonderful ambiguity [that] provides language with so many tremendous powers.[45]

His evident enthusiasm for language's inescapable and "wonderful ambiguity" is undoubtedly why Simon chooses to exacerbate, in order to make visible, writing's linguistic dimension, which usually remains repressed in writing about history.

The return of language's literal dimension into a text about history poses knotty problems, however, for when language rises to the surface of the text, the past fades. Is the dead horse a signified or a signifier, for example, and is Corinne a figment of Georges's (the narration's) imagination, produced in part by memories of an ancestor "cuckolded by his ideals"? Corinne puts a stop to the wild proliferation of the linguistic imagination by refusing to be the object of a fantasy, the product of someone else's text. But she leaves the novel at that point, leaving Georges oscillating between the horns of his dilemma, and the narration between language and history. Finally, he is reduced to asking not only "Comment savoir?" but also "Que savoir?" (306).

When the opacity of language returns to historiography, the historical signified fades, and when history returns, language seems once again transparent. (This is as true of critical discourse as it is of historiography and the novel.) The linguistic sign is a sphinx, a hybrid of sound and sense, and the historical novel a contradiction in terms. History and the signifier are each other's repressed; the abrupt return of either disrupts our confidence in both. Neither history nor the signifier may be uncanny in itself, but when they occur together, each represses and threatens to chase the other away, as in the oscillation of a figure-ground optical illusion.[46] When we think we have grasped the novel's language (or its history), its history (or its language) returns to dismantle our understanding. Most critics of this novel have dealt, implicitly or explicitly, with one dimension or the other. Readers of Simon's historical novels can fall into one of two traps: language without history or history without language. What I have tried to do is fall into each pitfall in turn, hoping to emerge with a description of the trap.

Georges knows that books imitate events. He also suspects that events imitate books. ("You read too much," retorts Blum, when Georges declares he would not mind dying of love.) Shoved into a cattle car headed for a concentration camp, he wonders if he has been turned into an animal, if he and his companions are "men changed with a tap of a wand into pigs or trees or stones all by reciting some Latin verses" (77). Life is mediated by books—as Emma Bovary never found out—and not only by Ovid but also by all the plots of novels and other cultural texts we use to tell ourselves reality. Usually we are unaware of this process. By showing the power and processes by which texts can produce and erase events, Simon shows the deadly importance of the (hi)stories a culture tells.

BEYOND CONCLUSIONS

Echoing some of the plot configurations I have outlined, Frank Kermode proposes that the minimal model of plot can be found in *tick-tock,* with life (or the novel) as the structured interval between. Having survived *tick,* he says, we live in the expectation of *tock.*[47] This is not the case in *La Route des Flandres:* at the end of the last page, the novel just continues ticking. Novels constructed on pictorial principles, stories that can be reemplotted in an endless array of genres, or plots that follow the turning and returning of words suggest that when death arrives it should arrive in the middle, and not constitute a conclusion or a resolution of puzzles and questions. Since Flaubert at least, novelists have looked for alternatives to the well-wrought ending. Simon's (and other New Novelists') inconclusive endings and the spatial configurations that structure their plots can be seen as directly challenging views of the novel or of history that consider a tale flawed if it fails to conclude. Camus too suspected that full consciousness of absurdity would mean renouncing a "wild longing for clarity" and instead assuming the task of beginning over.[48] It is worth wondering whether postwar novelists' search for new models of plot might not be a response to theories of history that envision a Final Solution. Such theories have been conceived by those who have had or have taken the power to impose their own versions of narrative closure. Apocalyptic ideologies that postulate the advent of utopian empires justify all sorts of ironing out of tangled paths. It is surely no accident that at the end of *La Route des Flandres* the wandering soldiers turn into horsemen of an uncanny anti-apocalypse, bringing no final resolution or resplendent Transcendent Signified or Holy Kingdom, but simply wandering lost and afraid in a forest of images, returning back over the same ground.

3. Figuring Out: *L'Année dernière à Marienbad*

We just don't discuss that . . . I can't tell you why we don't discuss it, because then I'd be discussing it. – Defense Department spokesman Pete Williams, on American military strategy in Iraq, February 1991

L'Année *dernière à Marienbad,* scripted by Alain Robbe-Grillet and filmed by Alain Resnais, seems to offer few similarities with either *Hiroshima mon amour* or *La Route des Flandres.* Where the Duras-Resnais film and Simon's novel provided multitudes of crisscrossing and sometimes contradictory anecdotes, *Marienbad* sustains only a very minimal, skeletal story: X tries to convince A that they loved each other last year. "The whole film, as a matter of fact, is the story of a persuasion," says Robbe-Grillet.[1] The visual austerity and starkness of the *Hiroshima* decor contrast with the baroque excesses of *Marienbad*'s setting, and the progressive uncertainty of Simon's narrator about the reliability of his memory is quite unlike X's confident voice. X is sure of his memories, and what he remembers is not a traumatic encounter with death but a love affair. Nor is this a tale told by a survivor. In fact, more than one critic has postulated that these characters are already dead! Another striking difference, of course, is that *Marienbad* has virtually no historical content.

Released in 1961 and quickly attaining cult status, *Marienbad* is one of the most visibly, even excessively, structured works of the Nouveau Roman or the Nouvelle Vague, and it is the most purely formalist of those to be examined here. Next to the hesitant, serpentine, and ramified narration of *La Route des Flandres, Marienbad* seems cold and mechanical; the very randomness of Simon's novel produces a "reality effect" compared with the studied unreality of Robbe-Grillet and Resnais's film. Sympathetic critics have seen the film as a manifesto of an art that knows no other reality than its own surfaces, its manipulation of words and images, and that is conscious of the material limits of its medium, be it film or writing. Unsympathetic critics have had a field day. They say that the dead, robotlike characters of *Marienbad* are symbolic (or symptomatic)

83

of the deadness of Robbe-Grillet's writing. They say, Who cares? I can't get involved with this; I can't get excited about it. This is irrelevant, solipsistic, has nothing to do with the world, is not worthy of my attention. A more constructive but still negative approach, coming from Lucien Goldmann, says that the affectless characters and the unreality of the setting are an expression of the depersonalization and reification of modern life.[2] All these views are valid to a degree, but they are too sweeping. In particular, they fail to account for *Marienbad*'s specificity or its fascination. In their haste to evaluate, whether negatively or positively, they also fail to give us a way to read the text as anything but a manifesto on aesthetics.

MARIENBAD SI!

Two shots in Chris Marker's 1961 film *Cuba si!* about the Cuban revolution suggest a model for the kind of attentiveness I want to bring to *Marienbad*. The first shot frames the front page of *Le Monde*, 16–17 April 1961. Immediately the camera zooms to a closeup focus on an article about Cuba. But in the split second between, it is possible to catch a glimpse of an article in the adjacent column, "The Leaders of the NLF," about the French conflict in Algeria and the hopes for negotiations at Evian.

Several points are in order. First, Chris Marker is both a self-conscious and a politically committed Nouvelle Vague filmmaker.[3] Although most of *Cuba si!* is devoted to praise of Cuba's revolution and its accomplishments, the film also contains a distinct but more covert criticism of American interventionism there, culminating with the Bay of Pigs at the film's end. By means of the two *Le Monde* shots and its criticism of the United States, *Cuba si!* also contains a drastically understated comparison with France. There is another brief moment in the film where the possibility arises that Cuba functions as a displacement of the ongoing French crisis in Algeria. A car drives into a tunnel toward what the voiceover narrator surmises is "a new world." The voice continues: "And we, 8000 kilometers away, we have only a memory of confidence, and before us, only false news." That is all.

Cuba si! was banned in France. This censorship was due not to a few oversubtle allusions to Algeria but to the film's favorable (now we would say romanticized) view of revolution. In 1961 France did not want to hear about revolution. Chris Marker did not make a film about Algeria, but he did suggest that his story of Cuba has its frame of reference elsewhere. This "elsewhere" is both literal (Cuba for the United States compared to Algeria for France) and rhetorical, expressed in displacements and gaps (in the film's title, for example, the first half of a graffito—"Cuba si! Yankis no!"). The phrase "false news [*fausses nouvelles*]" also identifies an epistemological angst: while *Cuba si!* does not address the French-Algerian crisis in any direct way, it does point to the difficulty of doing so.

These are also the rhetorical strategies of *Marienbad*. In fact, *Cuba si!* even contains two allusions to Resnais and Robbe-Grillet's film, released earlier in the same year. At one point the camera takes a slow and sweeping look at an elegant estate surrounded, like the castle in *Marienbad,* by gardens and statuary, while a languorous voiceover contrasts the poverty prevalent in Havana with the life-style of a few rich people who live in luxury, as in a dream where nothing happens (or where real life happens "elsewhere"). Earlier, the narrator introduced the film saying, "It was last year in Havana [c'etait l'année dernière à la Havane]."

What is fascinating about *Marienbad* is that it too, more ostentatiously than *Cuba si!* points to its own displacements and lacunae: the motive for X's desire to persuade; the source of A's apprehension; shadows of trees in a garden where everything else has shadows; the second half of a proverb; even last year. These absences, in particular the lack of a historical setting, are not a reason to alter our method of reading. Once again, clues to elusive connections between text and world are to be found in forms as much as in subject matter. *Marienbad* too is characterized by ironies and reversals and is open to analysis through its many abyssal figures—a matchstick game, a statue, certain enigmatic statements—and through its gaps, holes, and missing links. The film never does tell what happened in the past, but it does show how a discourse about the past is constructed. If the film is about anything at all, it is about the processes by which Meaning is created, not the meanings themselves. *Marienbad* thus paradoxically *inscribes* a historical discourse without *describing* historical events.

The "elsewhere" of *Marienbad* is not another place but another time, most explicitly last year. But immediately a problem arises: we have already learned that for the writers of the Nouveau Roman and the filmmakers of the Nouvelle Vague, as for psychoanalysts and historiographers, history is not in the past; rather, it is actualized in the present. Robbe-Grillet pushes the inherent limitations of cinema to their logical extreme; it is in the very nature of film, he reminds us, to create an immediate presence that appears and then vanishes. Using *Marienbad* as an example, he says:

The universe in which the entire film occurs is, characteristically, that of a perpetual present which makes all recourse to memory impossible. This is a world without a past, a world which is self-sufficient at every moment and which obliterates itself as it proceeds.

This man, this woman begin existing only when they appear on the screen the first time; before that they are nothing; and, once the projection is over, they are again nothing. Their existence lasts only as long as the film lasts. There can be no reality outside the images we see, the words we hear.

Even flashback that is aware of itself as filmic convention is excluded here. Anything that appears on screen is "present" in both senses of the word: neither what is past nor what is absent can be evoked. Robbe-Grillet continues:

The entire story of *Marienbad* happens neither in two years nor in three days, but exactly in one hour and a half. And when at the end of the film the hero and heroine meet in order to leave together, it is as if the young woman were admitting that there had indeed been something between them last year at Marienbad, but we understand that it was precisely last year during the entire projection, and that we were at Marienbad. This love story we were being told as a thing of the past was in fact actually happening before our eyes, here and now. For of course an *elsewhere* is no more possible than a *formerly*.[4]

It would seem then that not only A's recall of last year but also the faculty of memory itself must be excluded from consideration. The film's title points precisely to what it cannot be "about," so that *L'Année dernière à Marienbad* is the film's name, not a description of its contents. For Robbe-Grillet, the concepts "screen" and "memory" are by definition mutually exclusive.

For Freud, on the other hand, the concepts "screen" and "memory" are compatible. In fact, a screen can represent a memory. Observing in an 1899 article that certain of people's most vivid childhood memories had trivial or negligible content, Freud hypothesized that such scenes, and, by extension, memories in general, might not be passively recalled so much as actively constructed by unconscious mental processes, "almost like works of fiction."[5] His analysis of "screen memories" resembles his study of dreams; in both cases, the mental image is strangely incomplete. Often what is most significant is left out and replaced by something inconsequential. This seemingly trivial anecdote arouses an affective response disproportionate to its content, however, a clue that the dream or memory image is a kind of "compromise," as Freud puts it, between the memory itself and a resistance to the censor. He asks "why it should be that precisely what is important is suppressed and what is indifferent retained." His answer to that question is relevant to *Marienbad:* "It [the remembered scene] will seem incomprehensible to us because we are inclined to look for the reason for its retention in its own subject matter, whereas in fact that retention is due to the relation holding between its own subject matter and a different one which has been suppressed." The image's meaning, in other words, lies neither in the manifest memory nor in a latent memory, neither in a surface text nor in a non-text, but in a structured (rhetorical) relationship between the two.

While Freud and Robbe-Grillet disagree about the possibility of representing the past, their approaches are not as different as they might seem. Neither considers content to be of primary importance. Freud is not disturbed by "incomprehensible" subject matter, and Robbe-Grillet says we should not be thrown off the track by it. In the introduction to *Marienbad* we read that meaning may very well be lodged elsewhere: "This is precisely what makes the cinema an art: it creates a reality with forms. It is in its form that we must look for its true content" (7). I think we can retain Robbe-Grillet's observations about film as a medium and about this film in particular while keeping in mind Freud's demonstration that a text can exclude something while revealing it surreptitiously. We can also use Freud's analysis of censorship, with the rhetorical operations it implies, and his conception of the images as a scene of conflict. For both Freud and Robbe-Grillet, I want to argue, a text (or screen) can bear inscribed on its surface meanings that are alien to it. I propose that we take Robbe-Grillet absolutely seriously, perhaps more seriously than he takes himself, if that is possible. By taking the film itself and certain of Robbe-Grillet's pronouncements about it strictly literally and at the same time asking questions about history in or and the text, we will be led to an uncanny effect: some of the time-worn clichés about this film—such as the missing link or gap, play and game structures, abyssal features such as a statue and a matchstick game, formalism, and literality itself—will have to be radically reevaluated.

OPEN TO ALL MYTHS

Marienbad systematically teases its viewers by preventing them from piecing together any single coherent narrative that would exclude the competing presence of numerous other potential stories. For readers of the *ciné-roman* the characters' "names"—A, X, and M—facilitate the circulation of many meanings. As an aid to understanding the characters' polyvalence, it is helpful to see X (*l'inconnu,* or "the unknown one") structurally, that is, not as the unknown of a *chemical* formula—a substance whose identity can be determined experimentally—but rather as the x of an *algebraic* formula, a fixed relationship with variable values. Details in the text suggest a multitude of archetypal plots, but none is complete, and each contests the others. Is M the husband [*mari*] from whom X attempts to steal A away? M's sad lament, "Where are you . . . my lost love . . . " (157), would seem to suggest that he knows he will lose her. Or is M a doctor [*médecin*] who supervises his patient and her cure, as he suggests by his admonition to her,

"You should get some rest. Don't forget, that's why we're here" (133). The decor is open to both these plots: the sumptuous castle might serve as a resort hotel where wealthy and slightly bored vacationers indulge in flirtatious escapades, but it might just as well be an elegant sanatorium. Is A ill? Is she mad? One critic even goes so far as to suggest that the whole film takes place inside A's head, as she tries to get a grip on reality in order to choose between two men.[6] The many scholars and journalists who have reviewed the film have offered an astonishing variety of interpretations, but whatever their readings, all seem to feel strongly about the film, and most concede that it invites multiple interpretations.[7]

Specific identifiable stories emerge too, in the form of fragmentary subplots that the text teasingly holds out to us as possible means of interpretation and then promptly takes away. A gong that sounds at midnight marking a deadline for departure evokes Cinderella. The presence of this fairy-tale quotation might be confirmed by a scene in A's bedroom in which she tries on many different shoes. Furthermore, a glass slipper is suggested by means of a juxtaposition of A's broken shoe and a smashed drinking glass. At the same time, X plays equally well the role of a Prince Charming, arriving in the castle's stifling and deadly atmosphere to rescue his Sleeping Beauty and awaken her into a new life. But if A's departure with X at the film's end can represent survival or triumph, these values can be reversed. A's departure just as easily suggests death. This possibility brings into focus A's pleading for a year's reprieve; the matchstick game recalls Ingmar Bergman's *The Seventh Seal* (1957), whose hero plays chess with Death in order to outwit him and postpone departure on a one-way journey. The same values spotlight the presence of the Orpheus myth already mentioned: A is already dead. "You looked alive," X tells her (63). Or again, "These days, worse than death, that we're living through here side by side, you and I, like coffins laid side by side underground in a frozen garden . . . " (31). X-Orpheus would then descend into an underworld where M [*la mort*] presides.

Each of these virtual plots is suggested by a series of allusions and then subverted by its own fragmentation in the presence of other, contradictory plots, themselves incomplete. Not one of them is sufficiently developed to be of much use, and none can be a reliable foundation for interpretation as some critics have supposed. Nothing privileges one subtext over another; none is confirmed definitely, but none is rejected either. They simply coexist, a collection of crisscrossing semantic series, the building blocks of potential but unrealized stories. They retain all their contradictions and incompatibilities, as in a dream. *Marienbad* is a model of what Umberto Eco called "the open work."[8] Or as Resnais remarked, "The film is open to all myths."[9]

All of *Marienbad*'s potential stories—especially when taken together—are produced by another kind of "opening" that is one of Robbe-Grillet's favorite structuring devices, what Olga Bernal calls "a perpetual openness, a gap"[10] and what Robbe-Grillet calls "a hollow at the heart of reality [un creux au coeur de la réalité]."[11] In virtually all of his works there is a gaping hole somewhere in the story, a lacuna that functions as textual generator, interpretive aporia, and Orphic loss all at once, providing a motive for invention. The narrator of *La Jalousie*, for example, fills the space left by his wife's absence by imagining her infidelities. *Le Voyeur*'s Mathias is forced to invent activities and record them in a diary in a frantic attempt to fill in a suspicious gap in his day. In *Marienbad*, the absence of last year (whether due to A's failure to remember or the film's inability to show the past) is the pretext for X's verbosity.

To a certain extent, this Orphic design refers us to the commonplaces of postmodernism: the generative blank page, the play of absence and presence (*fort/da*) that makes language necessary and of which it is composed. But there is more. In every case the gap is the source not only of the narration itself but also of a pervasive anxiety or guilt. The gap in *Le Voyeur* is especially instructive, in that it prevents us from knowing whether a crime has been committed. A rape and murder may have occurred, but then again maybe not. That missing hour in Mathias's day and the anxiety it provokes induce him to weave a tangled web of words to prove his innocence. He needs to prove that he was "elsewhere"; his narrative, confused as it is, has the status of an alibi. But as Jeffrey Kittay argues, Mathias's alibi is in itself suspicious, because if he feels he needs one, he must not be innocent. Even though there may in fact be no wrongdoing, an alibi suggests a crime.[12] Similarly, *Marienbad* poses a problem concerning the past, but only the present can be shown. X's alibi fails because he is not elsewhere. He cannot be. He is here and now, or nowhere. But the gaping space carved out by his alibi construction remains. It alone has meaning. And if there is a crime, it is taking place before our eyes.

YOU KNOW THE PROVERB

This conspicuous narrative gap or aporia has the effect, then, of destabilizing the text, making it susceptible to reversals in signification. Such reversals are discernible in several important abyssal moments that are themselves characterized by reversals and missing pieces. These moments prevent us from formulating a story, while they force us to contemplate a potentially infinite regress of formal puzzles. The film's many mirrors are the most visible but not the most productive of these emblems. Another is the game played repeatedly by X and M, which reverses the ancient game known as Nim: traditionally, the last token goes to the winner, whereas in the film the player who takes the last token loses.[13] A correlated reversibility of winning and losing is played out in the film's most explicit plot, its love story. In the game parlor M always wins and X always loses. "I can lose," says M enigmatically, "but I always win" (39). He wins the game, but in the end he loses A. X, on the other hand, loses the game but wins the lady by persuading her to depart with him. In one scene A even establishes an explicit comparison between herself and the Nim tokens by idly laying out photos of herself in the triangular formation of the game. She is the prize in another contest between X and M that is the reverse of the one they play in the game parlor.

This kind of irony is often found in proverbs and dictums of the type Cold hands, warm heart. The idea of a proverb is suggested by a fragment of background conversation: "One of the other characters present then says to A: 'You know the saying [*le proverbe*]: from the compass to the ship . . .'" (46). As in the case of *Cuba si!* a slogan is suggested here by means of a fragment, suggesting that a missing piece would complete the message. It matters little, however, that the proverb is truncated or incomprehensible; we recognize proverbs by their form, irrespective of their content.

The hole in the proverb suggests in turn the possibility of the proverb as hole. A brief excursion into the literature "of another century" (as X describes the castle decor) reveals a connection with a theatrical genre, the "dramatic proverb [*proverbe dramatique*]," popular in the boulevards and salons of seventeenth- and eighteenth-century France. In its primitive form, the dramatic proverb was a parlor game resembling charades. Actors presented a short play or sketch, and the audience was invited to guess the play's missing title by determining what proverb was being dramatized.[14] Like *Marienbad,* the dramatic proverb enlists audience participation by means of a game format that calls attention to what is lacking. To supply a title for the games played by X and M, we might guess that X is "unlucky at cards, lucky in love," or use the expression "C'est à qui perd gagne [roughly, Loser takes all]." X might even be aware that his activities are structured like these dictums: he seems pleased enough to lose to M at the gaming table.

The proverbs just proposed are never stated in the film, and naming them does not constitute a solution to any puzzle. In fact, the rhetoric of reversibility and the gap or aporia prevents solving any puzzles without creating new ones. In any case, the viewer is not invited to fill in missing links, but simply to *notice the lack as lack.* The fragmentation of a proverb casts a shadow of doubt on received knowledge. Like the fairy tales mentioned earlier, proverbs have the form and status of collective wisdom. They are part of a generalized cultural heritage belonging to no one and everyone. As A. J. Greimas points out, they are un-anchored from temporal chronology and refer to an indeterminate past. "The archaic character of proverbs constitutes . . . a putting-outside-of-time [*une mise hors du temps*] of the meanings they contain."[15] They seem also to enjoy an unde-served innocence, one might say a sort of *mise hors du discours*. As dictums (or *dit-on*) they have the authority of general knowledge or revealed truth. Because of their presumed innocence, they provide a perfect ploy for persuasion. Or for a seducer.

"HAVEN'T I SEEN YOU BEFORE SOMEWHERE?"

Robbe-Grillet claims that *Marienbad* is the story of a persuasion: X attempts to persuade A that something occurred last year. But while X argues that he and A loved in the past, he in fact describes what is happening before our eyes. X's dis-course is double, even duplicitous. He simultaneously tells A what supposedly happened last year and describes their conversation as it happens. His narration is simultaneously descriptive and performative. When A laughs, for example, X incorporates her laughter into the "remembered" scene, a maneuver that puts his past tense in doubt and suggests that he is inventing the past from the raw materials of the present. The film thus literalizes the material limits of filmic rep-resentation as Robbe-Grillet has described them. It says, Nonsense, never mind what might have happened last year; something is happening now. "Last year" turns out to be what Alfred Hitchcock liked to call a MacGuffin: an excuse for a story, like the papers that the spies are after but that are ultimately beside the point. And as François Truffaut remarked, defending Hitchcock from the charge that he had nothing to say, "The only answer to that is that a film-maker isn't supposed to say things; his job is to show them."[16] What *Marienbad* shows might very well be called a persuasion or a seduction, but it could more accu-rately be called something else: a rape.

Because of its narrative implications, rape is the perfect crime for the purposes of this film. Rape differs from other violent crimes in terms of the kind of alibis it permits. To prove his innocence, a murder suspect must show that he was else-where or that the murder was committed by another person; he cannot claim that no crime occurred. Murder is not a crime whose noncommission can be narrated. Rape, on the other hand, can be transformed into another kind of story. This is exactly the sort of thing that happens in real life when rape is re-written retrospectively into "persuasion," "seduction," or even "romance." It also happens in fictions such as Renoir's *Une Partie de campagne* (1936; *A Day in the Country*), in which the viewer witnesses a rape and its subsequent retroactive reinterpretation by the young woman (with the film's complicity) into a nostalgically remembered romantic moment.

Missing links, ironic reversals, and displacements to an "elsewhere" are the rhetorical strategies that keep the rape in *Marienbad* from being immediately apparent. For X they serve the functions of an alibi in its etymological sense: he desperately and repeatedly turns the discussion to a "formerly" and an "elsewhere"—last year, perhaps in Frederiksbad or Baden-Salsa. He also emplots the description of what happened (or is happening) in the mode of a love story. To the extent that his voice is the film's (as in his opening question, "Are you coming?" [22], and his injunctions to "Follow me, please" [66], ostensibly addressed to A but encompassing the spectators), the fact that many stories are possible works to his advantage. But the film also works against him: his love story is full of holes, through which peek fragments of another tale that is its mirror opposite. In this light, *Marienbad* is the scene of a conflict or tug of war between its protagonist, who wants to turn the viewer's attention to another time, place, and story, and the film medium, which shows the here and now. Rape in *Marienbad* is neither remembered nor forgotten. Rather, it is shown. Although it is not described, it is nevertheless inscribed. But as in a screen memory, it is rendered incomprehensible because it is fragmented and scattered about the film in inconsequential details, leaving a hole in the center.

Where is it, then? First, it is in the very necessity of an alibi that calls attention to its own inauthenticity. X's story is thoroughly unconvincing. Like the French woman's memories of Nevers ("I'm becoming reasonable. They say: 'She's becoming reasonable'"), X's "memory" is patched together from fragments of surrounding conversations. His very presence in the chateau seems called forth by mention of a mysterious Frank, discussed disapprovingly by the other guests (or inmates, or whatever they are): "It was all anyone talked about last year. Frank had convinced her he was a friend of her father's and had come to keep an eye on her. It was a funny kind of eye, of course. She realized it a little later: the night he tried to get into her room, as though by accident and with some ridiculous excuse, anyway. . . . The fact that he had a German passport didn't prove much. But his presence here has no connection" (37). By far the longest fragment of background conversation, this statement outlines quite precisely X's maneuvers during the course of the film. The fact that Frank was already a subject of conversation "last year" suggests the possibility of an infinite regress of repetitions and imbrications that multiply the film's undecidability. Is X Frank? Is he this year's intruder, as his foreign accent (and the slippage into the present tense in the last sentence quoted above) would seem to suggest?

Rape is suggested as well in the fragments of violence scattered throughout the film. Apparently incoherent juxtapositions of scenes of guests engaging in a marksmanship game with scenes of A in her bedroom give rise to the possibility that A has been shot: first a sequence showing a shooting range, then a cut to A lying crumpled on the floor of her bedroom. But as the camera moves closer, we see that her eyes are open and her finger is placed coyly on her mouth. The combined effect of the two scenes is that of a violent event represented as an erotic one. The tone of the pistol shot remains, however, in the film's mood, its restrained violence, and its suspense, which seems to come from elsewhere.

Even less innocent is X's interpretive strategy concerning a statue in the castle garden. While A wants to know whom the two figures represent, X prefers multiple meanings, an approach that clearly applies to the film as a whole: "Then you asked me the names of the characters. I answered that it didn't matter.— You didn't agree with me, and you began giving them names, more or less at random, I think. . . . Then I said that it could just as well be you and I. . . . (A silence.) Or anyone" (63–65). A, who has less to lose from definitive interpretation, suggests two possible identities for the couple depicted by the statue: Pyrrhus and Andromache, Helen and Agamemnon. Her suggestions are not chosen "at random" as X supposes; each of the couples represents a case of kidnapping and rape. Furthermore, the two couples stand in inverse symmetry to each other: Pyrrhus captured Andromache, while Agamemnon set out to rescue Helen. A does not yet know whether X is her captor or her rescuer, and neither do we.

Then there are the two alternative versions of a scene whose juxtaposition allows X to revise his story. Each of the sequences apparently follows from his ominously symbolic earlier statement "I [penetrate into] your bedroom" (110). In the first version, X advances along a corridor toward A's bedroom. Hearing his approach, A retreats, seems trapped, makes self-protective gestures, is obviously frightened. Then—cut—the scene begins again, but this time A advances to meet X, whom she greets with open arms. Fear is thus rewritten as welcome, terror as joy, and assault as romance.

In the scenario (but not on the screen) the first version is described explicitly by X: "Finally . . . I took you, half by force," and then, "Oh no . . . Probably it wasn't by force" (115–16). He then revises his statement more emphatically: "No, no, no! (violently:) That's wrong. . . . (calmer:) It wasn't by force" (147). Deletion of these remarks from the finished film not only revokes the reference to coercion but also obscures the fact that it is X who deliberately rewrites the story. At another point the scenario's filming directions are even more explicit than the dialogue: "X appears in the foreground, seen from behind. Rather swift and brutal rape scene. [. . .] A struggles, but without any result. She opens her mouth as though to scream; but X, leaning over her, immediately gags her with a piece of fine lingerie [. . . .] The victim's hair is loose and her clothes in disarray" (146).

This scene, one of typical Robbe-Grillet sado-maso-eroticism, which he envisioned in an interview as "a rape that is 'realistic' in the style of the *Grand Guignol,* full of exaggerations and theatricality,"[17] disappeared between the scenario and the screen. Resnais may have sensed that an explicit rape scene violated the already established rhetoric of gaps and incompletion. Whatever the reason for its excision, the scene is not needed. Although (or because) it is not described at any specific point, the rape is inscribed in the film's entire texture.

As Robbe-Grillet himself said about the lacunae in all his works: "Everything, up to the 'hole' is told—then told again after the hole—and we try to reconcile the two edges in order to make this annoying emptiness disappear. But what happens is the exact opposite: it's the emptiness that overruns, that fills everything." And about *Marienbad:* "The event refused by the young woman has, at the end, contaminated everything. So much so that she hasn't stopped struggling and believing she won the game, since she always refused all of it; and, at the end, she realizes that it's too late, that in the final analysis she has accepted everything."[18] Another game of "qui perd gagne," or "qui gagne perd," it would appear. Astonishingly, Robbe-Grillet's comments execute the same maneuver as the film itself. (Theory is, after all, another form—or another layer—of fiction.) He points without naming it to an "event" that is missing, thereby postulating its existence.

The event is not really missing after all. It is elsewhere, but elsewhere *on the screen.* Like Poe's purloined letter, the event is simply not in its expected place in a coherent story, but while we contemplate the MacGuffin, the missing event is in plain view. If rape as an event has been suppressed from the story, it is present as discourse, dispersed in multiple thematic codes. It is represented symbolically by a series of broken things: a glass, A's shoe, later a balustrade over which X escapes being seen by M. It is present in a theme of penetration (into rooms, into thoughts). It can be seen in the fear A's face displays and in her repeated and increasingly frantic refrain, "Please [more literally, I beg of you] . . . let me alone . . ." (102). It is there in the various manifestations of X's pursuit and A's flight. And it is visible in the actress's self-protective gesture, arm held diagonally across her torso, which becomes her character's signature. Dramatic music in crescendo intensifies the anxiety surrounding these elements, which are relatively trivial in themselves. These are thematic analogues for fractured montage and incomplete narrative. The broken drinking glass is especially significant; A's panic in response to the event and the scream she cannot stifle are clues that the

2. *L'Année dernière à Marienbad*. A (Delphine Seyrig) makes "significant but incomprehensible" gestures.

glass breaking functions like a repressed memory. This object first appears in two rapidly alternating decors. In one of these, A stands with others at a bar. Frightened or startled by the appearance on the scene of X, she inadvertently knocks her glass to the floor, where it shatters. Interspersed in increasingly frenzied alternation is a scene that conforms to the cinematic conventions of a subliminal memory or a mental image: A in a bedroom hears someone approaching, is startled or afraid, and knocks a glass from a dresser.

These two parallel scenes are joined by A's scream, which has no apparent cause. Perhaps it is the cry that X successfully suppressed in the rape scene (which was itself removed from the film) resurfacing in another place. Those around her agree that A suffers from a "malaise," and her scream does function like a hysterical symptom. Freud writes that "the symptom is formed as a substitute for something else which remains submerged,"[19] or for our purposes, a substitute for something that is elsewhere (but still within the film). Even more instructive is Lacan's view that the symptom is behavior whose motive is absent, censored by the conscious mind; it is a signifier whose signified is repressed and displaced.[20] A's scream is thus an empty, aberrant signifier that refers to an absence. In each of these juxtapositions a violent scene is revised or expunged, but the process of revision itself remains visible. Knowledge is shown in the context of its disappearance. Symbols are obvious, but they are dispersed, subordinated, displaced, and can be dismissed. In other words, memories may be latent, absent, expunged, impossible, or a MacGuffin, but the process of censorship is on the screen if we care to see it. If we apply to the film Freud's analysis of screen memories while keeping in mind Robbe-Grillet's injunction to look for content in form, we can conclude that the story depicts not a rape but a rhetoric of rape, and the image's meaning is neither in violence nor in its absence but in the relationship between the two. The rape has not been covered up; the film has no secrets. What we see is the process of revision and rewriting—the mechanisms of censorship.

A DISCOURSE WITHOUT CONTENT

The unconscious is that chapter of my history that is marked by a blank or occupied by falsehood: it is the censored chapter. But the truth can be rediscovered; usually it has already been written down elsewhere. – Jacques Lacan, *Ecrits*

To describe a rape and its censorship in *Marienbad* by reference to psychoanalytic understanding of screen memory, neurotic symptoms, and the like itself actually involves an interesting irony. The currency of psychoanalytic discourse has turned a metaphor into a catachresis, a metaphor that has forgotten its origin. This process appears in literary critics' understanding of censorship but also, and perhaps consequently, in the widespread (mis)use of psychological categories to explain phenomena that would more properly be seen as social or political. (Kurt Vonnegut satirizes this process in *Slaughterhouse Five,* when his Billy Pilgrim, hospitalized with war-related shock, is told he suffers from pre-Oedipal frustration.) When Freud uses the term *censor,* however, he uses a metaphor self-consciously to describe psychic repression in terms of social and political phenomena. He even invokes press censorship as a model to explain psychic functioning. Describing dreams, he states: "Now where will you find a parallel to what has taken place here? In these times you have not far to seek. Take up any political paper and you will find that here and there in the text something is omitted and in its place the blank white of the paper meets your eye: you know that this is the work of the press censor." The visual image of a whited-out space represents censorship in the French term *carré blanc,* as on an anticensorship poster declaring, "No blank squares for an adult public [Pas de carré blanc pour un peuple adulte]." Freud goes on to say that the gaps in your newspaper are not the only evidence of the censor's work but that in some cases "there are no blanks, but from the roundabout and obscure mode of expression you can detect the fact that at the time of writing, the author had the censorship in mind."[21]

Freud is making explicit here what I want to suggest about *Marienbad*'s "formalism": that the final aspect of the image, in Freud's example a newspaper page, must be understood in the context of the pressures exerted on it from the outside. Whether the formalization of a single work or an entire school of works (such as the Nouveau Roman or the Nouvelle Vague) takes the form of an artist's conscious decision to hide thematic content or, on the other hand, and this is more likely, the form results from self-censorship or from the mentality of a historical period, the pressures function in the same way. The rhetoric of censorship thus suggests a possible meeting ground for psychoanalytic and social interpretation.

Leo Strauss justifies the leap I want to make here between Freud's "roundabout and obscure mode of expression" and the form of a literary work. In Strauss's view, "The influence of persecution on literature is precisely that it compels all writers who hold heterodox views to develop a peculiar technique of writing, the technique which we have in mind when speaking of writing between the lines. This expression is clearly metaphoric. Any attempt to express its meaning in unmetaphoric language would lead to the discovery of a terra incognita, a field whose very dimensions are as yet unexplored."[22] *Marienbad* does leave clues regarding what material might be written between the lines. What is crucial at this point, however, is that this rhetoric of censorship presents the film's tortured and abstract aesthetic. Robin Wood, for his part, makes a similar point when he links the incoherence of many American movies of the 1970s to a "blockage of thought."[23]

In his analysis of Dora, Freud describes hysteria as both "an inability to give ordered history" and "unreadable,"[24] both remarks reminiscent of critics' opinions of the Nouveau Roman and the Nouvelle Vague and of these artists' expressed goal of breaking with narrative representation. "The symptom is formed as a substitute for something else which remains submerged," he writes elsewhere,[25] and Lacan elaborates that a symptom is behavior whose motive or signifier has been repressed, displaced, and censored.[26] This form of representation, which speaks through screens and symptoms, where the body speaks what the tongue cannot, can best be described as a hysterical discourse. Accordingly, *Marienbad* can be understood as a case in which the history repressed from explicit representation speaks through the bodies of characters and in the body (or form) of the text.

Censorship is itself one of the more carefully hidden notions in Western civilization.[27] In France this double suppression reached a kind of paroxism in 1960 and 1961, the year during which *Marienbad* was being written and filmed.[28] For example, during those years there were three times as many police seizures of newspapers and periodicals as in the year before (1959) and about twice as many as in the following year (1962).[29] During 1960 and 1961 the Algerian conflict reached a turning point and an antiwar movement of decisive proportions developed in France. Information about antiwar sentiments and activities was strictly banished from the daily news. Revelations of atrocities and stories of torture appeared in articles and in books (many published by the Editions de Minuit, Robbe-Grillet's publishing house)[30] only to be promptly seized, suppressed, and punished. Moreover, whereas books and articles tended to be suppressed after initial publication, films could be controlled preventively, before they appeared. The censor's "visa," required since 1938 of any film appearing in France, is itself an ironic euphemism in that to impose the necessity of a "permission" presupposes the power to deny it.[31]

Official suppression was exercised during this period not only on published material but also on individuals. The active resistance of intellectuals to continued French presence in Algeria took two forms, both of which reached crisis proportions in September and October of 1960, while Robbe-Grillet and Resnais were working on *Marienbad* in a Paris studio. The first was the circulation of a petition expressing solidarity with those who used illegal means to oppose continued French presence in Algeria. This statement was later known as the "Manifesto of the 121," although more than three hundred prominent intellectuals, film stars, and other public personalities eventually signed. The document expressed solidarity specifically with draft resistance and with those who supplied direct aid to Algerian rebels. Such aid, in the form of money and safe passage, was supplied via what became known as the "Jeanson network," a resistance network headed by philosophy professor and Sartre biographer Francis Jeanson. In September 1960 several of the network participants who had been arrested were brought to trial for treason.

Apparently certain literary forms are in themselves considered safe. After all, if a work has no content, or obscure content, or if it "only" tells a love story, how could it possibly be subversive or dangerous? This false proverb gives rise from time to time to some odd formulations. One has only to think of the curious double negative in Resnais's description of *Hiroshima mon amour* as "a love story [. . .] from which atomic anguish would not be absent." A similar example can be found in a poem written by Paul Eluard during the German occupation. The poem is very long, and like a *proverbe dramatique,* it has no title. Apparently the official censor glanced at it and concluded that it was a love poem. The poem begins:

In my pupil's notebook
On my desk and the trees
On the sand on the snow
I write your name

Twenty monotonous stanzas later the name of the beloved is revealed:

And by the power of a word
I start my life again
I was born to know you
To name you

Liberty.

When the poem appeared in the window of a Parisian bookshop in 1942, a more literary German propaganda officer read through to the end and ordered the book removed from the shelves![32]

Formalism too is considered safe. In some cases it even causes censors, as well as more ordinary literary mortals, to overlook content altogether. According to Marcel Ophuls, such was the case when his *Le Chagrin et la pitié,* which was hardly a formalist document, appeared before the Censorship Board in the politically charged atmosphere of post–May 1968 Paris. Ophuls confesses that he does not understand how his film finally made it past the censors after a series of delays, obfuscations, and refusals. He even reports a rumor that for the screening before the Censorship Board a sympathetic projectionist ran some of the reels backward! Finally, *Le Chagrin* was given the green light. Ophuls's observation about successfully surmounting this obstacle is instructive in its irony: "The fact remains that the members of the Censorship Board, no doubt persuaded that they were dealing with one of those obscure and inaccessible films, an avant-garde work that posed no risk of stirring up the crowds, agreed to give us the government's imprimatur."[33]

Another document reveals the underside of Ophuls's statement. In September 1960 an article in *L'Express,* a weekly that was frequently suppressed at the time, reported on its "survey" concerning Algeria and censorship. Journalist Michèle Manceaux interviewed ten French filmmakers, asking the following questions: "(1) If there were no censorship, would you want to make a film about the Algerian war? (2) If so, how do you think the cinema could approach this subject?" Nearly all the respondents declared that they would indeed make such a film if they could. Roger Vadim said yes, he would make a film resembling Malraux's *L'Espoir* (*Man's Hope*) but he would call his *Le Désespoir*. Jacques Doniol-Valcroze reiterated at length the impossibility of such an undertaking and finally declared that "French Cinema is condemned to irrealism."[34] The irony, of course, is that films (and novels) of the period were later condemned *for* "irrealism." Manceaux's questionnaire creates the same sort of metadiscourse I find in *Marienbad* (and in the epigraph to this chapter): forbidden to discuss a subject, Manceaux asks instead about the impossibility of talking about it. With its content censored, *L'Express* publishes articles about censorship. Censorship of the news *is* the news.

Marienbad very indirectly alludes to this power of censorship to shape a text. On a corridor wall can be seen a poster announcing the evening's theatrical entertainment: a play entitled *Rosmer*. Ibsen's *Rosmersholm* (*The House of Rosmer*) concerns a man who must decide whether he will make his true political beliefs public in defiance of threatened punishment.[35] Obviously, such directness is not Robbe-Grillet's approach of choice. He insists that in any case art rarely acts directly to influence political questions: "Art should make an honest effort to acknowledge its powerlessness to resolve urgent social issues." But he goes on to sketch out an alternative to—or perhaps it is the value of—"pure" irrealism: "The only opportunity I have to intervene in the social arena is to invent a free discourse that seems to put the world in parentheses, while really speaking about it nonetheless."[36] With the world between parentheses (or perhaps better still, outside parentheses, leaving a hole in the middle), a discourse thus liberated can reveal not the content of reality but the forms in which it is constructed.

INSIDE OUT: A DISCOURSE WITHOUT CONTEXT

The stories people tell . . . do not tell us simply and unambiguously what the situation is. These stories are part of the situation. – R. D. Laing

In spite of itself, however, *Marienbad* is not as totally antireferential as Robbe-Grillet claims it is. Although formal content is the film's most marked social and historical dimension—"It is in its form that we must look for its true content"— I want to conclude my analysis of the film by showing that *Marienbad*'s discursive content is historical as well, albeit in a very roundabout fashion.

One of the reasons the discourses in (and of) Marienbad have no coherent content is that they are never allowed to take root in a context. In the *ciné-roman* this dislocation is conscious. Robbe-Grillet's filming directions specify that the secondary, background characters, as they mingle and converse interminably in the castle's corridors, make "a few gestures, significant but incomprehensible (out of context [*privés de leur contexte*])" (28). This distinction between significance and comprehensibility is crucial. The gestures—and the whole film can be called a gesture or series of gestures—are incomprehensible to the spectator or reader, but that does not imply that they do not have meaning that could be understood if a context were restored.

The film's own production context can now once again be viewed in the light of its internal organizing principles by asking what patches or fragments of the surrounding discourses of 1960 and 1961 *Marienbad* appropriates to itself. Of course the film does not assimilate surrounding context willy-nilly in an unproblematically mimetic way. If this were so, it would not have been necessary to describe at such length the film's rhetorical machinery. It should be possible now to extend our understanding of the relationship between interior duplication and its context in order at least to speculate about the processes of exterior duplication that are a part of the film's texture. As in the case of *Hiroshima mon amour,* the film's internal form reflects contextual pressures. By performing a final reversal of content and context, it becomes possible to see that what is missing from *Marienbad* is not indicated by a hole at its center, but by a void around its edges. Meanwhile, Freud's view that screen memories seem "incomprehensible" only when one looks too simply at subject matter, and not at the relation between subject matter and what has been censored, should be kept in mind. This view turns the text inside out: following the rhetoric of the *creux* and the text's ironies, *Marienbad* itself is the aporia (the *carré blanc*) in a larger social discourse. Or to adapt a statement from R. D. Laing, *Marienbad* does not—cannot—tell us simply and unambiguously what was going on in 1960 because the film itself is part of what was going on.

If the film itself does not designate explicitly the context in which it was created, Robbe-Grillet and Resnais have not been so reticent. Both have discussed the pressures of the milieu in which they worked. Resnais responded to Michèle Manceaux's interview in *L'Express* with the reply that if there were no censorship, he would make a film about a couple whose marriage disintegrates as a result of the Algerian war. The interviewer reports Resnais's response, and she concludes: "But, giving up like the others, Resnais left for Germany to make an apolitical film that, he says, we have, 'to look at as if it were a sculpture.'" That film was indeed *L'Année dernière à Marienbad,* as Resnais confirmed a year later when he declared that *Marienbad* was a documentary about a statue.[37] The *Ex-*

press interview thus shows that this particular retreat into formalism devolved directly from censorship. It is misleading, however, to describe the film as apolitical; as we have seen, its formal mechanisms are very political indeed.

Robbe-Grillet, whose *oeuvre* is more purely formalist than Resnais's, is, paradoxically, more interested than the filmmaker in problems of politics and art, and his approach is characteristically more theoretical. At a 1971 colloquium Robbe-Grillet spoke of *Marienbad*'s "gestation": "*Marienbad* was made in the middle of the Algerian war and precisely at the moment when intellectuals were taking stands publicly for the first time." Robbe-Grillet continued his remarks about *Marienbad*'s genesis by addressing the question of political engagement inside and outside literary texts. It was on this point that he and Resnais differed most sharply:

Now the New Novel was generally seen as deliberately detached from politics, whereas Resnais was considered extremely involved politically. [. . .] In our first discussion, Resnais came right to the point, he wanted to induce me to address current events openly. He would have particularly liked the conversations in the hotel to refer to the Algerian war, and, while preserving the form I chose, that they have for their subject the issues with which everyone was preoccupied. I was categorically opposed. I preferred not to make the film at all rather than to utter even once the word Algeria and this precisely for political reasons.

Robbe-Grillet did not say in what way his reasons were political, but he did reiterate his belief that while literature could not grapple directly with social issues, it could restructure the categories in which we think:

I felt that it was not reasonable for an intellectual to intervene politically in his works. We had other weapons at our disposal: direct aid to the NLF or even the manifesto of the 'Hundred twenty-one.' Rather than manipulating a political content known in advance (for example, the problems of colonialism), the revolution to which literature (or the cinema) aspires would be a generalized revolution in meaning.[38]

In short, this is a kind of revolution where formal content and the categories of thinking (the politics of form) take precedence over thematic content.

It does not suffice, however, to suggest that the Algerian conflict is important to *Marienbad* because it has been omitted or even because it preoccupied its authors during filming. I have claimed that the film has no secrets, and it is by means of its own rhetoric that we can read the inscription of the surrounding social text. In the passages above, Robbe-Grillet accepts the self-censorship inherent in the exclusion of social allusion of any kind. This position betrays his unwillingness to consider the presence of society's *texts* within his creations, a presence he has not hesitated to flaunt when the topic was eroticism. For example, asked about the presence of typically masculine erotic fantasies in his novels and films, he responded as follows: "All my books are organized around a kind of panoply of stereotypes that are carved out of the language society provides me. I live in society, I am part of that society, I am myself inside its ideology, and not exterior to it. But I see a system for maintaining my freedom within this ideological prison. The system is born of the New Novel and of all modern art [. . .]. It consists of detaching fragments from society's discourse and using them as raw materials to construct something else."[39] Similarly, much as *Marienbad* performs instances of cultural intertextuality by incorporating proverbs, myths, and allusions to archetypal stories, it also "reads" the events, lexicon, and public preoccupations of 1960, which it weaves into its own narrative and discursive fabric.

There is, for example, a referential dimension to *Marienbad*'s proper nouns. Marienbad, Carlsbad, and so on, are or were fashionable spas: there exists a real Marienbad in Bohemia, now Czechoslovakia. What distinguished Marienbad from the others was its clientele: as early as the 1820s, well-to-do Russian and Polish Jews would travel there to reside in its elegant hotels, imbibe the waters, and engage in intrigues, gossip, and flirtations.[40] All of this ended in March 1939, when the German army invaded the town, arrested or executed the Jews who had not managed to flee, and established an occupied protectorate.

It is not necessary to leap to the conclusion that the Marienbad in Resnais and Robbe-Grillet's film is the real town of the same name to read the resonances that reverberate between literary and historical texts. The story of the Bohemian spa, like the film's other subtexts, organizes certain fictive elements and brings new details into focus. The film's decor lends itself to comparison with the hotels of Marienbad; the "already dead," ghost-town atmosphere takes on new significance; and A's memories, or refusals thereof, open to the collective. Remembering yesterday's violences while reliving them today becomes a historiographically charged activity, as does the attempt to rewrite a rape (of yesterday or today) as romance. Like the Boulogne of Resnais's *Muriel* (which I examine at the end of this chapter) and the Hiroshima of *Hiroshima mon amour,* Marienbad is a phantom city (and word) uprooted from its past and covered over by the screens of fiction or memory.

The fact that Marienbad is a *ville d'eau* might bring to mind many such towns in France, from Biarritz to Aix, from Lourdes to . . . Vichy. And if Marienbad evokes a historical theme, if only in embryonic form, its opening scene, in which X wanders through deserted corridors evoking a past that can only be imagined, is uncannily similar to the opening scenes of Resnais's *Nuit et brouillard* (also censored), in which another disembodied narrating voice invites the spectator to follow him down the deserted alleys between the empty, moss-covered block-houses of today's Auschwitz. That voice too recounts the impossibility of re-membering, while narrating a memory reinvented in and for the present. In fact, viewed from the perspective of its production in 1955, a year after France's de-feat in Indochina and just as the Algerian conflict was beginning to loom, Res-nais's emphasis on the dangers of repeating the past and the possibility that Nazi atrocities could easily recur constitutes a covert editorial on France's contempo-rary behavior.

A more complex historical (or pseudohistorical) allusion is suggested by the "documentary about a statue." A documentary is the most ostentatiously refer-ential and historical of cinematic genres, but like other film genres, it can only show history as "presence" (see chapter 1). After X and A have debated the iden-tities of the figures, M intervenes to identify them "once and for all" as follows: "Excuse me, sir. I think I can supply you with some more precise information: this statue represents Charles III and his wife, but it does not date from that pe-riod, of course. The scene is that of the oath before the Diet, at the moment of the trial for treason. The classical costumes are purely conventional . . . " (69). Trying to identify the statues by means of the offered details, we are brought up once again by the film's antireferential strategies and reminded that we have to read the statue as a screen. M's gesture apparently violates the openness of inter-pretation pursued by X and the film as a whole, but what he actually says, if it is examined closely, reestablishes that openness. Although the three historical markers given—Charles III, an oath before the Diet, a treason trial—sound au-thentic enough, there is no such historical personage. M's intervention is a fic-tion invented out of historical materials, a historical discourse without historical reference. The stone figure is thus also a rhetorical figure, the fictional sum of historical parts.

The name Charles is of course rich with associations. Although no Charles III quite fits the bill, this name, like the name Marienbad, is no more accidental than Pyrrhus and Andromache. Reference to a treason trial might make us think of Charles I of England, who lost his case and his head in a treason trial that marked the temporary end of a dynasty. Another Charles whose reign signaled a re-gime's end was Charles X of France, the last of the Bourbons and the last gasp of the Restoration monarchy. Finally, the best-known Diet is the Diet of Worms, over which yet another Charles presided: Charles V, Holy Roman Emperor from 1519 to 1558 was also known for, among his other deeds, his unsuccessful attempt to invade Algeria in 1541. Were one to trace the European involvement in North Africa to its earliest roots, one would unearth Charles V.

While these details form a most unlikely mosaic of disjointed allusions, as historical discourse in *Marienbad* they make sense. They make sense, that is, if one keeps in mind that history is in the present and stories are constructed with (and by) the film as a *bricolage* of surrounding textual fragments. The pseudohistorical allusions in *Marienbad* and, even more importantly, the film's formal procedures are drawn from a vast network of images available to the collective imagination in 1960 (or more accurately, to a segment of Parisian intellectual society who shared a broadly defined social and political outlook). These images, constituting what Fredric Jameson calls a work's "referential preconditions,"[41] constitute a bridge between *Marienbad* and its context, providing a site where formal and social interpretation meet.

The word *treason* was everyday currency in 1960. The signatories of the "Manifesto of the 121" and especially the defendants in the Jeanson trial were accused of wartime treason in a conflict it was forbidden to call a war. There was another Charles in the news during that period, the one Sartre called "Charles XI," that is, Charles de Gaulle. De Gaulle's return to power in 1958 was experienced by many as simultaneously an anachronistic restoration monarchy and a bewildering reversal of the symbolic value he had had twenty years earlier. In fiction, journalism, and cartoons of the time, critics of his presence and of his style of personal rule return again and again to two images of de Gaulle, both of which are picked up and transformed in the discourses and structures of *Marienbad*.

A pervasive image in the jokes and cartoons of 1960 is that of "Le Roi Charles." For example, the satirical weekly *Le Canard enchaîné* spoofed de Gaulle's legendary royalism and autocratic pretensions by portraying him in powdered wig and kingly garb. In the fall of 1960 the editors launched a column entitled "La Cour" to report, with appropriate preciosity, the doings at the court of "Mongénéral."[42] In later issues problems of presidential succession were satirized in a series of articles under the headline "Who will be Mondauphin?"

The use of irony, underlined in the cartoons and journalism of 1960, highlights the unstable reversibility of winning and losing, and the figure of de Gaulle as both liberator of France and oppressor of Algeria. This is the factor that contrasts the film's two actual historical allusions—the name Marienbad and King Charles—and the same irony that is dramatized without political content in *Marienbad*'s game of Nim. The Jeanson network and its sympathizers were particularly aware of this historical reversal: their network's success depended on its organizational framework, whose structures of communication were already in place, left over from the Resistance. Even some of the actors were the same.

Another image that reappears in the journalism of 1960 is rape. If rape ap-

3. *Le Canard enchaîné*. De Gaulle's royal persona, July–September, 1960. – Courtesy *Le Canard enchaîné*.

— Nous préférons Notre Sévigné...

1960 : UNE ANNEE PAS CARROSSABLE
Les pavés du Roi

4. *Le Canard enchaîné* spoofs de Gaulle in a regular column entitled "The Court." *Above,* the President/Sun King prefers Madame de Sevigné's letters to news about a critical "Letter from J.-P. Sartre," 28 September 1960, during the Jeanson trial. *Below,* de Gaulle takes a rough ride in 1960 over *pavés,* which are both paving stones and, colloquially, scandals or shock waves, 28 December 1960. Courtesy *Le Canard enchaîné.*

pears as a frequent metaphorical usage in the literature of resistance, this may be because, as Robin Morgan points out in another context, "the violation of an individual woman is *the* metaphor for man's forcing himself on whole nations."[43] In wartime, rape has always been more than a rhetorical figure, but in its literal application it has also been one of the forms in which the concept of conquest is expressed. When in 1963 it finally became possible for Resnais to make his film about Algeria, he used the rape and murder of an individual Algerian woman, Muriel, as a microcosmic representation of the relationship between two nations. But during the filming of *Marienbad,* rape was already part of the public discourse about Algeria, particularly surrounding an event that preoccupied Paris in June 1960: the scandal, brought to public attention by Simone de Beauvoir, of the torture, rape, and murder of an Algerian woman, Djamila Boupacha, by French paratroopers in Algeria.[44] From that time, journalistic references to "the rape of Algeria" proliferated, for, in the words of one historical source, "the rape of Djamila became the symbol of Algeria violated [*violentée*]."[45]

As for X, during this same period there were several attempts to bring individual cases of military mistreatment of Algerians before the courts. In most instances the individuals responsible were not known, and such trials were more successful in bringing cases of torture to public attention than in achieving any judicial resolution. In French juridical language, when one sues or brings to trial an unknown individual, this situation can be expressed as a suit against "X." Whether the X in *Marienbad* is an unknown criminal and A is Algeria, or whether A, X, and M form a geometric representation of mediated desire and violence, *L'Année dernière à Marienbad* bears the rhetorical and even thematic impact of the historical moment of its creation.

AFTERMATH: LE TEMPS D'UN RETOUR

After the most intense censorship peaked in 1960 and 1961 and began to subside, displacement to an "elsewhere," whether to Cuba or Marienbad or an exaggerated formalism, became less necessary. A few filmmakers began to allude to Algeria and even to incorporate explicit references to the conflict in their plots. The year 1962 saw the release of both Chris Marker's *La Jetée* and Agnès Varda's *Cléo de 5 à 7.* The former is a lyrical photomontage with a science-fiction plot, but it raises the topic, utterly proscribed a few years before in any context whatsoever, of torture. Varda's film is another love story, but from which, we could say, adopting Resnais's remark about *Hiroshima,* the anguish of Algeria is not absent: radio broadcasts, newspaper headlines, and overheard conversations mention the conflict in Algeria. Varda's story brings together a woman awaiting the verdict that she has cancer and a soldier savoring the final hours of his leave before he must return to combat in Algeria. The juxtaposition implies a comparison: whether facing cancer or the war, both protagonists are living with fear, and Varda's film is heavy with malevolent omens and morbidity. *Cléo* is a self-conscious film as well. It reflects on the limits of representation and even speculates on possible causal connections between political pressures and artistic form, as in a café scene where we overhear a lament about the stupid mess in Algeria: "Our literature, you can't understand a thing in it," the voice opines. Everything is affected, even painting. As the conversation continues, the camera sweepingly surveys a display of paintings on a wall; they are all abstract. Literature, music, and painting have all become, the voice remarks, "incompréhensibles."

Jacques Demy's 1964 *Les Parapluies de Cherbourg* is also a love story framed by the Algerian conflict. A young couple are in love and want to marry, but he is drafted and must leave for Algeria. During his absence she marries and has a child. Years later they meet and realize their romance is a thing of the past. So much for the plot. A large portion of the film is devoted, however, to the young woman (Catherine Deneuve) and her anguished waiting: she waits for her soldier to write, but he never does. Once again, the Algerian conflict is associated with an inability to write, a breakdown in communication, an imposition of silence. This is perhaps what Resnais had in mind when he responded to Michèle Manceaux's survey, mentioned above, by stating that he would like to tell the story of a couple whose marriage breaks up because of the Algerian conflict.

In 1963 Godard's *Le Petit Soldat* was finally approved for distribution, after its suppression in 1960 on the grounds of its confusing plot involving references to torture. Also released in 1963, Resnais's *Muriel: Le Temps d'un retour* is by far the best of the films that touch on France's identity crisis over the Algerian conflict. Resnais's next film following *Marienbad, Muriel* can be seen as a replay of the representational strategies of *Marienbad,* but this time the historical context and content are restored.[46] *Muriel* interweaves two stories that in turn bring into play two historical periods: in the foreground plot, Hélène reestablishes contact with Alphonse, who was her lover during World War II. In a secondary plot, Bernard, Hélène's stepson, has just completed military service in Algeria. When asked what he does in life, Bernard replies: "I return from Algeria [Je reviens d'Algerie]." In actuality, however, one could say "Il n'en revient pas" ["he doesn't return," or idiomatically, "he can't get over it"]. As a result, repressed Algeria returns to him in the forms of bizarre hysterical symptoms, unintelligible and antisocial behavior, and, ultimately, violence. But this time a character's hysterical discourse does not entirely repress Algeria from the film as a whole.

"How to remember in 1963?" wonders the preface to *Muriel,* where scenarist Jean Cayrol notes that Bernard's months in Algeria have "disfigured" him.[47] Bernard is tormented by his past, and he is disfigured literally as well—in photographs where his face has been cut away, in a peculiar mask he wears to dinner, and especially in an image of his face refracted through a teleidoscope, a device that resembles a kaleidoscope but fragments, rearranges, and disperses, not bits of colored glass, but segments of the surrounding reality. If we take Bernard's disfigurement figuratively, it becomes clear that his memories of Algeria distort his texts as well: he functions as another *mise en abyme* of the impossibility of speaking coherently about Algeria. The teleidoscope can itself be taken as a figure of the kind of representation that *Muriel* achieves. By working with Bernard's and Alphonse's guilty Algerian memories, this film inscribes what *Marienbad* can only perform without content: the reassembling of surrounding discourses in an attempt to represent France's guilt over the Algerian conflict.

What Bernard cannot get over in particular, what attempts to get represented through his own and the text's hysterical symptoms, is the rape, torture, and murder of Muriel. When a friend asks whether Bernard is troubled because he wants to "recount Muriel," Bernard replies: "Muriel cannot be recounted [Muriel, ça ne se raconte pas]." In fact, Muriel herself does not appear in the film; she is its empty center, more an event than a character, and her story can only emerge in fragments around a blank space refracted through the teleidoscope of the text. That text tells the story of the failure of narrative, or, in Freud's description of hysteria, its "inability to give ordered history."

It is significant, however, that although Bernard's behavior and the film as a whole are distorted and fragmented in ways similar to those of *Marienbad* (reversals, mysterious proverbs, abyssal self-consciousness, enactment of the mechanisms of censorship and hysterical discourse, an epistemological gap at the center, and so on), the story of Algeria does eventually get told. Bernard's attempt to cope with his memories leads him to make a film about his experience. Muriel and the central event are absent from his, and consequently from Resnais's, film. Appropriately enough, Resnais uses Bernard's film as an interior duplication to dramatize the transmission of history disfigured by (self-)censorship and hysteria. While he tells fragments of his tale, Bernard's film shows something else, another scene, elsewhere: soldiers laughing and having a good time, removed from their wartime context. After his film ends, Bernard stands in front of the white square of light formed on the wall by the projector. The image's resemblance to a police lineup conveys Bernard's self-accusation. His story has not been told by his film after all, as this visual pun of the *carré blanc* of censorship indicates. Later Bernard shoots his pistol at the blank square, perhaps in an effort to destroy the memory itself or perhaps as another attempt to erase censorship and get the story told, to lift the repression in order to allow his story to return. The "return" of the title is multidirectional, an unstable, reversible movement: Bernard's return *from* Algeria cannot be complete until Algeria (and Muriel) return *to* his consciousness, until his experience can be figured literally in his discourse rather than hysterically in his body.

In spite of its totally different thematic content, *Marienbad* has more in common with *Muriel* than a first glance would suggest. Whereas *Muriel* manages to talk obliquely about a case of torture and murder, however, *Marienbad* can only stage a discourse of rape and violence, a discourse in the context of its disappearance. Both films share the disfiguration that is the trace of that suppression. In *Marienbad*, the pressure of the political, although displaced, is acute. Nonetheless, we are left with an understanding of historiography (in fiction and elsewhere) as the construction of a discourse about the past for use in, and using, the materials of the present. The discourse spoken by X and by the entire film could be called a metahistoriography; it does not tell history, but it does demonstrate how history is and can be told, and even, perhaps, how its day-to-day texts are experienced. With respect to the surrounding "significant but incomprehensible" gestures, *Marienbad* functions as a kind of empty allusion or teleidoscope, open to all myths, offering itself as a mechanism that can organize, write, and rewrite society's stories without telling them.

4. Signs of the Times: Fictions of May 1968

Rock and roll has become respectable. What a bummer. – Ray Davies, of the Kinks

About three-quarters of the way through *Alice's Restaurant* (1969), Arlo Guthrie is called in by the army for a preinduction physical examination. When those in charge discover that he has a police record for littering, they undertake an FBI background check, beginning with fingerprinting. At this point Arlo turns to face the camera in extreme closeup: with a smirk, he extends his inked middle finger toward the authorities in an obscene gesture of defiance. Then, turning his hand, and with a puckish expression on his face, he adds a second finger to present the peace symbol. This moment documents the conjunction of at least three semiotic fields. First, his inked finger is a kind of signature, pointing to Arlo's inevitable insertion into social institutions, in this instance, judicial and military. Second, the lone and angry finger can literalize its oppositional stance by means of a visual pun: *manifestation*, the French term meaning "protest," derives from the Latin *manus*, "hand," and *festus*, "hit" or "struck." Thus, like the related words *offend* and *defend*, *protest* is both palpably evident and inherently belligerent. Finally, Arlo's second gesture marks a subtle shift from unacceptable defiance to hip, from challenging authority to complicity with what singer Joni Mitchell a few years later called "the star-making machinery."[1] Peace signs, even in the 1960s, were bought and sold, turned into a highly visible commodity on the fronts of tee shirts, on the seats of bluejeans, on earrings, patches, and bumper stickers. Produced in grand Hollywood fashion, *Alice's Restaurant* continues to provide an enjoyable nostalgia trip into American sixties counterculturism. Arlo's gesture and his *geste*, that is, his song and story, have become mainstream spectacle.

This scene—this shift from one sign to another—can serve to identify a dilemma confronting those radical artists in France who wanted to reflect *within their art* on the stakes, successes, and failures of "Mai '68." Arlo's shift from hostile to sheepish and from the obscene to the chic is indicative of a double bind that lies at the heart of the 1968 cultural rebellion: artists who question authority also subvert the authority of authorship. Art as practice may be incompatible with art as institution, and thus to challenge the legitimacy of institutions (including sign systems, such as language itself) is to risk either silencing oneself or becoming totally incomprehensible. Arlo's two gestures thus point to an opposition between art as institution and art as praxis, and they are emblematic of opposing esthetic responses to a countercultural impulse: simply put, alienate everyone or be coopted. For many writers, filmmakers, and cultural critics at the time, the urgent question was how to clear a precarious path between the two, in other words, how to practice "countercultural art." Was this ultimately a contradiction in terms?

WRITING "ABOUT" MAY 1968; OR, "JE N'AI RIEN À DIRE
[I Have Nothing to Say]" (Censier)

The most comprehensive literary study of May 1968 available to date is *La Littérature et le Mouvement de Mai 68* by Patrick Combes.[2] Combes examines novels, criticism, graffiti, and the activist participation of writers in or against the movement. Observing from the standpoint of 1984 that "traces of the movement of 1968 are still many and obvious today, in everyday life and in the imagination [*dans le champ quotidien, dans l'imaginaire*]" (9), he tries to identify and circumscribe those traces in post-1968 cultural production. As a way of gauging the relation between the events of May and novels about those events, he surveys a corpus of fifty or so novels that represent some aspect of the rebellions. After detailed analysis of characters, the events portrayed, the stereotypes deployed, the ideological positions that can be discerned, and so on, Combes expresses disappointment that with respect to the phenomenon of May the novels are able finally to offer only "reductive explanations." He classifies these explanations into four general types. Each of the novels attributes the events of May to one of the following: (1) a "crisis in civilization" of worldwide proportions, often taking the form of generational conflicts or revolt against the alienations of consumer capitalism; (2) the nefarious intervention of a bunch of immature student and intellectual misfits, outside agitators, and troublemakers; (3) a collective psychopathology on the part of maladjusted misfits desublimating their sexual or other frustrations in an orgiastic free-for-all; and (4) a metaphysical quest to affirm a new morality or create a new utopian form of human nature.

This classification system is based entirely on the novels' thematic emphases and cognitive statements. Its categories parallel analyses of the events by social scientists, who have arrived at similar taxonomies.[3] But Combes's sociological categories are fundamentally unsuited to address his initial question, namely, "Did May give rise to new forms, to esthetic innovation?" His methods and even the selection of his corpus have to do with the novels' themes, their content, their status as representations of the events of 1968, and so the answer he finds to his question is a resounding no. Fictions about May, he concludes, are generally traditional in form, and rather mediocre at that. He laments the failure of the novels to generate new discourses, but his corpus excludes precisely those works whose primary interest lies in their work with forms of expression.

If Combes concludes that May cannot be found in the novels "about" May, he is aware that the esthetic questions raised by the movement could possibly be addressed elsewhere. Speaking from within the horizons of socialist realism, seen as the only legitimate reflection in fiction of revolutionary movements, he declares literature's failure to "cover" the event,[4] but he fails to address the fact that the Communist Party was not sympathetic to the uprisings in the cultural sector and that the insurgent students were abandoning socialist realism as a revolutionary methodology in favor of surrealism. Over and over again, Combes refuses to see representation itself as problematic.

And yet the study is interesting and intelligent because Combes asks the right questions and makes potentially useful distinctions. He wants to look, but does not know *where* to look, for works that would prolong the creativity of the "inscrivains," those ebullient, spontaneous, and insurgent scribblers on walls, posters, fliers, and even the human body. He distinguishes between the novel *about* May ["le roman *sur* Mai"] and what might have been a novel *of* May ["le roman *de* Mai"] (emphasis added); he speculates that "the only possible works about May are the ones that don't talk about it" (253). He concludes sadly that works in which May is not the object of description but rather the "enunciating subject" of the fiction have yet to be seen (193).

I disagree. Combes's failure to find such works illustrates my observations about the risks, even the definition, of countercultural art in the wake of May 1968. In addition to his confusion of esthetic with sociological issues, Combes misses the point in two ways: he fails to see the risk of cooptation, the double bind I mentioned at the outset (*récupération* was the buzzword in Paris at the time); and he does not look at cinema. In sum, he never asks the questions that will be my own point of departure here, namely, What sort of fiction was subsequently produced by the active participants in May? If Sarraute or Duras, or Godard or Truffaut, did not write about May, why didn't they? What *did* they produce? Can the effects of May 1968 be perceived in their works, and if so, where? This chapter considers in detail the concept of recuperation or cooptation and then uses it as a lens through which to examine two very different examples of counterdiscursive esthetic practice: *Tout va bien,* directed by Jean-Luc Godard and Jean-Pierre Gorin, and Marguerite Duras's *Nathalie Granger.* It should be possible to determine in what ways these are fictions of, but not "about," May and to appreciate both their strategies and their limits.

"NOUS REFUSONS D'ÊTRE RÉCUPÉRÉS
[We Refuse to be Recuperated]" (Odéon)

Daniel Cohn-Bendit was the most visible leader of Les Enragés de Nanterre, the student group that launched the revolt at that university in March 1968, and he subsequently became a sort of symbol of the entire rebellion. Immediately following the events of May, Cohn-Bendit published a book that begins as follows:

Had I decided to write a book on the French political scene and on the chances of a revolutionary uprising only two or three months ago, no publisher would have taken the slightest notice of me. But such was the impact of the events of May and June and so wildly has the name of Cohn-Bendit been bandied about that, far from my having to go down on my knees to them, the publishers now come chasing after me, begging me to write about anything I choose, good or bad, exciting or dull; all they want is something they can sell—a revolutionary gadget with marketable qualities.

In any case, all self-respecting publishers are falling over themselves to cash in on the May events. In our commercial world, individual capitalists are perfectly willing to pave the way for their own destruction, to broadcast revolutionary ideas, provided only that these help to fill their pockets.[5]

Throughout the book, this risk of selling out the revolution (by literally selling it in book form) is a source of palpable unease. Cohn-Bendit worries about the narrowness of the gap between two hand gestures. The phenomenon he describes was also of interest to Tom Wolfe, who in 1970 baptized it "radical chic." Wolfe explains the term by recounting a social occasion he calls "Panther night at the Bernsteins," a fundraising event sponsored by Leonard Bernstein and his wife ostensibly to raise money for the Black Panthers' legal defense. Wolfe lingeringly and acidly describes Panther leaders nibbling miniature hors-d'oeuvres and engaging in polite chitchat, while the New York best-dressed elite consumes a titillating mélange of terrorism, exoticism, voyeurism, and liberal racism. His satire shows how a revolutionary impulse can be reduced to a question of "the tricky business of the fashionable new politics."[6]

I believe that radical chic is an inevitable, often fatal by-product of countercultures.[7] The thirst for stories about crises combines with a strong collective and conservative need to "manage" them (in the psychological sense, that is, to assimilate them and defuse their threat), to mystify them, and ultimately to dismiss them.[8] It would appear that most of the novels Combes included in his survey, and especially the categories he established to classify them, accommodate this impulse. It is not surprising, then, that he finds in the novels either unsympathetic or romanticized versions of the events. Conversely, adherents to social movements who want to extend their counterculturism into their artistic expression attempt, with varying degrees of success or even conscious awareness of the process, to resist such recuperation.

Thus, on the part of countercultural artists, and even a political writer like Cohn-Bendit, there appears to be a self-imposed ideological pressure, a sort of anxiety not of influence but of legitimacy, that keeps them balancing between two unacceptable extremes. On the one hand, one can assume the voice of authorship and thus of authority, which is precisely what had been targeted by the revolt (as in the slogan "Question authority") and which had come, in the heat of events, to be associated with the paternalistic and patriarchal state, the police, and retrograde aesthetic tendencies. The alternative is to reject authority entirely, and along with it authorship. Since anything that can be understood can be coopted, this might mean rejecting even the arbitrary laws whereby language produces meaning, resulting in either a form of self-censorship that leans toward silence or the creation of works that no one will want to buy or be able to understand. In the best cases, it can motivate construction of counterlinguistic practices, of counterdiscourses. The two films to be studied in this chapter are explorations into the modes of this kind of practice. Their relation with the events of May is not metaphoric, or not simply metaphoric, but metonymic: they are not trying to "explain" May, reductively or otherwise, but to continue its explorations into the relations between aesthetics and politics.

"L'IMAGINATION AU POUVOIR [Power to the Imagination]";
"A BAS LE RÉALISME SOCIALISTE. VIVE LE SURRÉALISME
[Down with Socialist Realism. Long Live Surrealism]" (Condorcet)

Many analysts of May 1968 have concluded that if the upheaval ultimately failed as a political movement, it did have a lasting impact on culture. They show the various ways in which the events culminated a process of redrawing the intellectual map with respect to the political domain. Keith A. Reader, for example, speaks of a "dethroning of economism from its place at the center of left-wing thought" in favor of a new and broader understanding of what constitutes the political.[9] The definition of the target of social transformation and intellectual investigation was enlarged from *la politique* to *le politique,* from "politics" to "the political." This shift moved language and cultural production closer to the center of the political sphere and provoked more widespread appreciation of the political impact of discourse. It also put the spotlight of the moment on the kind of experimental research on form and discourse that the New Novelists and New Wave filmmakers had been pursuing all along, legitimizing their work and moving it closer to the center of the broader cultural stage.

Of course for thinkers like Jacques Lacan and Michel Foucault, as well as Roland Barthes, Jean Baudrillard, Julia Kristeva, and Jacques Derrida, this emphasis, with its attendant investigations into the links between language and power, was nothing new, but the period gave new energy and a new public to their investigations. Tracing the lines of force linking the work of these thinkers to the spirit of May 1968 would be a massive study on its own. It will, however, be helpful to examine here a few crucial sources of important perspectives on this problem of cooptation or selling out and its impact on cultural production after 1968.

By 1968 the term *recuperation* was already prominent in the lexicon of the situationist group, whose influence on the events and "style" of May 1968 cannot be overestimated. Their outlook could be summarized by the observation that social change is rendered impossible, is already preempted or pre-recuperated, by ossified structures of social interaction, including everything from the suffocating conventions of literature, painting, and the cinema to the layout of urban centers and the codified expression of sexuality. Their writings—in pamphlets, books, and especially in their journal, the *Internationale situationiste,* launched in 1958—are the source of many of the wall slogans of 1968. Their emphasis on the liberating power of play and their overall *style contestataire* shaped the strategies and styles associated with 1960s counterculturism in France. The group's agenda was a complete overhaul of modern life, a revolution in daily life [*la vie quotidienne*]: they called for a redesign of cities that would give rise to a more communal, less privatized social space; their art, like a stroll through their utopian cities (several of the members were painters and architects), was constructed on free or random, and often "manifestly" hostile, expression and a principle of *dérive,* which might be translated as "going with the flow," reminiscent of Rimbaud. The similarities of their goals, if not their style, with those of Zen Buddhism and other means of altered states of consciousness are readily apparent, as are the situationists' connections (downstream) with punk and (upstream) with dada and surrealism.[10] Although the *Internationale situationiste* is in many ways modeled on the *Révolution surréaliste,* published periodically by the surrealists between 1924 and 1929,[11] the situationists repudiated these forerunners (along with everything else), putting forth their program

j'aime ma caméra
parce que
j'aime
vivre

j'enregistre les
meilleurs moments
de l'existence

je les ressuscite
à ma volonté
dans tout leur éclat

LA DOMINATION DU SPECTACLE SUR LA VIE

5. Alienated desire is transformed into commodity spectacle. "I love my camera because I love life. I record the best moments and relive them whenever I wish, in all their freshness." *Internationale situationiste*, 11 October 1967.

instead as a *reversal* of surrealism, as in their slogan "The point is not to put poetry at the service of revolution but revolution at the service of poetry," a slogan eagerly adopted by the *soixante-huitards*.

For our purposes in studying the texts in this chapter, it is important to stress the broad implications of the situationists' remarkably coherent critique of consumer capitalism. A book by the group's leader served as a handbook for many participants in the events of May. In *La Société du spectacle* (1967; *The Society of the Spectacle*), Guy Debord follows the strategy outlined in the journal he controlled. He puts culture at the center of its theory by redefining consumer capitalism in terms of "spectacle." Debord mercilessly attacks the moribund, reified, and coopted forms of spectacle to be found in the commercial cinema, on television, and at the theater, identifying them as an opiate of the masses. He argues that capitalism systematically alienates people from their own lives, which are then sold back to them in the form of spectacles (for example, advertising, television sit-com narratives, and so on).[12] People thus become spectators of their own desires, which are taken away from them and transformed into commodities. The alternative Debord proposes is the spontaneous improvisation of disruptive theatrical "situations" (in the United States these were called "happenings") that would radically subvert habitual social interactions and provoke new forms of subjectivity.[13] Resistance to recuperation by consumer capitalism thus requires a transformation of interactions that can be accomplished through a heightened awareness of the power of consumable objects, whether the object is a book, a house, a lipstick, or an idea.

The situationists devised elaborate strategies for avoiding recuperation. They systematically proscribed ownership of any kind, especially of ideas. Plagiarism, as one of capitalist consumer culture's police tactics, was among the icons the situationists strove to overturn. The implications of this stand can best be illustrated by an anecdote. When I attempted to obtain the complete *Internationale situationiste* through my institution's interlibrary loan service, I discovered that only a few copies exist in this country and no library would lend it. I asked a colleague at one of the universities that has it to copy the entire volume, almost seven hundred pages. The photocopying office there was unwilling to do so until confronted with the notice printed on each issue of the journal: "All the texts published in the 'Internationale Situationiste' may be freely copied, translated, or adapted, even without indication as to their origin." I got my photocopies. But recuperation is, as I said, an unavoidable by-product of subversion: the book in which the facsimiles are published bears a copyright![14]

Debord's redefinition of capitalism in terms of spectacle and politics in terms of desire intersects nicely with the Nouveau Roman's reputed chosisme and the self-conscious attention to the limits and effects of visual representation on the part of the Nouvelle Vague filmmakers. Moreover, his insistence that bourgeois art sells us back our own alienated desires prefigures the insights of psychoanalytic (Lacanian) film theorists such as Christian Metz and Laura Mulvey, who have investigated how cinematic images shape viewers' desires and hence their subjectivity. Since it was a specific goal of the situationists to forge new forms of subjectivity (a version of altered states of consciousness), it was to be expected that they would show considerable interest in the cinema. Debord first mentions the concept of spectacle in the inaugural issue of the journal, in connection with cinema, and the *Internationale situationiste* contains several articles that discuss the work of New Wave filmmakers. The journal recognizes its own strategy of self-subversion in *Hiroshima mon amour,* which it considers an important "appearance in the 'commercial' cinema of modernist self-destruction." *Marienbad,* on the other hand, is considered too "precious" to have much effect. Debord himself made several minimalist films (along the lines of Andy Warhol's), one of which was entitled *Contre le cinéma (Against Cinema,* 1964). His journal as well as his brief and self-aborting film career also address the political dilemma of the artists studied here. In the words of the *Internationale situationiste,* the goal of art should be to "put an end to the separation that arose around 1930 between avant-garde artists and the revolutionary Left."[15]

It apparently has not been necessary to credit the situationists, and indeed many have failed to do so, because their style is so recognizable.[16] Their writings attempt to circumvent recuperation with a style that is outrageously and indiscriminately offensive. This offensiveness takes the forms of obscenity, scatology, hostility, and general grossness. In their lives and in their writings, paintings, films, and architectural and urban designs they attacked the foundations of culture by flaunting their transgression of behavioral taboos and verbal niceties. They systematically avoided publicity, disrupted the codes of civilized daily life, steered clear of popularity, and tried to contradict themselves as much as possible. They also attacked anyone who praised their work, including insiders, who were often excommunicated. Their diminishing numbers, their disdain for publicity or success, and their very success itself as evidenced in the widespread "plagiarism" of their work and its infiltration into public discourse ultimately led to their disappearance from the scene. The *Internationale situationiste* ceased publication in 1969, and the group disbanded in 1972. Its leader, Guy Debord, permanently withdrew his creative works (mostly films) from circulation, and several other members drifted into obscurity, insanity, or suicide. Their influence can be recognized, however, in the goals, the tactics, and the playful "spirit" of the student uprisings of May 1968 as well as in the antirepresentational tactics and antispectacular spectacles of many post-1968 works, including *Tout va bien* and *Nathalie Granger.*

Situationist echoes, in the form of hypothesized causal links between readability and cooptation, can also be seen in the post-1968 work of Roland Barthes. Barthes had always been interested in the politics of language and in capitalism's mystifications (or mythologies) of everyday life, but after May 1968 his work became more intensely lyrical and personal, less overtly didactic or theoretical. A stance similar to that of the situationists but more gently expressed can be discerned in his 1970 account of his trip to Japan in *L'Empire des signes.*[17] In that book, he resists indulging in tourism as a form of consumerism by evoking his efforts to resist appropriating the cultural Other in the name of a humanistically imposed sense, an interpretation. Rather, he uses the signs, the spectacle he finds in Japan, as a sort of "situation" to transform his own way of thinking.[18] Also understandable in the aura of the situationists is his 1968–69 seminar at the École pratique des hautes études, published in 1970 as *S/Z*. There Barthes makes his famous distinction between the readerly text [*le texte lisible*] and the writerly text [*le texte scriptible*]. The readerly text repeats existing discourses and serves them up as a consumer commodity. It is designed to be *récupérable*, that is, easily understood and thus easily put to the service of dominant ideologies. The writerly text, on the other hand, resists representation and consumable meaning. When Barthes says that "what is at stake in literary work (of literature as work), is no longer to make the reader into a consumer, but into a producer of the text,"[19] his description of the text parallels the neo-Marxist situationist redefinitions of the liberated city, or game, or sexuality, or spectacle.

As a final guideline in delineating the problematics of cooptation in and of cultural production, it is useful to keep in mind Louis Althusser's 1970 essay "Ideology and Ideological State Apparatuses."[20] In that essay, which contains a neo-Marxist redefinition of the work of cultural representations, Althusser defines ideology as a "system of ideas and representations which dominate the mind of a man or a social group" (149). Those representations mediate individuals' relations to the "real world" of political and social institutions.[21] While his perspective is more broadly theoretical and does not address textuality directly, Althusser's views of culture are neatly congruent with those of Barthes and of the situationists. His conception of culture as semiautonomous (that is, his insistence that the relation between "superstructure" and the economic is not a simple mimetic one) opens the way to the possibility of defining ideological work in terms of discourse, or what we might call discursive "situations." His definition of ideology once again resonates with an understanding of filmic images as formative of subjectivity. Althusser thus provides the theory for what the New Novelists and the New Wave filmmakers claimed was their goal all along: to forge a representational regime whereby it might be possible to imagine political commitment not *in* writing but *of* filmic or novelistic *écriture* itself. Cultural production might thus not be limited to reflecting the economic sphere, but it might be an arena where consciousness could be transformed directly. Althusser's essay legitimizes for the political Left the view that cultural representations and semiotic systems are not simple reflections of some already constituted "reality"; rather, they are entities that engage in ideological struggle by mediating one's experience of reality (shaping one's subjectivity and institutions) and through which social change can be wrought.

"JE SUIS MARXISTE TENDANCE GROUCHO
[I Am a Marxist of the Groucho Tendency]" (Nanterre)

Before finally examining the two texts to be studied in this chapter, I want to look at Patrick Combes's second error. He may have found no "new forms" or "esthetic innovation" in the fictions about May 1968 that he studied because he elected to exclude the cinema from his investigation. And yet May 1968 and the cinema go hand in hand. Even before the formation of the March 22 Group (with Cohn-Bendit) at Nanterre, the earliest rumblings of revolt in the cultural sector were heard in February at the Cinémathèque, with the notorious Langlois affair. That scandal began when Malraux and the ministry of culture took note of Langlois's eccentric and disorganized manner of running the Cinémathèque française and peremptorily replaced him with one Pierre Barbin, who was widely considered a bureaucrat and hostile government agent. The focus of the conflict quickly shifted from evaluating Langlois's real or imagined short-comings to defending the autonomy of cultural institutions.[22] The entire international cinema community, galvanized by Truffaut, Godard, Gorin, Rivette, and others, rose in defense of Langlois. Walking in two directions once again, Langlois was returned to his post in April. Later, the momentum gathered over the Langlois affair was responsible for the tumultuous closing of the Cannes Film Festival in May in sympathy with the student revolt and in protest against Gaullist repression.

The confrontation over Langlois was thus a harbinger of what was to come in May. A group called the Etats généraux du cinéma began to rethink the entire gamut of institutional practices relating to cinema: production, distribution, spectatorship, relation to the political and the social. As many commentators have pointed out, this first incident showed that the the will of the Gaullist state could be resisted. It was possible after all to reject bureaucratic control of culture. The self-regulating autonomy (*autogestion*) of creativity could score victories against the governmental control of culture and its use as commodity. Idiosyncratic genius could stand up to bureaucratic bullying.

It is important to note, in relation to the issue of recuperation, that not one of the filmmakers involved in the defense of Langlois or the revolts of May and June 1968 made a film "about" May. (Godard came the closest with *La Chinoise*, but that film appeared in 1967!) Truffaut, one of the leading defenders of Langlois, was in the process of making *Baisers volés* (*Stolen Kisses*) when the trouble erupted. That film, released later that year, bears one small sign, a signature of sorts, that never carries over into the narrative but rather takes the form of a single still shot of the lowered iron gate of the Cinémathèque. Significantly, this shot is projected behind the credits, as if Truffaut were listing the events of 1968 as co-creator of the film (or, in Combes's words, as if May were not the object but the subject of enunciation). This is borne out by Truffaut's comments about the way the spirit of the events infused the film's production: the filming team (crew, actors, technicians) transformed the structure of their interactions and became a sort of collective. Later Truffaut chose to recount that *process* in *La Nuit américaine* (1972; *Day for Night*), his film about filmmaking, where he documents a transformation in the means of production, if you will, but with nary a mention of 1968.

A second way that May 1968 can be seen as inherently cinematic is in the fact that as a revolt *about* (as well as *in*) culture, the rebellions often took language, especially written language, as their target. There developed a widespread and systematic suspicion of the book, of the document, of written authority. Value was shifted instead to transgressive uses of language, for example, the innovative syntax of the wall slogans, such as "L'anarchie, c'est je," which normally would be written, "L'Anarchie, c'est moi," after the authoritarian Gaullist "L'Etat, c'est moi." The transgressive force of the graffiti is especially noticeable if one keeps in mind that in France it is against the law to write on public walls. It is important as well to underline, or rather, to emphasize, that here I am talking about writing not as a material format but as a mode of language use, and so at this juncture emerged distinctions between literature (the Work) and *écriture* (the Text, or simply textuality) and between writing and "l'inscription de la parole."[23] It was *la parole* (perhaps best translated as "speech act," "speech as act," or even as "speech as violence"), even when written, that was most transgressive, thus most liberating, as Barthes outlined in an essay written during the events entitled "L'Ecriture de l'événement."[24] The ambiguity of his title turns on the preposition *de:* the essay contains both a refusal to write *about* the events (to consider them an object of interpretation) and a taxonomy of the ways in which the events themselves constituted an unmediated *subject* of *écriture,* as in *la parole sauvage* of graffiti, wall posters, speeches, images, and even violent acts. By positing the varieties of *la parole* as the most effective mode of language, Barthes once again intersects with the situationists, who claimed that violence was the only form of expression capable of successfully resisting recuperation.

Barthes thus sees the significance of the events as a *"Prise de la parole* (comme on dit: *Prise de la Bastille*)." One could call this a kind of *autogestion* of speech, which declares its independence both from written language and from puritanical rules requiring that before one speaks one must have something to say. It was thus also, more intricately, an *autogestion* of the signifier, liberated from the hegemony of the signified, seen as a mechanism of social control. The freely playing signifier was cast as hero in a drama of political resistance. Writers and filmmakers, like and among the demonstrators in the streets, made the point that speaking was not about *making a point*. It was about play, about carnival, about the freedom to be poetic. The right to speak without having something to say also became the battle cry of the Nouveau Romanciers, who began to call themselves Nouveau Nouveau Romanciers and to pay even closer attention than they had before to the forms and microcontexts of expression rather than its contents. Jean Ricardou and the *Tel quel* writers were the most vociferous theorizers of the novel as a site where the linguistic worker could take control of the means of production not of consumable meaning but of pleasure, of the use of language not as an instrument but as a material.[25] Texts that aim to continue the momentum and spirit of May will be writerly ones.

The cinema is an even more promising place than the novel to look for such experimentation with language use. Books, after all, however avant-garde they may be, are associated with school and with the law (of the land, of the Father). Moviegoing, on the other hand, is reserved for leisure time, which is, according to the situationists, the most fertile ground for transformation of mentalities. In fact, after 1968 both Robbe-Grillet and Duras make a marked shift from the novel to film.[26] As Madeleine Borgomano points out in a discussion of Duras's post-1968 emphasis on filmmaking, the living speech and images of a film destroy themselves as they proceed.[27] They are self-consuming and thus resistant (before the advent of video rental, in any case) to classical exchanges such as purchase, ownership, and display, as with the coffee-table book, the gift book, and so on. And Fredric Jameson could have been describing the situationists when he argued that performance arts are more readily adaptable to a revolutionary aesthetic than are reified forms like the novel. This is because "what is real is precisely not the isolated script or text itself but rather the work-in-situation, the work-in-performance, in which for a brief moment the gap between producer and consumer, between *destinataire* and *destinateur,* is momentarily bridged, and the twin crisis of a missing public and an artist without social function is temporarily overcome."[28] In short, seeing filmic *écriture* as a site of ideological struggle and cultural transformation (as Althusser theorized it) meant reclaiming the spectacle as "happening," as event or "situation," rather than remaining its passive consumers in the sense that Debord understood the term.

In light of this emphasis on language as performance, as spectacle, and as signifier, then, it is not surprising that 1968 has itself been described in terms of cinematic spectacle. Writing in *Le Monde* on 15 May 1968, for example, Bertrand Girod de l'Ain alluded to the iconography of both the French Revolution and the more recent Chinese one when he invoked the Cultural Revolution climate in the Sorbonne. Noting that the Sorbonne had become a "temple to culture," he grandly announced that the night of 13 May, the night the Sorbonne was opened to the crowds, was "an extraordinary night of exalted liberty." "Inside," he added, "one would have said it was the Revolutionary Assemblies as seen by Abel Gance." Edgar Morin makes a similar unmediated jump from the streets to the cinema when he speaks of "la Sorbonne-Potemkine."[29]

"NE NOUS ATTARDONS PAS AU SPECTACLE DE LA CONTESTATION MAIS PASSONS À LA CONTESTATION DU SPECTACLE

[Let Us Not Linger on the Spectacle of Contestation but Let Us Move on to the Contestation of the Spectacle]" (Odéon)

These multiple but intersecting perspectives can now be used to look briefly at two films, one by Godard and Gorin (the Dziga-Vertov Group), the other by Duras. Both Godard and Duras were participants in the successful effort to reinstate Langlois, and both joined the Union des écrivains, another ad hoc group of artists organized during the events of May. Godard and Gorin's *Tout va bien* and Duras's *Nathalie Granger* appeared in 1972. Both films systematically attempt to foreclose the recuperation of cinema, and of revolt itself, as radical chic objects for consumption. In other words, both demonstrate an attempt to circumvent spectacle-as-commodity in the situationist sense (see the slogan that heads this section) and instead to reclaim spectacle in the spirit of 1968, thereby making May 1968 the subject rather than the object of their enunciation.

Tout va bien follows a season in the life of a Parisian couple in the wake of 1968. Yves Montand plays Jacques, a disillusioned former New Wave filmmaker who now produces advertisements for television. Susan DeWitt (Jane Fonda) is an American journalist sent to cover a strike who comes to fear that she is simply covering it up. She later begins a different sort of article that will investigate the political meanings of the phenomenon, new at the time, of the hypermarket. The plot, such as it is, takes place in three arenas: the couple's progressive alienation from their work; their dissatisfaction with their sex life, which they characterize as a monotonous round of "cinéma, bouffe, baise [movies, meals, screwing]," a formula to which I will return shortly; and their day sequestered with the boss of a sausage factory in his office during the strike Susan is there to cover. There are some final intimations that their experiences are part of the broader changes taking place in national life.

Nathalie Granger follows a day in the life of a middle-class suburban family. After two little girls (Nathalie and Laurence) have left for school and the man has departed for work, Isabelle Granger (Lucia Bose) and her friend (Jeanne Moreau) occupy themselves with routine household tasks. Most of the film's plot is made up of non-events. Dismissed from school because of her uncooperative behavior and violent outbursts, Nathalie will not go to boarding school after all. The mail and a newspaper are delivered but will not be read; rather, they are torn up or burned. The family will not buy a new washing machine from an itinerant salesman. In the meantime, Nathalie and Laurence return from school to take their piano lesson, and throughout the day can be heard radio broadcast fragments about two adolescent murderers hiding out in a nearby forest.

Other than their year of release, at first viewing the two films would seem to have little in common. Yet both stories actually evoke a failed or incomplete revolt. More significantly, both try visibly to subvert established cultural forms at the same time that they (inevitably) reproduce them. With the explicit aim of transforming society, the makers of both films took a multilayered materialist approach to filmmaking. First, they strove to transform the process of artistic production. Duras shifted her emphasis from writing to filming (although she continued to write novels as well), and she reports how *Nathalie Granger* evolved from an unspoken harmony between director and actors. With Jean-Pierre Gorin, Godard formed the short-lived Dziga-Vertov collective for revolutionary filmmaking, of which *Tout va bien* is among the last (and most accessible) productions. Both films attempt to be political by situating themselves in the context of their production. Each film says "where it's coming from [*d'où il parle*]," to use the jargon of the times. In addition, the filmmakers' materialist approach meant that they would aim at the creation not of new forms per se but of "situations" that would in turn produce new relations and new forms of subjectivity (changed consciousness) on the part of characters and audiences alike. *Tout va bien* is, as Godard claims, both a "film about politics," though not directly the politics of 1968) and a "political film."[30] *Nathalie Granger,* on the other hand, *enacts* but does not *recount* the broader issues it raises; it presents the behavioral, linguistic, and visual codes of 1968 but not their narration or representation. By defining themselves as cultural *processes* rather than *products* for consumption and by thematizing their critiques of consumerism, both films participate in the larger aesthetic project of seeking film forms consonant with the politics they espouse.

Tout va bien begins with Godard's voiceover narration announcing, "I want to make a movie," to which a female voice answers, "To make a movie, you need money." The opening credits unroll against the backdrop of a hand writing checks for lighting, camera crew, stars, and so on. Paralleling this self-conscious display of filmmaking's material apparatus, the narrator describes its narrative unfolding, moving outward (as the characters themselves will subsequently do) from the personal to the collective: first you need "she and he," then a love story, some conflicts, and finally, history.

In more covert ways, *Nathalie Granger* is also about the social and material conditions under which discourse is produced. While the film's visual horizon is the limit of the house itself, bordered by walls, forest, and street, the family's non-events are seen within their framing institutions: marriage, school, the media (newspaper and radio), consumer society, parenthood. Different perspectives, particularly the masculine and the feminine, are shown as they are shaped by spheres of activity and work. Women's lives in the home, being inherently antispectacular, are better placed to resist representation as visual or verbal commodity. In fact, *Nathalie Granger* mounts a far-reaching critique of any sort of intellectual activity, including language, dialogue, and filmmaking. The fact that *Nathalie Granger* is almost a silent film is itself the logical enactment of its female characters' privileging of music and silence over speech.

Autoreflexivity in both films, then, far from signaling a mere narcissistic "film d'esthète" as Jacques/Montand pejoratively puts it (and as much New Wave criticism takes for granted), is actually in itself a political positioning. In the context of a *mise en question* of culture as a whole, the highlighting, or *mise en abyme*, of filmmaking as process is in itself a critique of consumer values. Godard's characteristic Brechtian estrangement techniques and Duras's pure eccentricity (spatial, verbal, and esthetic) foreground the films' processes, their materiality, preventing identification with a single unproblematic point of view or consumption of a message or story. One could even suggest that here *autogestion* takes the form of self-conscious, self-designating, and self-regulating textuality.

To trace this critique of consumerism, and particularly of cinematic language and images as objects of consumption, I want to organize the rest of my discussion around a few consumer goods in each film. This *leçon de choses* [object lesson] will include the sausage, vegetables, and dessert in *Tout va bien* and a newspaper, a table, a baby carriage, and a washing machine in *Nathalie Granger*. Tracing the displacement of values onto material objects will make it possible to see how these objects reshape the individual's relation to production and consumption, thereby transforming economic and semiotic exchange and moving toward new forms of subjectivity. It will also turn out that the objects themselves have certain gendered meanings that prevent the film (as they prevented May 1968) from achieving closure.

Tout va bien invites analysis around the polyvalence of the French term *consommation*. The term is to be understood as consumerism, of course, but also as food and sex: the suburban lifestyle of "boulot, métro, dodo [work, subway, sleep]" is reworked for the purposes of the film's contestation to include *cinéma,* along with *bouffe* and *baise,* as facets of daily life that need to be transformed. Observing the meat processors' strike, Jacques and Susan begin to see how their subjectivity in relation to work and to sexuality has been manipulated by capitalism, and they are led to re-theorize the politics of their private life.

Sausage

Most of the film takes place in a sausage factory, where the screen is dominated by two activities: incessant talking and eating. These two themes intersect in ways that bring to light a critique both of writing and of gender relations. In one of Godard's characteristic monologue scenes, the boss gives a prepackaged speech analyzing the strike along the lines of the "disruption-by-a-handful-of-agitators" explanation of May 1968. Speaking with a written discourse, a discourse of (false) authority that could never be considered *parole* in the way Barthes defined it, he concludes his comically patronizing "analysis" of the factory situation by expressing his confidence that he will be home in time to greet his dinner guests. In another sequence, a striker reminds the viewer of the politics of gender and of women's double work day, in which she is responsible both on the job and at home: she argues on the telephone with her husband, begging him to "let" her stay at the factory, promising that he will find his supper in the refrigerator, ready to heat up.

So much ostentatious eating (and talk about eating) evokes the role of Maoism in fashioning the discourses of 1968. In a famous 1927 speech, Mao explained to Party intellectuals the differences between their theories and the messy realities of peasant revolt, declaring aphoristically: "A revolution is not a dinner party."[31] Among the most notorious and problematic policies of the Chinese Cultural Revolution was the campaign to reeducate intellectuals by transplanting them to work in factories and fields. Godard's Jacques, according to his monologue a former New Wave filmmaker, infused by the more radical political analyses brought to the project by Gorin, mentions this policy in passing to help explain his estrangement from intellectuals and from "les Gauchistes" [the Leftists, i.e., the Communist Party]. The film enacts this policy visually as well. When Jacques and Susan are finally released from the boss's office, the workers wish to explain their grievances to the press. Although Susan protests that she already understands it all, it becomes clear that she does not as several workers in turn describe conditions in the factory—the pervasive sexual harassment, the ludicrous and unhelpful agendas of the Party and the union, even the nauseating smells. During these narrations the visual backdrop shows Montand and Fonda among workers on the assembly line, stuffing and loading sausage. Addressed didactically to an audience of intellectuals, the film sets itself up as a surrogate reeducation of just this sort. And Fonda, as the spectator persona within the film, will ultimately come to the knowledge that her journalistic practices not only betray the understanding she has begun to achieve but also reproduce that false consciousness for consumption by a wider public.[32]

Sausage is not a gratuitous choice, if at least three other post-1968 films can serve as evidence. The heroine of Alain Tanner's 1971 film *La Salamandre* also works in a sausage factory, and in his 1975 *Pour Jonas qui aura 25 ans en l'an deux mille* (*For Jonah Who Will Be Twenty-Five in the Year Two Thousand*), a high-school teacher punctuates a lecture on the politics of historical periodization by dramatically slicing a sausage with a cleaver. In Michel Drach's 1974 *Les Violons du bal,* the protagonist (Jean-Louis Trintignant) helps a 1968 rioter escape the police and offers him a meal of bread and sausage. When Trintignant sarcastically points out that the "bourgeois sausage" certainly tastes good, his guest retorts proudly that "sausage isn't bourgeois, it's proletarian." These images take on the character of institutional allegory in the light of Daniel Cohn-Bendit's account of the university, which he compares to a "sausage machine, which turns people out without any real culture and incapable of thinking for themselves, but trained to fit into the economic system of a highly industrialized society."[33] By means of the image, Godard and Gorin have illustrated the ways in which the factory (re)produces consciousness even more effectively than it produces sausages, as the workers themselves are literally transformed into the product they ostensibly produce.

Vegetables

One of the better-known scenes of *Tout va bien* takes place in a hypermarket, one of those giant French supermarkets that sells every imaginable product, from camembert and instant soups to automotive parts and power tools. While Fonda paces back and forth with her notebook, the camera sustains a tracking shot lasting more than six minutes that takes in the full sweep of the huge market, with its endless row of checkout registers. As the scene unfolds, the hypermarket comes to stand for the society itself. An incident erupts that centers on a man peddling books about the Communist Party platform. When he is unable or unwilling to answer the questions posed to him by a group of stereotypical young people, probably students, he grows hostile and tells them they should just buy the book. One of the shoppers protests that one cannot sell ideas as if they were vegetables. The film here offers a composite image that might be called the "supermarketplace of ideas." Hawking ready-to-wear liberation clichés, the communist "militant" is himself a figure of alienated and alienating intellectual discourse, and the book he sells—that "revolutionary gadget with marketable qualities" (Cohn-Bendit)—is added to the speeches by the factory boss, the union leader, and Jacques himself (recounting how he became an advertiser) to construct the film's critique of the word. The scene underscores public discontent not only with the circulation and exchange of goods (no one is buying the book) but, more importantly, with cliché-ridden and ultimately empty political language itself. Contrasting with the canned discourses of these figures is the film's highlighting of spontaneous speech, in the form of printed signs, subtitles and intertitles, songs, slogans, graffiti, protest chants, and so on. As the butt of this comparison, the intellectual himself (and intellectual discourse wherever it appears) is here the primary culprit, turning his own production into commodity.

Mao's essay continues: "A revolution is not a dinner party, or writing an essay [*comme une oeuvre littéraire* in the French version], or painting a picture, or doing embroidery; it cannot be so refined, so leisurely and gentle, so temperate, kind, courteous, restrained and magnanimous. A revolution is an insurrection, an act of violence by which one class overthrows another."[34] The film itself is thus to be contrasted with the book sold in the supermarket. Godard and Gorin use clichés in order to criticize and situate them. This film is neither a slick, sugar-coated supermarket bestseller nor easy to consume. Its resistance to narrative closure and pleasure, its distancing strategies, and its constant turning in upon itself and its own materiality shift the burden onto the spectator, who must renounce the position of comfortable consumer in order to enter into the work of producing meaning. In short, *Tout va bien* strives to be a writerly text.

Moreover, the spectator's working conditions are abominable: in parallel with the sausage worker's description of the disgusting factory odors, which cling to her clothing and hair long after she has left the premises, the spectator's job of listening and viewing is hampered by excessive, intrusive noise, imperfectly discernible objects, off-centered and out-of-focus framing, and disjointed tracking shots. It could be said that after 1968, through the Dziga-Vertov period and the influence of Gorin, Godard wants to make art more and more indigestible. The viewer's feeling that he or she is being assaulted by the film is part and parcel of the attempt to make a cinema that will refuse to be "leisurely and gentle, temperate, kind, courteous, restrained and magnanimous." Godard and Gorin are attempting instead to make film into "an insurrection, an act of violence," that will *be* as well as *depict* a revolution—and it should be noted in passing that *Le Petit Robert* lists among the meanings of *sausage* "a stick of dynamite."[35]

"Cinéma, bouffe, baise." The film withholds the rewards. In the context of a class analysis, what makes narrative closure problematic is the way that issues of gender and sexuality cut across the issues of the workplace. When Susan DeWitt argues that work and home, public and private, cannot be thought separately, she undercuts both classic narrative expectations and classic Marxian analysis. And so at the end, when the narrator announces that protagonists are beginning to learn how to "think themselves historically [*se penser historiquement*]," it is clear that their new self-reflexive subjectivity will include a new (post-1968) awareness of conditioned sex-role behavior. The notion that "the personal is political" (as it was expressed in the United States) was closely related to the situationists' call for a transformation of everyday life, but it took the events of the late sixties, and especially the collective retrospection about those events, to reveal the gender implications of these insights. In short, the film allows issues of gender and sexuality to problematize the narrative of revolution in the same way, it turns out, that the emergence of the feminist movement problematizes any analysis of May 1968.[36]

This is where *Nathalie Granger* comes into the picture. While the two films share the project of constructing counterdiscourses that might prolong the contestation of May without necessarily recounting it, in many ways they move in opposing directions. *Tout va bien* and *Nathalie Granger* can be contrasted according to a distinction between proliferation and erasure. Everywhere that Godard's contestation takes a dialectical form that brings into play *more* elements—more discourses, more (and more contradictory) points of view, more color and noise, and a surfeit of meanings—Duras proceeds to reduce, to minimize, to evacuate meaning. The two films contrast as active struggle and passive resistance can both disarm an attack; as direct address and no address at all can both frustrate cinematic voyeurism and specular identification; as noise and silence (or music) both repel the imposition of a dominant language. Both films systematically disorient the spectator by avoiding subjective shots and the spatial logic of shot-countershot alternation, but while Godard achieves this through deployment of multiple and split points of view, Duras tries to eliminate point of view entirely: her camera wanders through the house like an anonymous intruder. Both are exquisitely self-conscious filmmakers as well, but where Godard subverts narrative and visual conventions from within, making the elements of their construction evident, Duras evacuates narrative altogether. Both deny the pleasures afforded by mainstream spectacle, but where Godard conceives of revolution as an act of murder and challenges the identification offered in commercial cinema by showing the reality of class struggle, Duras undermines the pleasure principle by going beyond it, to suicide and extinction of narrative, point of view, and speech itself. In short, where Godard disrupts by means of *ex*plosion, Duras proceeds *im*plosively. Or perhaps it is the difference between Mao and Zen.

The most striking and important differences between the two can be found in the ways they approach the problems of gender. The most salient areas in which the two address this issue are the interrelated politics of space and of language. *Tout va bien* elaborates a universe in which the masculine is associated with separation of workplace from intimate spaces and in which men and women (Montand and Fonda) speak different languages. Duras places language in its entirety on the side of men. And if Godard and Gorin see theorizing, the two protagonists learning to "think themselves historically," as the solution to conflicts between the sexes, for Duras theory is part of the problem. Her film is consonant with the by now well-known position, elaborated among French feminists of the early 1970s, whereby as soon as a woman speaks she becomes a ventriloquist, speaking a language that is not her own and does not express her reality. Women's marginality in language is correlated visually and on the soundtrack of *Nathalie Granger* by means of the women's silence and the way they inhabit the space of the house.

Because Duras is interested not only in foiling recuperation of the revolts of 1968 (that is, in refusing to turn revolt into a consumable commodity) but also in rethinking those revolts in terms of gender, the objects on which she focuses her critique have less to do with consuming and eating than with cleaning up. By locating her "story" in a houseful of women performing traditionally feminine tasks in the near-total absence of men, she thus adds to a critique of consumer capitalism the complication that objects, especially household objects, have gendered meanings. They are there to be destroyed, rejected, erased, wiped away. The film systematically demonstrates the superiority of silence over speech and the desirability of making a clean sweep, both literally and figuratively. The problem here is how to use language to revolutionize language, and use images to reject received cultural imageries.

A Newspaper

Tout va bien, as I have shown, establishes a distinction between liberating and oppressive uses of language [*parole*]. Duras puts all language on the side of mystification, falsehood, and oppression. Perhaps the film's most explicit act of logocide occurs when Isabelle Granger collects the newspaper and carefully tears it into shreds (with a sound that is "gratifying" and even "intoxicating"). Isabelle's act repeats her earlier gestures of burning first the mail and then a pile of leaves in the yard, and it mirrors the crime for which Nathalie has been expelled from school (and for which she becomes a sort of heroine in the mode of May 1968): willfully blotching up her writing lesson [*leçon d'écriture*]. The impulse at work here is very different from Susan DeWitt's gesture of discarding the script of her news report, but the motives are similar: in both cases (and in the case of the vegetable-book) the written word is worthless, empty, because it is alienated production, dictated by the marketplace and not by the ideas or ideals it may have sought to embody. It is the act of destruction that is most creative. This paradox was expressed by one of the best-known images of May 1968, in a slogan attributed to Duras: "Sous les pavés, la plage [beneath the paving stones, the beach]."[37]

A Baby Carriage

The project of cleaning away language gives weight to the objects Duras chooses to depict and makes her visual puns important and subversive. In one of these, Nathalie, home from school, tries to take her cat for a ride in a baby carriage, but the cat repeatedly escapes. Finally, in frustration, Nathalie throws the empty carriage against a tree and abandons it. As the only evidence given of Nathalie's alleged violence, this action seems insignificant, and yet, coming from within a nurturing gesture, it shocks. The obvious allusion to Eisenstein's image, in *Potemkin,* for the failed Odessa revolt of 1905 adds to the weight of Nathalie's revolt. In juxtaposition with her defiance of school (and its rejection of her), Duras's film stages visually Morin's remark about the "Sorbonne-Potemkin." But it does so in a way that does not recount May 1968 in any way other than by making the events the subject of the film's discourse and its visual and verbal play.

A Kitchen Table

A kitchen table is the third object and second visual pun it will be useful to examine. One of the most critically celebrated (and derided) scenes in the film consists of a very long sequence during which Isabelle and her friend clear away dishes after their meal. We watch the two women in medium shot, busy in the kitchen, and we also see closeups of their faces. Most striking are the extreme closeups of their hands, slowly sweeping the crumbs from the surface of the table. The scene is slow, hypnotic, and silent, the image rich and ambiguous. What emerges is a brutally blunt but, paradoxically, soothing account of the rhythm, the repetition, the mindlessness of housework, the very antithesis of social change, a movement that is no Movement. But the scene is also infused with tranquil rhythm and peacefulness. Through the visual pun inherent in the notion of clearing the table—*tabula rasa* (etymologically, erasure)—one can begin to appreciate how portraying this routine but often invisible task in the context of art (and performed by a famous actress) makes the sequence become subversive precisely because its very plotlessness overturns narrative and visual expectations. It is thus not coincidental that both baby carriage and kitchen table are usually and here associated with femininity. Duras seems to say here that history and analyses of the Marxist or situationist types have concentrated their attention on the work of *producing* the table. The work of cleaning it up has remained invisible, even from within a revolutionary rhetoric.

The utter silence of the scene is also a particularly feminine mode for the Duras of 1972. As she put it in an interview at the time, women's writing is always translated into language from a nondiscursive darkness.[38] Silence in *Nathalie Granger* is a strong force, not simply an absence of speech or noise. "Men prevent the silence from being heard," says Duras.[39] Duras's post-1968 literary efforts, particularly *Détruire, dit-elle* (1969; *Destroy, She Said*), are informed by an angry and profoundly pessimistic vision of the bankruptcy of all language. This was presumably what turned her away from novel to film and, within film, her emphasis on nonverbal communication (e.g., Nathalie's piano theme, which haunts each of the characters in turn, including the spectator). Film itself, erasing itself as it proceeds, offers both a method and an emblem for the destruction of language.[40]

Language comes from outside the house, silence inhabits within, and the dividing line between outside and inside the domain of the house, including its garden, is several times emphasized. When the man (who is never given a name and hardly has a face) departs, presumably for "work," the house can almost be heard to emit a sigh of relief. During the day, the women isolate themselves from the outside and from chronological time, and they feel its eruptions (a ringing telephone, the arrival of a salesman, delivery of a newspaper, radio broadcasts about a murder) as violent intrusions or curious irrelevancies. For Duras, borders are sacred and dangerous: her privileged characters—like Lol V. Stein, the inhabitants of the hotel in *Détruire, dit-elle,* or the beggarwoman in *India Song*—live on the margins and borderlines of forests and towns, of violence and madness. The two women in *Nathalie Granger* are presented iconographically as sorceresses: garbed in long dark cloaks, they sweep leaves and burn them, and they stir the leaves in a pond with long poles, all in ritually and hypnotically slow motion. A black cat glides across the frame from time to time. Duras describes the house as a grotto, a cavern.[41] Later on, a dog skitters away in panic, afraid to approach the house. The suggestion is that feminine spheres of activity have a subversive potential precisely because of their silence and resistance to narrative. I think we can understand this hint of witchcraft in the way that Hélène Cixous and Catherine Clément relate the sorceress to the hysteric: "The heart of the story linking the figures of sorceress and hysteric lies in the subversive weight attributed to the return of the repressed."[42] In *Nathalie Granger,* that repressed takes the form of feminine silence and of the associated discursive modes that have been repressed from mainstream spectacle. Duras thus produces a hysterical cinema that acts out in silence the ills of the body politic. One can also understand why her film enacts revolt without recounting any history, 1968 or otherwise: "For the hysteric does *not* write, does *not* produce, does nothing—nothing other than make things circulate without inscribing them."[43]

The film also suggests, however—against the grain of Duras's insistence on a feminine essentialism that many commentators have found problematic—that discursive modes, including silence, are less a matter of gender identity than of spatial and institutional placement. It shows how this countertemporal, counternarrative potential can be learned or unlearned, and this because it is a function of the individual's location relative to institutions. The schoolmistress, for example, speaks a decidedly "outside" language of authority, while a salesman gradually, by means of the aura surrounding the two women and through experience of their silence, is able to enter the feminine sphere, with its specialized forms of liberation and resistance.

A Washing Machine

The two discursive models are confronted when the salesman (Gérard Depardieu) wanders into the house, selling the final item I want to examine: a washing machine. As is made clear in his later monologue about all the jobs through which he has passed (including, significantly, typesetter and launderer's apprentice [*apprenti blanchisseur*]), washing and erasure are everywhere thematized. Revolution is envisioned not as a transformation of discourses and objects but as their removal, their erasure, leaving a blank or *blanc* (as in *blanchisserie*) that is not, this time, the *carré blanc* of censorship but rather the reverse. It is a radical cleansing, a stripping bare, a reduction to the essential condition where the voice of the unconscious and the sounds of silence can be heard.

As the salesman recites his sales pitch, it is clear that his logorrhea is borrowed and he has no investment in it. He is drawn to the rhythm of the house, and perhaps this is why the women have not objected to his presence in a space that Duras describes as a feminine "closed space [. . .] free—cleansed [*nettoyé*]—of any oppressive presence."[44] Finally, after his prepared speech reveals its futility and awkwardly dwindles to silence in the face of the women's friendly but passive nonresponse, he discovers that the household is already equipped with the very machine he has been promoting. It is understandable that the women do not need a washing machine: Durasian women, we might say, always already have one. It is also no surprise that the salesman's opening statement—"I represent [*je représente*] the Vedetta Tambour brand"—is progressively revealed to be an alienating position. The washing machine is trying to take his place, become his spectacle, the projection of his own alienated desires. Instead, it represents *him,* as its language stands in for his own. Finally, he declares in despair, "I give up"—"J'abandonne [la représentation]"—a remark that I think we can take as a double rejection: on his part, of his role with relation to the commodity market of washing machines and language as well; and on Duras's part, of a manner of cultural production. The salesman, like Godard and Gorin's film, talks about the bankruptcy of institutional discourses. At the same time, however, both salesman and filmmakers persist in trying to sell something. Whether their wares include a household appliance or the fetishized images of radical chic stars Jane Fonda and Yves Montand, they explain the impossibility of explaining. Duras, on the other hand, quietly refuses to talk about it.

"VIVE LA DÉMOCRATIE DIRECTE
[Long Live Direct Democracy]" (Sorbonne)

In retrospect, one of the most significant developments to emerge from May 1968 has been the women's movement. Both films examined here extend the signifying practices of 1968 in their use of the imagery and commodities of domestic economy to dramatize the inseparability of the domestic and the economy. In both, as the political dimension of everyday personal life comes to light, gender leaves the class analysis problematic, the revolution unfinished, and the narrative open. Susan DeWitt theorizes possible new relations between the sexes and new ways in which gendered perspectives must be brought to bear on the analysis of class conflict; Duras too explores feminine spaces and modes of interaction, what we might now call a women's culture, and with it alternative modes of narrativity and representation. In both cases, it is through consciousness of the gendered nature of discourse that a counterdiscourse becomes imaginable. Similarly, by the end of *Alice's Restaurant* Arlo Guthrie has moved into the center, that hegemonic and eminently recuperable position, and it is Alice who is literally on the margins of the screen, standing on the porch of her home in a deconsecrated church turned commune, looking toward a future—perhaps the women's movement—where it will be her turn to fabricate the new signs of the times and, in turn, face the task of extending those gains by resisting commodification of the very practices that were so subversive.

This analysis also suggests, I think, covert links between rejections of representation (or mediation) in two domains: in the streets, the *soixante-huitards* followed a strategy of direct or participatory democracy and a revolt against representation by the codified and authoritarian (and patriarchal) discourses of unions, bureaucracies, and an increasingly remote Gaullist government. The films studied here critique the reigning social and cultural codes—the representational regimes in both politics and culture, including language and the image—responsible for the alienated and dispossessed society of the spectacle described by the situationists. Both sought to create situations in which no one element would speak for or in the place of another, reducing it to powerlessness. It is not surprising that both were utopian: mediation—of institutions and sign systems—is as inevitable as it is frustrating. The real heritage of May 1968 lies not in what can be said about it but in what it made it possible to say.

5. Truffaut's Otohistoriography

After all, the fundamental question of philosophy (like that of psychoanalysis) is the same as the question of the detective novel: who is guilty? – Umberto Eco

In 1987 Marguerite Duras was subpoenaed to testify for the defense in a trial that was notorious before it began, that of former ss Obersturmführer Klaus Barbie (alias Altmann) for crimes against humanity. Duras, a personal friend of François Mitterrand, whom she knew as Morland when the two worked together in the Resistance; Duras, whose husband, a political prisoner because of his activities as a communist and a Resistance fighter, was spirited back from a concentration camp just in time to prevent his death from starvation and whose painful recovery she documents in excruciating detail in the title story of her 1985 book, *La Douleur* [literally, Pain];[1] Duras respectfully declined the court's invitation. Citing article 331 of the penal code, which limits witnesses' testimony to the facts of the case and the personality of the accused, she declared that she had no firsthand knowledge of the facts and that she was pleased never to have met Klaus Barbie.

It was not the story about her husband that inspired the defense attorney, Maître Jacques Vergès, to request Duras's testimony, however, but rather another piece in *La Douleur,* a piece in which Duras describes the inner turmoil of Thérèse, a young Resistance fighter presiding, just after the Liberation, over the interrogation and torture of a petty informer. Thérèse is fictional, but Duras makes no bones about admitting that the incident is drawn from personal experience. Maître Vergès no doubt hoped that her testimony, along with that of others, such as Regis Debray and Raymond Aubrac, would demonstrate that Barbie's atrocities should be classified not as crimes against humanity but as war crimes beyond the statute of limitation and, moreover, that as such, they resembled acts committed by many French people during the Occupation, the post-Liberation Purge of collaborators (the *Epuration*), and the Algerian conflict. He thus insinuated that if Barbie were to be found guilty, then a large number of

French men and women would be implicated as well. Vergès had clearly not read Duras's story closely enough to perceive its suggestion that torture, no matter who inflicts it, is a horror, even for the perpetrator. Nevertheless, he was all too well aware of the collective uneasiness about other possible revelations that made the Barbie trial such a focus of anxiety and scandal.

It is not difficult to discern the elements in the widespread, if ambivalent, return to (or of) the period 1940–44 in French public life and cultural production of the 1980s. Those changing but always uneasy national memories of World War II have never been far below the surface. Their presence has been perceptible in the form of echoes and ironies during the crises of the Algerian war and of May 1968. In addition to Barbie's trial (preceded by his sensational extradition from Bolivia), we can cite as evidence of this return the Mitterrand government, the first socialist government since Léon Blum's, and of Mitterrand himself, the first president of the republic to have bona fide Resistance credentials without the investment (or with a negative investment) in continuing to endorse the official Gaullist myth of the Resistance. Records about the Occupation have been largely inaccessible, and those about the Purge became available only in the 1980s. Then there was the publication of revisionist histories, most notably by Robert Faurisson, claiming that the Holocaust was a fabrication of Allied propaganda.[2] Books like Faurisson's were soon countered by the appearance of Claude Lanzmann's film *Shoah,* which the director called an oral history of the Holocaust. Later in the decade, there was the reopening of debate about Heidegger's Nazism. All this occurred in a climate of renewed anti-Semitism and the emergence on the political scene of ultraconservative racist Jean-Marie Le Pen and his National Front Party.

In his influential book *The Vichy Syndrome: History and Memory in France since 1944,* Henry Rousso situates this recent and intense phenomenon within the evolution of national memory since the Liberation.[3] Using a psychoanalytic framework to diagnose the ills of the collective psyche and asking why memories of the Occupation and the Vichy government, or L'Etat français, were so slow to come to the surface, Rousso identifies four stages or sets of symptoms in the postwar period. First came a period of "unfinished mourning" (roughly 1944 to 1954), when no satisfactory resolution, no acceptable representation of recent memory, could be found. The war's immediate aftermath, characterized by purges, amnesties, and internal division, paralyzed a nation incapable of dealing fully with the trauma, desiring only to forget and heal. This was followed by a phase of "repressions" (1954–71), during which amnesia was institutionalized under the banner of comforting national mythologies, particularly "resistancialism," a belief in nearly universal heroic resistance, consciously constructed as a "founding myth of the post-Vichy period" (16). This phase extended through the losses of colonies and wars in Indochina and North Africa, during which, as the first part of the present study shows, comparisons with past crises had to be carefully managed by selective recollection and false analogies (for example, de Gaulle's 1940 and 1958 returns to prominence).

By 1971–74, the "broken mirror" phase, the reflecting myths in which the nation had become used to contemplating itself had begun to crack. Memories were awakened by the death of de Gaulle in 1970, by a new generation asking questions, by the appearance of countermyths, such as the implication in *Le Chagrin et la pitié* that the majority of the French public did not belong to the Resistance but rather, either actively or passively supported collaboration. Finally, after 1974 began a period of full-fledged "obsession" and the return of the more deeply repressed issue of genocide. The title of a recent issue of the review *Esprit*—Que faire de Vichy? [What to make of Vichy?]"—captures a prevailing mood in which, as Rousso remarks, Vichy has become "a best-selling subject."[4]

Historians have not been alone in their preoccupation with resurfacing wartime memories: music, clothing, both high and popular culture reflected the same themes, as the general public was caught up in the momentum of the widespread mood that has been called the *mode rétro*. Pascal Ory has confirmed Rousso's analysis with his careful and extensive documentation of the rise of "la consommation nostalgique" as an important leisure-time activity. Ory coins terms like *rétrophilie* and *archéphilie* to capture the significance of the dramatic rise, between 1968 and 1981, of visits to the historical monuments and to museums, of interest in historical novels and films, and of use of national and local archives.[5]

Rousso's observation that Vichy has become a best-selling subject and Ory's discussion of nostalgia consumption alerts us to the possibility that the new fashion may be yet another attempt to manage or recuperate a troubling past by turning it into a commodity. In the films and novels discussed in this section there is evidence of a strong ambivalence, consisting of a familiar mixture of desires to remember and wishes that the whole problem would simply go away. The persistence of anxiety deriving from memories of the Occupation period is discernible even in the 1989 Bicentennial, which showed signs of having been mediated by memories of history more recent than the Revolution. The celebration incorporated a mock trial, a replay of the Revolutionary Convention, in the form of a televised public referendum on the execution of Louis XVI. Louis fared better this time around: the good citizens of Paris voted to acquit the king. Their collective gesture of revisionary historiography can be seen, I think, as a ritual of self-accusation and self-forgiveness for national crimes in Revolutionary times and since. For as Robert O. Paxton remarks in another context, "The government of Marshal Pétain and its policies were, after all, [among] the most controversial events in French public life since the execution of Louis XVI."[6] In the light of renewed interest in collaboration and the Purge, it was as though the *ancien régime* and its passing could only be glimpsed through the memories of a more recent crisis in national identity. Such an interpretation is suggested by the fact that the king's defense was argued by none other than Jacques Vergès. By comparing World War II with the Algerian conflict (during which Vergès had defended members of the Jeanson network) and the Purge and then, implicitly, with the Terror, the Barbie trial and Vergès's surrounding theatrics (including the launching of a committee to rehabilitate Robespierre) strategically played to a complex web of public anxieties, thus blurring categories, glossing over historical differences, and making it more difficult than ever to come to terms with France's collaboration with Nazism.

These incidents form a backdrop to the peculiar dynamic of confession and invention, of guilt and desire for absolution, of evasion and a will to knowledge to be found in some recent fictions that are trying to construct a discourse about World War II and France's murky role in it. The obsessive insistence with which memoirs and fictions return to stories about the war makes it clear that national and individual collaboration with Nazism (and in particular with anti-Semitism, the deportations, and the Holocaust) remains a scandal, understood both as an outrage and in its etymological sense of *skandalon,* or stumbling block. The fear of being suspected or accused of complicity with the Nazi program remains an important stumbling block in French identity and in scholars' attempts to understand postwar French history. Deriving from religious usage and designating a temptation or leading astray by example, this scandal is also usefully identified as a recurrent trope that suggests the presence of a historical disease or contagion. Looking backward remains a dangerous enterprise fraught with the risk of contamination by guilty secrets.

This return to the period of the Occupation is particularly remarkable in the work of New Novelists and New Wave filmmakers, who between the mid-seventies and the eighties might seem to have drifted away from the experimentation and self-reflexivity upon which they had built their reputations toward an overtly historical mode. In this section and in the conclusion, I will examine four of these. Duras, whose work has always been intensely personal, became more explicitly autobiographical with the appearance of *L'Amant* (1984; *The Lover*) and *La Douleur;* Alain Robbe-Grillet published two volumes of memoirs in 1984 and 1987, in which he discusses his family's Anglophobia, anti-Semitism, and admiration for Pétain.[7] Among the filmmakers, most notable returns to the period of the Occupation are François Truffaut's *Le Dernier Métro* (1981; *The Last Metro*) and Louis Malle's *Au revoir les enfants* (1987). Moving through the eighties from the earliest of these works (Truffaut's film) through the two novel-ists' memoirs and to the most recent (*Au revoir les enfants*), one finds progres-sively less labyrinthine mediation through fictional plots and characters in favor of more explicitly autobiographical confrontation of the issues of personal in-volvement in and responsibility for historical events.

None of these works analyze or comment directly, however; nor do they evoke public events on the panoramic scale of the Barbie crimes and trial or the Revolutionary Convention. Rather, they are stories of private guilt and doubt, betrayal and loss, recounted against a historical backdrop that is sketchy at best. In spite of Robbe-Grillet's aggressive assertions to the contrary (see the intro-duction to this volume), however, it would be a mistake to receive these texts as a return to some unproblematic realism. While they have always been highly self-conscious creators of often self-reflexive films that foreground experimenta-tion in form, genre, and mood, Truffaut and Malle have always shown more concern to reach a wider public, and so they have never aimed to be as egregiously theoretical or avant-garde in their formalism as Resnais and Robbe-Grillet were in *Last Year at Marienbad*. Nor have they been as committed as was Godard or the Duras of *Nathalie Granger* to the quest for a revolutionary es-thetic. Nevertheless, *Le Dernier Métro* and *Au revoir les enfants,* like the memoirs of Robbe-Grillet and Duras, are far from being readable as transparently auto-biographical. Rather than reinterpretation of the remembered events them-selves, what seem still to be at stake in such stories, as in the earlier work by the same artists, are the problematic nature of representation and questions of how the self constructs itself historically and, conversely, how historical knowledge is shaped by private circumstance and mediated by writing or filming.

In many fictions of World War II, from Elie Wiesel's *Night* (1960) and Wil-liam Styron's *Sophie's Choice* (1979) to the books by Robbe-Grillet and Duras and the Malle and Truffaut films, memories are organized around a focal scene that appears in some ways to be the origin or crux of the story. Similarly, in Freud's theory of the primal scene, most notably in his "Wolf-Man" case, he traced his patient's symptoms to a single repressed childhood memory, specifi-cally the child's inadvertent observation of a scene of sexual intercourse between his parents, an event the child understood to be violent. Freud approached his patient's symptoms and dreams as metaphors of a memory so mysterious as to evade representation.[8]

For the purposes of reading historical fictions, it is helpful to turn once again to Robert Jay Lifton's study of Hiroshima survivors, noting this time his re-working of the Freudian primal scene into what he calls an "image of ultimate horror." Lifton moves away from Freud's concept of the primal scene by restricting the image's origin to neither specifically childhood nor specifically sexual memories, but he retains Freud's understanding that a repressed trauma remains the ground from which spring the individual's subsequent symptoms (or for our purposes, representations). Observing that most of the Hiroshima survivors he interviewed suffered from the perseveration of "a specific image of the dead or dying with which the survivor strongly identifies himself, and which evokes in him particularly intense feelings of pity and self-condemnation," Lifton describes such images as "a type of memory which epitomizes the relationship of death to guilt." Further on, he renames such obsessive (but repressed or forgotten) scenes "residual images" and describes them as "the pictorialization of [the individual's] central conflict in relationship to the disaster."[9] Lifton's formulation, to which I will refer repeatedly in the chapters ahead, lends itself to use as a model of the relationship between fiction and memory, a model in which the disaster is not pictorialized directly but mediated by rhetorical conventions and personal psychic configurations.

In the case of the films, the disaster is also significantly mediated by the cinematic apparatus itself, which makes the primal-scene model particularly applicable. As Jean-Louis Baudry points out, film more closely resembles dream than any other art form, including theater. He suggests that as the spectator watches the images from a position of darkness and isolation, the apparatus brings about a state of "artificial regression."[10] Christian Metz goes further in exploring affinities between film watching and primal scene. For him, the projector aperture and the screen's borders produce a "keyhole effect," and the crucial element in cinematic voyeurism consists in an "unauthorized scopophilia," the furtive thrill of watching without being watched in return. Cinema is thus inherently transgressive, because it is based on the institutionalization of an otherwise prohibited practice. As Metz puts it, "For its spectator the film unfolds in that simultaneously very close and definitively inaccessible 'elsewhere' in which the child *sees* the amorous play of the parental couple, who are similarly ignorant of it and leave it alone, a pure onlooker whose participation is inconceivable. In this respect the cinematic signifier is not only 'psychoanalytic'; it is more precisely Oedipal in type."[11] Keeping Metz's analysis in mind, it will be less surprising to find, in the films of Truffaut and Malle, and even in the texts by Duras and Robbe-Grillet, that the traumas of history are filtered through and represented by means of the family romance. It will also be possible to identify and evaluate components of subjectivity in historiographic fabulation.

With the works studied in this section, the artists of the Nouveau Roman and the Nouvelle Vague come full circle. In the early years it was their referential dimension that was most consistently overlooked or discounted. Now it is their mediated, textual dimension that is most easily eclipsed: there is celebration that the artists have "finally" decided to tell the story straight. While it is true that the works examined below seem more accessible than the earlier works because they are not characterized by the tortured representation of hysterical discourse, they are not literally autobiographical either. Truffaut does not even claim that his film represents an anecdote from his own life, and Malle states specifically that the crucial scene in his own film is invented. That they include a historical past does not make them transparently readable, any more than *Hiroshima mon amour* and *La Route des Flandres* were. Rather, their autobiographical venture is more in the nature of a primal scene. Each is a *mise en scène* of a witnessed crime or crimes. That scene is shaded, screened, and transformed, but it is central. Whether the primal scene turnes out to be fiction or truth is a matter of indifference. Autobiography here serves as a *mise en abyme* of historiography. At work is a personal mythology or phantasm, a haunting, that has been present all along in each artist's work and serves as the ground for historical representation.

Dream this umbilicus: it has you by the ear. It is an ear. – Jacques Derrida

In *La Nuit américaine* (1979; *Day for Night*), Truffaut's movie about moviemaking, in which he acts the part of Ferrand, a filmmaker, there is a scene where an agent accosts Ferrand to propose a script about pollution. Flanked by two actresses, one specializing in political and the other in pornographic roles, the agent asks Ferrand aggressively, "Why don't you make political films? Why don't you make erotic films?" The moment is both humorous and autobiographical: undoubtedly the most discreet as well as the least overtly political of the artists studied here, Truffaut himself has been asked the same questions on numerous occasions, and his relation to politics has always been enigmatic. Even before he became a filmmaker himself, Truffaut was associated with "apolitical" filmmaking: he began his career as a scriptwriter by writing the scenario for Godard's *A bout de souffle*. Then, during the events leading to May 1968, Truffaut divided his time between activism and filmmaking, but unlike Godard, he never incorporated the events into a film.

Although perhaps more than any other Nouvelle Vague artist, Truffaut desires to please, to entertain and to be loved, this does not mean that he steers clear of sensitive subjects or seeks to avoid controversy. It would be absurd to advance such a claim concerning an artist who has made a film about a man's obsession with the dead (*La Chambre verte* [1978; *The Green Room*]) and another in which child abuse is a central issue (*L'Argent de poche*) and who conceives of his career as a series of problems or wagers. Rather, Truffaut does not believe in political filmmaking, and he rejects *engagement* for reasons he claims are autobiographical. Asked in an interview whether he thought art could change people's lives or the structure of society, he replied: "Only very slowly. And the slower it is, the more effective it is. Such changes are not spectacular. What's more, if you think that in twenty years a film with political content will offer a clearer image of the society in which it was made than a non-political film, you are completely mistaken. . . . The idea that we should try to reflect the society we live in is false—we will reflect it in any case, intentionally or not."[12]

The tasks we bring to *Le Dernier Métro*, then, are similar to those we addressed in connection with *Hiroshima mon amour:* to locate the historical dimension of this film that seems at the same time both historical and evasive and to identify the level and angle of Truffaut's investment in it. Can *Le Dernier Métro* be considered a film about the Occupation? Is the Occupation integral to the film's vision, or is it, as Don Allen states and as Truffaut's own remarks seem to confirm, "little more than a backcloth to the central drama of a theatrical troupe"?[13] How are we to read Truffaut in relation to the war, especially given the highly charged return to it in the eighties?

Le Dernier Métro was the second part of a projected trilogy: the first was *La Nuit américaine;* the third, to be set in a music hall, was never completed. Rather than following a tightly constructed dramatic plot and like *La Nuit Américaine,* which documents the myriad activities on a movie set, *Le Dernier Métro* portrays life on and behind the stage of a theater. The story begins in the Theatre Montmartre in October 1942. The theater's artistic director, Lucas Steiner (Heinz Bennent), a Jew, has reportedly fled to South America. In his absence, the theater is being run by his wife, Marion (Catherine Deneuve), who is also an actress, and rehearsals are being directed from Steiner's notes by the assistant director, Jean-Loup Cottins (Jean Poiret). The story charts a full range of responses to the Occupation: the action opens with the arrival of a new actor, Bernard Granger (Gérard Depardieu), who is also an "actor" in the Resistance; during the course of the film, the collaborationist critic Daxiat will attack the theater's new play, *La Disparue* [The vanished woman], of which fragments are shown; one of the actresses will be criticized by her colleagues for her willingness to further her career by accepting roles in collaborationist plays; Martine, who dates German soldiers and who traffics in black market goods through her friend Raymond, the prop manager, will be suspected of the theft of several actors' personal belongings and identity papers; Jean-Loup, a homosexual, will be harassed by Daxiat as the latter threatens to assume direction of the theater himself.

Meanwhile, Marion Steiner coolly keeps the Nazis at bay to the point of appearing to condone their policies (by refusing to hire a Jewish actor, for example). The reason for her intransigence is known only to herself and to us: her husband is actually hiding in the theater cellar. The couple's drama centers on the Steiners' attempts to secure Lucas's exit from France via a Resistance network (which collapses on the eve of his departure, with the invasion of the *zone libre* in November 1942) and on the growing romantic tension between Marion and Bernard, of which Lucas seems to be aware. During a surprise search of the cellar by Gestapo agents, Marion is forced to share her secret with Bernard, to whom she turns for help. How Lucas Steiner's predicament is resolved is not clear, although we do learn at the end that he survived the war.

Le Dernier Métro is not the first of Truffaut's films set in a specific historical moment or incorporating wartime events: *Jules et Jim* (1961) spans the years from before World War I to the beginnings of World War II, and *La Chambre verte* begins in the aftermath of a massacre (World War I) and deals with a survivor's obsession with his dead young wife and his comrades lost in battle. But Truffaut has never, not even in *Le Dernier Métro,* made historical events the central topic of a film, nor has he used semiallegorical characters, direct address, or other techniques, as Godard has done, to theorize politics and ideology directly. His emphasis is always elsewhere: on the personal, the private, and on characters. Like all his films, *Le Dernier Métro* is the story of how individuals respond to an extraordinary situation. His emphasis is on "actors" in the theatrical and historical "stage," and this is how we must understand the Occupation: as the setting against which individuals feel, behave, and choose. Truffaut's choice of emphasis does have both esthetic and political implications, however: any stand he might take is filtered through the behavior of various characters, none of whom is cast exclusively as hero or villain, and the film's center of gravity, like its plot, is dispersed. Thus, *La Disparue,* the play being rehearsed in the theater, serves as an important interior duplication of the historical setting. As spectators of both, we are never given a whole coherent plot or a unified perspective on the topic, but we do come to understand how the multiple characters feel and what motivates their behavior. Because of the abyssal constructions—a play within a film, with actors playing the role of actors—once again, what remains unclear throughout is the location of the boundaries between art (the plays) and "reality" (the film).

In keeping with Truffaut's professed dedication to the primacy of characters over setting and plot, then, *Le Dernier Métro* is about the effect of events on characters—how they behave in situations—not about the events themselves. As in Camus's *La Peste* (*The Plague*) and Ophuls's *Le Chagrin et la pitié,* the full spectrum of responses to the Occupation is shown and many positions are represented. In fact, Truffaut conceived his film as a fictional counterpart of Ophuls's documentary.[14] Like *Le Chagrin, Le Dernier Métro* builds a portrait of an era out of fragmentary vignettes of individual behavior. Spectators of these films are not meant to identify with a single character, but to appreciate the subtle complexities of political behavior, the varieties of heroism, and the motives of villainy in a stressful and treacherous situation.

But while Camus and Ophuls ultimately do take a stand, Truffaut's own position is unclear. *Le Dernier Métro* ends with a a sleight of hand, a theatrical trick. We are led to believe that Marion and Bernard meet years after the war, in a hospital where Bernard is recuperating in a neck brace and with abrasions on his face. The two share their regrets that their love affair never worked out, even after the death of her husband. At the last moment, the camera moves back to reveal a painted backdrop, and we realize that we are watching another play. There is applause, and Marion, Bernard, and Lucas join hands for a final curtain call. This ending is troubling: is the war no more than a stage trick, a play? Deneuve was cast in the role of Marion, Truffaut says, because of her ambiguity, her cool exterior, and her ability to hide her inner feelings and motives.[15] It is as if history has been a dream or an illusion, part of a play that ends, much to our relief, freeing us to go home. This possibility justifies the setting: it is as if theater and history were indistinguishable.

In light of the ending, it would appear that in spite of its historical setting, or even because of it, *Le Dernier Métro* must be seen as a belated Nouvelle Vague film. Like *Hiroshima mon amour,* it has a historical setting, but the focus on characters and their private dramas makes it unclear whether the war is integral to the plot or simply a backcloth. The lack of coherent plot or closure, the absence of clear heroes or even protagonists, and the evasiveness of the narratorial voice all evoke New Wave films made two decades earlier. Reality is figured as theatricality: everyone is acting in one or more roles. Even within the interior play characters are playing roles, in a dizzying (but familiar) series of interior duplications. Is Marion and Bernard's brief tryst, for example, part of yet another play, as its artificiality and Lucas's role in "directing" it would seem to suggest? The pervasive use of mirrors, *mises en abyme,* and autoreflexivity, together with the trick ending, suggest an infinite regress into fictionality. Such procedures blur any referential dimension and cause the spectators (and the characters) to lose sight of the boundaries between "reality" and fiction.

One feature of the film's theatricality is its emphasis on surfaces and external realities. As Patricia Mellencamp argues in an essay about musical comedies, the presence of spectacle in a film interrupts narrative, "awakening the spectator to the fact of filmic illusion."[16] Truffaut loves intensely visual filmmaking; this is what he admired about Hitchcock. The presence of stars like Deneuve and Depardieu underscores the film's status as performance and its show biz glamour. The drama is not located in the film's dialogue or its auditory dimension, but in the glances, the electricity that passes between characters, so that if the sound is turned off, it is still possible to follow the story. Marion glances guiltily at Martine in the Gestapo headquarters, where she has gone to plead her husband's case. Daxiat's menace is palpable in his use of social space. The erotic tension between Bernard and Marion is reflected in glances deflected by mirrors. The special importance given to these mirrors is very reminiscent of *Marienbad*, as is the use of a play within the film.[17] The cumulative effect is of art as a dream (or drama) from which we can awaken. At the very least, this is a form of wish fulfillment and evidence of Truffaut's optimism and sweetness. His preference for complex motivations and his inability to portray evil (even Daxiat has his pathos) make it extremely difficult for him to make a strong film about World War II. Even Ophuls's careful documentary has its villains.

We can begin to identify the film's perspective on the historical events it portrays by noting that the basic premise of *Le Dernier Métro*—that everyone is an actor hiding behind a role at all times—is paradoxically consistent both with the narrative aesthetic of the Nouvelle Vague and with the historical reality of the Occupation. Truffaut has said that in *Le Dernier Métro* the characters' actions are circumscribed by compromise. This distinguishes them from the "definitive" characters in his other best-known and most successful films: Truffaut's protagonists from *Jules et Jim* to *La Chambre verte*, through *La Femme d'à côté* (1981; *The Woman Next Door*), *La Mariée était en noir* (1967; *The Bride Wore Black*), *L'Histoire d'Adèle H.* (1975; *The Story of Adele H.*), and even in the Antoine Doinel cycle are characterized by their monomania.[18] Their personalities and their stories are defined by an all-consuming and often fatal passion—for freedom, love of the dead, jealousy, revenge, the quest for perfection. On the other hand, Marion and Lucas Steiner, Bernard Granger, and the others in *Le Dernier Métro*, even Daxiat, are "compromised" in that they cannot reach the limits of their obsessions. They are hemmed in on all sides, and their actions are censored by lived history: the presence of the German occupiers, who threaten to foreclose their livelihood and even their lives. This claustrophobia, contrasting with the broad range of Truffaut's other characters' spheres of action, goes a long way toward accounting for the inconclusiveness of *Le Dernier Métro*'s plot and the fuzziness of its characters' (like Truffaut's own) political perspective.

THROUGH THE EYES OF A CHILD

This circumscribed sphere of action and understanding is also part of the "child's-eye view" Truffaut attributes to the film. Truffaut was ten years old in 1942, the year in which the story of *Le Dernier Métro* is set, and although no single character in the film is autobiographical, Truffaut has said that he understands his film as a child's perspective on the Occupation.[19] Pursuing the implications of his remark, I want to show how Truffaut's representations of the period are shaped by private obsessions and developmental narratives as well as public events. Truffaut's film about the Occupation harks back to the beginnings of his career as a filmmaker: he had long planned to set a film during World War II, and he has stated that *Le Dernier Métro* was the realization of his oldest dream.[20] It is significant that he made his film about the Occupation late in his career, having already established himself as a well-loved filmmaker. Despite his aversion to political films and taking a stand, reading his career backward through *Le Dernier Métro* reveals that Truffaut's cinematic project has been both autobiographical and historiographic from the beginning, so that in *Le Dernier Métro*, as in the case of Malle's *Au revoir les enfants,* it is possible to gain access to the film's historical through its autobiographical dimension. The truth value is to be found not primarily at the level of the story itself, however, but rather at the level of its emotional tone, which harks back to childhood experience of the Occupation. That tone consists of a number of factors that can be isolated.

First is fear and the natural desire to escape from it. On the one occasion where Truffaut speaks at any length about his memories of the Occupation, in his 1975 introduction to André Bazin's *French Cinema of the Occupation and Resistance,* he talks about the period as contemporaneous (almost synonymous) with his initiation into moviegoing. He points out that during wartime there is a significant increase in the popularity of spectacles of all sorts: "After the Armistice, when the Germans occupied France, movie theaters became a refuge for all, and not only in the figurative sense of the word." Truffaut was too young to need escape from recruiters for the Service de travail obligatoire (STO) requisitioning workers for German factories, but he did experience the movies as double escapism: his "anguish" that the projection would be halted by an air-raid alert was exacerbated by the fact that by the time he was ten, like Antoine Doinel, he was sneaking out to see movies and needed to return home before his parents. As for the theater, he quotes a critic of the period who complained about one actor's slow delivery saying, "If you want to catch the last Métro, you'd better not go to hear Alain Cuny."[21] The title of Truffaut's film reflects that anxiety.

In addition to the desire to escape from Occupation realities and the fear of being caught by the STO, the curfew, or one's parents, there was the escapist content of the movie stories themselves. The dictates of the Censorship Commission (backed up by Nazi critics such as Lucien Rebatet and Alain Laubreau, the model for Truffaut's Daxiat),[22] reinforced by the public's psychological needs, created a cinema in which there was no place for subversion, protest, or political opinion of any kind. Instead, Truffaut remarks, it was "understandable that cinema took refuge in historical films and films of fantasy and enchantment."[23] Rejecting even the notion that some of these films nevertheless delivered a coded political message, Truffaut goes on to defend cinema of the Occupation period (and of the present) against those who criticize apolitical and escapist cinema. He points out that whereas "Italian cinema of 1940–44 was almost entirely pro-Mussolini and fascist, . . . 98 percent of French cinema during the Occupation managed not to be Pétainist."[24] Truffaut's view of the films of the period gives us an added perspective from which to understand the ending of *Le Dernier Métro*. The last scene, which is by any analysis "escapist," may be a reconstruction not so much of the events as of the films of the period. Marcel Carné's *Les Enfants du paradis,* by one account the best known of all the films made in France during the Occupation and "perhaps the most highly regarded French film of all time,"[25] is no doubt a specific antecedent for *Le Dernier Métro.* Made in 1943 and released in 1945, Carné's film is about a theater troupe and theatricality in life and on the stage, and it stars the famous Arletty, for whom Truffaut's character Arlette (Andréa Ferréol), the first character to appear on the screen as the movie begins, serves as a tribute. Ernst Lubitsch's *To Be or Not to Be* (1942), which also plays at the boundaries of theater, reality, and World War II, is another likely reference point. Such is Truffaut's characteristic style of interfilmic allusion, in which he uses the cinema and film history as the "reality" against which he tells his own stories.

Second, the normal childhood suspicion that adults are always playing roles was exacerbated by the clandestine and dishonest subterfuges of the Occupation. Truffaut remembers, for example, his aunt's purchase of under-the-counter copies of *Gone with the Wind* at a time when most American and English novels (and films) were forbidden. And he remembers (characteristically, through the mediation of a poem by Aragon) posters in the metro encouraging the denunciation of those wanted by the Occupation authorities.[26] Like movies, adult clandestine activities take place in the dark, and so Truffaut reports that it was in the interest of tone rather than of historical accuracy that the first forty-five minutes of *Le Dernier Métro* consist of nighttime scenes. Truffaut speaks in practical terms about this choice and about how, by isolating relevant details and leaving the rest in obscurity, spotlighting protected the film from inadvertent anachronisms. But this darkness can be seen both as a technical solution to a technical problem and also as a feature of the film's "child's-eye view," that is, both as a historical and a psychological milieu. This limited visual field and the fragmented narrative it embodies correlate with a child's limited understanding of contexts, connections, and causalities and a consequent foregrounding of isolated and sometimes inconsequential but nevertheless vivid details that acquire a menacing, hallucinatory, or symbolic aura. Truffaut's nighttime scenes convey a child's imperfect comprehension of a crisis that is both frightening and fascinating and in which adult activities take place in a mysterious twilight zone, or after the child has gone to bed.

All of these factors—claustrophobia, escapism, darkness, focus on detail, clandestineness, and dishonesty—add up to what Truffaut calls the film's "ambience." According to Truffaut, *Le Dernier Métro* is a period film more than it is a political film.[27] I think we can take his phrase "film d'époque" to mean both a film about the period and a film like those of the period. In fact, the second is more important than the first. Historical content is not the most important element in Truffaut's project of recreating the ambience, the emotional tone of the period. In addition, from the perspective of a child in the dark (at the cinema, at the parent's bedroom door, or more metaphysically, in relation to historical events), the mysterious, clandestine, and possibly threatening behavior of adults presents all the components of a primal scene.

To appreciate the historicity of *Le Dernier Métro*'s emotional tone and its "child's-eye view," it is helpful to read backward through an earlier film where, in the absence of events or setting, ambience is the *only* historical dimension. Truffaut often discusses the autobiographical origin and content of *Les Quatre Cents Coups*. That 1959 film, for which the young director received the Palmes d'Or at the Cannes Film Festival, tells the story of a young boy (Antoine Doinel, played by Jean-Pierre Léaud) who is an encumbrance to his mother, who would rather spend her time in flirtatious pursuits, and an annoyance to her husband, Antoine's adoptive father. Like the young Truffaut, Antoine has a best friend who plays hooky with him, and the two spend their time in the streets and at the movies. Also like Truffaut, he is expelled from school and spends time in a reformatory.

Given the autobiographical source of *Les Quatre Cents Coups,* and realizing that Antoine Doinel is about twelve years old, Truffaut's age during the Occupation, it is surprising that there is no historical reference at all—no explicit or allusive reference to the war, no stray German soldier, no fleeting shot of a newspaper headline, no overheard news broadcast. One can easily imagine the difficulty and expense of recreating an epoch in a low-budget film, and Truffaut was no doubt reluctant to mount so ambitious a project in a first feature-length project. But he also makes the following telling remarks about the absence of historical setting in *Les Quatre Cents Coups:* "In 1958, writing *Les Quatre Cents Coups* with Marcel Moussy, I remember regretting that I was unable to evoke a thousand details from my adolescence linked to the Occupation, but the budget and the 'nouvelle vague' spirit were incompatible with the notion of a 'period film.'"[28]

Whereas the Occupation setting missing from Truffaut's early film reappears in *Le Dernier Métro,* the two films share the ambience whose features are enumerated above. Many scenes in *Les Quatre Cents Coups*—in fact, the defining portions of the action—take place at night or in hiding: Antoine, on the run (the film's working title was "Les Fugues d'Antoine"), hides in a darkened room at his friend's house and then in a printer's office that appears to be in a basement or underground. The film is in black and white, which not only corresponded to Truffaut's budget but also conveys the sense of chiaroscuro and menacing shadows that Truffaut learned from the film noir genre so popular in the early postwar years and that he adapts to excellent effect in other films as well. Hitchcockian suspense and clandestineness are conveyed in the scenes in which Antoine sneaks into his stepfather's office to steal a typewriter and in which he escapes from school into the movies. Anxiety about getting caught pervades the mood. Even more significant for a comparison of *Les Quatre Cents Coups* with *Le Dernier Métro* is the behavior of adults. Antoine's father is alternately and unpredictably chummy and punitive, and his mother pursues her secret amours while playing a series of highly artificial roles (authoritarian, nurturing, conspiratorial) with Antoine. Both parents demonstrate pettiness, deception, and downright meanness. It is in these features that the film contains memories of the period that are both autobiographical and also historical and that correspond to the variety of responses to Occupation portrayed in *Le Dernier Métro.*

There are also similarities in the narrative shapes of the two films. Although he never explained the ambiguity of *Le Dernier Métro*'s ending, it resembles *Les Quatre Cents Coups,* about which Truffaut does take pains to explain the care he took to make sure that the end was neither optimistic nor pessimistic; he wanted neither to romanticize the child nor to indulge in fatalism or melodrama. Whatever else one might say about the ending of *Le Dernier Métro,* it is clear that Truffaut wants to avoid either romanticizing the period (by making it falsely heroic or martyred or pious) or condemning in hindsight behavior that was typical of the times he portrayed. The film noir elements of *Le Dernier Métro* are obscured, in large part precisely because of the historical content and the fact that the later film is in color. Nevertheless, its affinities with *Les Quatre Cents Coups,* by means of the autobiographical plot material, narrative structure, and ambience, are undeniable.

THROUGH THE EARS OF A CHILD

But the richest area the two films have in common with each other and with Truffaut's own biography is their thematics of eavesdropping. Early in *Les Quatre Cents Coups,* Antoine, playing hooky from school, stumbles across his mother kissing a stranger on the street. At home, he sleeps between two rooms, so that upon her return from her assignations his mother must step over him on her way to her room. Abed but wide-eyed, Antoine can hear his parents arguing. He hears (probably not for the first time) that his stepfather somewhat grudgingly gave him a name and that he himself is the product of his mother's promiscuity. Similarly, he overhears them discussing where to leave him while they go off on a holiday. In all these instances, what he overhears is that he is an intrusion and a hindrance to his parents' pleasures.

There is a child in *Le Dernier Métro*—Jacquot, the concierge's son. Although his role is small, any child in a Truffaut film is significant. Jacquot is early seen engaging in juvenile lawbreaking, on the same small scale as Antoine and the young Truffaut: he grows tobacco illicitly, under the back steps of the theater. Later, he is taken into the theater family by the director (as Truffaut was brought into the film world by surrogate father Bazin, and as Truffaut himself recruited the boy Léaud) to play a role in *La Disparue*. He will play Eric, the child of Héléna (Marion/Deneuve). From the fragments of the play that are presented, it is possible to piece together that years before, Héléna disappeared mysteriously for a time (hence the play's title) and returned with the baby, Eric. Now, as Eric overhears, the past erupts into the household with the arrival of a tutor (Bernard/Depardieu), who may be Eric's father.

We first see Jacquot in the film's opening scenes, where he sets rolling a series of visual and thematic relays that connect him to Antoine Doinel, to Bernard, to Lucas, and to Truffaut himself.[29] Through his role in the play as a child of uncertain parentage, Jacquot evokes Antoine and Truffaut. Jacquot's appearances as himself in the opening scenes are carefully articulated with those of Bernard, the new actor. At the end of the first scene, Bernard has just tried unsuccessfully to accost Arlette, the theater's costume director, just outside the theater. Immediately after her exit, Bernard crosses the path of a child "of about twelve,"[30] and the camera lingers on him as he plays alone in the street. A German soldier (the first Occupation indicator in the film) passes by and, by way of a friendly greeting, ruffles the child's hair. Immediately the child's mother appears and gruffly demands, "What did that [soldier] do to you?" After hearing that the German had touched her child, she announces that they will go home and wash the child's hair. And in case the spectator or the child might be tempted to understand her anger as simply rhetorical, in the next scene, when Bernard taps on the concierge's window to ask directions, we can see that she is indeed lathering her son's head.

The multiple relays in this scene, at the very outset of the film, introduce literally and forcefully the motif of contamination: the lathered head is an image of the ways in which Nazism is felt to be physically contagious, and the Occupation a contamination. The figurative or ideological analogue is introduced almost immediately, when the theater's manager, Raymond, explains that the French Gestapo came to search the theater. Whom you talk with, with whom you are seen fraternizing, whom you touch or look at, whose path you cross—all are clues about who you are and where you fit in the spectrum of responses to the political situation. The contagion motif finds a second variant in the visual articulation of the scenes, what I have called a relay. Bernard crosses Jacquot's path, and then we follow Jacquot. The two cross paths a second time, and we follow Bernard again. Thus the opening scenes begin to establish a connection between Bernard and Jacquot, the first link in a chain of interrelated "contagious" or echoing actions, of individual behaviors that implicate others and expand the film's autobiographical resonance.

So that not only Bernard as adult but also Jacquot and even Truffaut as child are immediately thereafter initiated into the contaminating mystery of anti-Semitism and complicity with Nazi policies. Bernard has just arrived at the theater and is awaiting an audience with Marion to sign his contract. Through the translucent window of a closed door, Bernard overhears a conversation between Cottins and Rosen, a Jewish actor who is being refused a role in *La Disparue*. Knowing that Lucas Steiner, a Jew, has gone into hiding contributes to the outrage that both Bernard and Rosen exhibit when the latter is sent away on the words of Marion Steiner: "Tell the truth: that Marion Steiner doesn't want Jews in her theater."

The choreography of this sequence is critical to understanding the film as a child's-eye, primal-scene view of the Occupation. It is dishonest from Bernard's point of view, since he does not yet know that Marion is protecting Lucas's hiding place in the theater cellar. A partisan of the Resistance, Bernard is now in the awkward position of accepting a job where a Jew had just been sent away.[31] It is mysterious that so beautiful a lady could be so hardhearted. But above all, it is clandestine, as the scene masterfully demonstrates with its play of doors and shadows. Like Antoine, Bernard eavesdrops on conversations that take place literally and figuratively between two doors [*entre deux portes,* a French usage that describes the way Rosen is sent away without having gained admittance]. The predominance of "off" voices and the views of Cottins's and Rosen's shadows against the backlighting on the closed glass doors underscore the fact that Bernard is eavesdropping and point up its status as primal scene. As in Antoine's Oedipal situation, Bernard is not only overhearing conversations but eavesdropping on a partially understood episode of betrayal that engages him personally. Unlike Antoine's, that betrayal is not only personal; it involves complicity with Nazism. The similarities between the two films highlight Bernard's role as a proxy between Antoine and Truffaut and between the earlier New Wave period and the later moment when the historical context or content, or both, have been restored.

More overt autobiographical resonance can be found in Lucas Steiner himself. Like Ferrand, the character in *La Nuit américaine* played by Truffaut himself, Lucas is the director and leader of a troupe of actors. He will be vilified by the collaborationist critic, Daxiat, for some of the same grounds for which Truffaut and Ferrand are criticized, notably for being "apolitical." Even small humorous details link Steiner to Truffaut: like Truffaut himself before the war, for example, Lucas Steiner only read the entertainment pages in the newspapers.[32] And like Antoine hiding out from schoolmaster and parents in a printing shop, and like Truffaut himself as a child AWOL from school and then from the army, Lucas Steiner is a man in hiding, a man on the run, a man seen as "illegitimate," if not in the patrilineal sense that applies to Antoine, Eric in the play, and Truffaut himself, then, even more significantly, in the broader social context of the Nazi threat that hangs over him.

Lucas's exile, his role in a drama of exclusion *entre deux portes* is marked here again by a thematics of eavesdropping. Lucas rigs a heating vent in order to listen in on the play being rehearsed on the stage above his hiding place so that he can participate secretly in the direction of the play and the management of his theater. In addition, through his understanding of the innuendos and nuances of his wife's voice as she inflects her stage role as Héléna, he understands the erotic tension between Bernard and Marion that will ultimately lead to a hasty, awkward, and rather artificially staged tryst. Thus it is that the romantic and the historical plot of the film converge when the two men finally meet face to face, when Marion is forced to ask for Bernard's help in hastily dismantling Lucas's underground hiding place before a Gestapo raid.

Lucas's other means of auditory connection with the outside—the radio—is equally important. Like Bernard eavesdropping on Rosen's dismissal, Lucas listens in on a rabidly anti-Semitic radio broadcast.[33] Their eavesdropping is an overdetermined form of overhearing in that they over-hear, that is, they hear too much. This is how Lucas expresses his heartfelt plaint about what he hears on the radio: "They say that it's better to hear this stuff than to be deaf. But sometimes I wonder whether it wouldn't be better to be deaf" (103).

I want to suggest that there is a primal scene in Truffaut's work, in that the whole film (and much of Truffaut's *oeuvre*) is a story of anxious over-hearing, with the concomitant theme of deafness and a desire not to hear. Truffaut himself was partially deaf, and the obsessively circulating images of hearing and

6. *Radio is an important image of both the Occupation and the Resistance, as was underlined by the French government's decision to commemorate the fiftieth anniversary of de Gaulle's 18 June 1940 broadcast from London launching the Resistance with the construction of a giant replica of a 1940s-style radio at the place de la Concorde. So aware was de Gaulle of the mythical value of the radio as a reminder of his own heroic role in the Resistance that in 1968 he rejected television and chose instead to announce on the radio his decision to hold a referendum.*

deafness in his work suggest that this theme constitutes both an autobiographical and a historical dimension of *Le Dernier Métro.* The importance of the links between childhood eavesdropping on parents' arguments and their erotic life, on the one hand, as in *Les Quatre Cents Coups,* and an imperfectly understood position as helpless witness of history, on the other, is suggested by a neologism coined by Jacques Derrida: *otobiography*. Derrida threads together many of the themes I am addressing here when he proposes that "the ear is uncanny. Uncanny is what it is; double is what it can become; large or small is what it can make or let happen (as in laisser-faire, since the ear is the most tendered and most open organ, the one that, as Freud reminds us, the infant cannot close)." Derrida advances the proposition that you are what you hear, that one's inner and outer life—or, for our purposes, one's psychic and historical life—are connected by the ear, and, as he makes clear in his analysis of Nietzsche, that the ear is what makes one permeable to institutions (such as schools) and ideologies (such as Nazism).[34]

The infant cannot close its ear, but it can fantasize deafness. I believe that just as Lucas Steiner would rather be deaf, Truffaut's autobiographical fictions are the product of what Frank Kermode calls the "narrative effect of sensory failure." Kermode identifies in certain novels instances of strangeness, opacity, or gratuitousness that could be explained as moments of sensory failure, such as blindness, deafness, forgetfulness, or any interruption in the normal processing of information. The result is that meaning is subverted and the text is rendered irreducible and resistant to reading. In *Le Dernier Métro* the desire to be deaf has such an effect, both for the characters and for the historicity of the work as a whole. Selective deafness is a permission to rewrite the past, to rearrange or deny the primal scene, and to remember it otherwise. The distance between otobiography and pure invention can be measured by the extent of such "willful narrative deafness."[35]

TRUFFAUT'S OTOFILMOGRAPHY

That the scene of overhearing (and the Oedipal will to deafness) constitutes a primal myth in Truffaut's work can be gleaned from the cumulative force of the theme throughout his *oeuvre*. A network of such scenes ties the films together by relay from one character to another who is deaf or deaf-mute, wants to be deaf, or is somehow cut off from communication by an interruption or defect in the hearing circuit. Modifying Lifton's formulation of the primal trauma and its fictional transformations, we can say that for Truffaut the residual image, the pictorialization of the central conflict in relation to the disaster, is the scene of overhearing or deafness itself. This myth exerts a shaping force on his representation of history. A retrospective survey of the theme shows the specific implications of (over)hearing in *Le Dernier Métro*.

L'Argent de poche (1976; *Small Change*) is Truffaut's composite portrait of childhood. Truffaut follows the lives of a group of schoolchildren in much the same way that he treated a film crew in *La Nuit américaine* and the theater troupe of *Le Dernier Métro*. One of the children, Julien Leclou, has been neglected and battered by his unstable, poverty-stricken mother and grandmother, who are squatters in an abandoned warehouse. Julien cuts himself off from communication (and from pain) by feigning deafness. When the concerned school proctor, receiving no answers to his questions, asks him exasperatedly, "Are you deaf, or what?" he draws attention to how Julien is both protected and damaged by his "willful sensory failure." At one point, a sympathetic schoolteacher makes a rather heavy-handed speech to the effect that children need to be protected from abuse because unlike adults, they cannot defend themselves. The ear cannot close.

Hearing and deafness are even more distinctly privileged in the four films in which Truffaut himself is an actor. More indirectly than the Doinel cycle, these films convey Truffaut's personal mythology.

La Chambre verte is the story of a man's attempt to remain in communication with the dead and his concomitant deafness to the living. Julien Davenne's aural disconnection (he refuses to answer the telephone, for example) is doubled by his visual fuzziness (he is often filmed through distorting glass). The film is based on two short stories by Henry James, but it includes a character, a deaf-mute child named Georges, who neither appears in the James stories nor is essential to the narrative. So incidental is he to the story that he does not even figure in plot summaries of the film. So why is he there? I think his very gratuitousness can serve as a clue to the overriding importance of the themes he brings to the film: he is partially deaf, and like Antoine in *Les Quatre Cents Coups,* he is superfluous. He is himself the narrative effect or personification of sensory failure.

Even in Steven Spielberg's *Close Encounters of the Third Kind* (1977) Truffaut's character, a scientist, has a privileged relation to hearing. If in *La Nuit américaine* Ferrand wore a hearing aid, in *Close Encounters* he wears an ear monitor, through which he can perceive sounds that others cannot hear. In the course of the film, he orchestrates a symphony of extraterrestrial vessels and converses with them in a special sign language of musical notes. As in *La Chambre verte,* he presides over rituals of communication with the dead, this time soldiers presumed to have died during World War II. It is as if deafness and the desire not to hear correlate with a refusal to acknowledge loss and with the compensatory presence of special inner voices (the auditory counterpart to "insight").

But it is with *L'Enfant sauvage* (1969; *The Wild Child*) and *La Nuit américaine* that the mythology of overhearing and deafness are most developed and suggest the most complex connections to *Le Dernier Métro*. In his story drawn from a real historical incident, the "wild child" is a mute and partially deaf boy who grew from infancy in the forest of Aveyron, until he was rescued in 1898 by one Dr. Itard (played in the film by Truffaut). The doctor's investigations reveal that the child has a scar from a knife wound on his throat. Did his mother (the film is explicit that it must have been the mother) attempt to destroy him and leave him for dead because he was handicapped? Or was his handicap the result of her attempt to destroy him? In either case, his condition is related to his abandonment. It is the trace of his originary trauma. That Truffaut plays the role of Dr. Itard underscores the autobiographical elements even in this pseudodocumentary: Dr. Itard adopts the child and acts as his surrogate father (even as Bazin had done for him, and as he did for Jean-Pierre Léaud, to whom the film is dedicated). The central philosophical issues of the film, which is a difficult one despite its captivating anecdote, are whether after his childhood spent in the wild this child can be civilized and, even more significant, whether he wants to be. Watching the excruciating scenes where Victor is captured, brought to town on a leash amid the taunts of village children, put on public display for sensation seekers in an asylum, and then subjected to rigorous and sometimes cruel "training" by Dr. Itard, one wonders whether Victor's "selective deafness," like Julien Leclou's, is not self-willed.

Finally, in *La Nuit américaine,* Ferrand (Truffaut) wears a hearing aid, and he explains that he (like Truffaut and like Doinel in *Baisers volés*) lost his hearing in one ear in the artillery. During the course of the film, Ferrand suffers a recurrent anxiety dream, broken into three separate sequences. In the dream, a child with a cane and top hat approaches an iron grill. It is the entrance to a movie house. In the third sequence, he uses the cane to reach through the grill in order to draw toward him a carousel, from which he steals several movie posters: stills from Orson Welles's 1941 classic, *Citizen Kane.* For all its artificiality, the dream is richly meaningful. The child's "crime" evokes the pranks of Antoine Doinel, his outfit recalls the little tramp, and his cane, while providing (in French as in English) a sight gag or dreamlike pun on the name Kane, also alerts us to the presence of other visual and verbal play. As the child escapes down the alley toward the main road, he runs toward a giant neon sign that spans the upper screen: SURDITE. Deafness.

What, if anything, motivates the presence of this "sign"? In a dream, as in the films of François Truffaut, no detail is arbitrary. I would like to suggest that, in the presence of the double Kane/cane icon, deafness is to Truffaut what Rosebud is to Charles Foster Kane. Welles's film, it will be remembered, is plotted around Kane's rise to power, his downfall, and his death, seen in flashback by a newspaperman seeking to decipher the significance of Kane's last word, "Rosebud." The spectator's quest, if not the newsman's, comes to fruition in the film's last frame, which shows a Rosebud-brand sled, along with Kane's other non-saleable belongings, slowly being consumed in the flames of an incinerator. Only the spectator can trace the sled back to an earlier moment in the film and in Kane's life, the moment when his mother sent him forcibly away to school. The opening scenes emphasize how he was painfully wrenched away from his sled and then from his loving but puritanical and powerless mother. It is clear that his mother sends him away to protect him from paternal abuse, a dimension that cannot have been lost on Truffaut.[36] Much has been made of the artificiality of the scene, its errors, and its cheap Freudianism and sentimentality, but it is clear that in *Citizen Kane* the sled and Rosebud are links in a metonymic chain leading back to a primal scene of maternal abandonment.

Similarly, in Truffaut's work, through the metonymic relays described above, each instance of deafness, voluntary or involuntary, can be traced to a scene of separation, exclusion, and abandonment: Antoine, overhearing his parents, is then sent away to reformatory;[37] Julien, abused by his mother, pretends to be deaf; Victor is abandoned, deaf, mute, and wounded, in the forest. Truffaut himself, abandoned by his parents and his first love, escapes first into the army (where he is made deaf in one ear by artillery fire) and then into cinema, first as a cinephile and then as a filmmaker, where he adopts hearing loss as his signature motif. Truffaut once remarked in passing that the hearing in his other ear had already been damaged since childhood (though whether this loss, like Victor's and Julien's, was a result of abuse he does not divulge).[38] Both the inner and the framing films in *La Nuit américaine* tell stories of intergenerational infidelity and betrayal. Childhood abandonment and war, two traumas, two ears. About the abandoned and deaf "wild child," Truffaut says that "that child's original wound [*blessure d'origine*] is irreparable."[39] The phrase *original wound* suggests a condensation of Edenic loss, Oedipal blindness (scar of the family romance), and umbilical separation into one overdetermined image: the (deaf) ear that the infant cannot close. In Derrida's words, "Dream this umbilicus: it has you by the ear. It is an ear."

Just as the child Truffaut is connected by relay to Jacquot/Eric, Bernard, and Lucas Steiner, Marion Steiner is both Lucas's wife and his mother. Disempowered and infantilized by the necessity of hiding, Lucas is dependent on her for food and other material comforts as well as for connection with the outside world. She is his umbilicus. Like the mother in *Citizen Kane,* she is obliged to send Lucas away (and in one scene she even has to bash him on the head with a pipe) in order to protect him from more serious harm. In his incarnation as a child, Lucas listens (from outside the play) to his mother's (his wife's) infidelity through the air duct at the same time that Eric (within the play) overhears the story of his own illegitimacy and parental abandonment. Bernard plays the interloper in both scenarios. Eavesdropping, Lucas becomes aware of his wife's (his mother's) infidelity and, more devastating, is excluded from his theater, proscribed from society, and sent away from his home(land) because his country is sleeping with Nazism. It is no wonder he would rather be deaf.

It seems clear, then, that Truffaut's representation of Nazism and the war is filtered through his private obsessions. His personal iconography is determined by his otobiography. Truffaut is not the first or only artist to link memories of war to real or feared separation from parents. This linkage, obvious from the point of view of a child, is best expressed by Anne Frank. Anne's account reveals that she is not afraid of being killed or of dying (these are not real to her anyway), but of being separated from her parents.[40] Such separation is for children the image of apocalypse, a metaphor or even a cause of death. All children are separated from their mothers. This is the sense of the family romance, which always concludes tragically. But only in some childhoods, due to the coincidence of age and history, is this separation associated with wartime. For Truffaut, already psychologically abandoned and still a child at the time of the war (about the same age as Anne Frank, in fact), the connection between the two seems obvious and necessary. This ear-umbilicus, where the personal and historical converge, becomes the ground for Truffaut's representation of the Occupation.[41]

It is also the basis for Truffaut's view of himself as an artist. His deafness motif authorizes several statements about the nature of his creative process. In particular, it is a figure of belatedness. In addition to being a belated New Wave film, *Le Dernier Métro* and its thematics of deafness suggests that imperfect hearing is a metaphor for the artist's relation to his precursors. In the sense that Harold Bloom terms "misprision" and in which Frank Kermode describes sensory failure as a gateway to creativity, Truffaut's selective and willful deafness helps answer the question of how he manages to be such a strong *auteur* himself while incorporating so many loving tributes to his cinematic heroes, from Lubitsch and Carné to Hitchcock and from Renoir to Bazin. This process is figured in *Le Dernier Métro* as the contrast between Jean-Loup Cottins and Lucas Steiner. As a director, Cottins is a complete nonentity: he receives his directions from his absent mentor, Lucas Steiner. Where Cottins hears perfectly—too well—well enough to be the transparent ventriloquist of his mentor's genius, Lucas's hearing is interrupted and distorted through the mediation of Marion and the air vent. The distance between the two styles of directing, figured abyssally in the film, signals a willful protection from assimilation into the work of precursors.

The hearing aid, part of a Truffaldian iconography of the self, establishes his own distinct identity as an artist.

A second form of belatedness inherent in the deafness motif is its weight as a sign of Truffaut's nostalgia for the silent or mute cinema [*le muet*], which represents for him a golden age of visual storytelling. His oft-repeated admiration for Hitchcock's visual narrative, for example, and the silent nature of the dream sequence in *La Nuit américaine* (which resembles the silent memory passages in *Hiroshima mon amour*)[42] indicate that the fantasy of deafness is a desire to return to the preverbal (maternal), that pre-mirror stage before abandonment, before the Oedipal separation from the mother. From this angle, the primal trauma can be understood as a brutal introduction into sound.

This brings us full circle to *Le Dernier Métro* and its perspective on the Occupation, particularly to its troublingly evasive ending. Jean Renoir remarked enigmatically that *Les Quatre Cents Coups* was "un portrait de la France."[43] *Le Dernier Métro* is also a portrait of France, but not only, or not primarily, the France of 1942: it is also a portrait of France in 1981. The film's title is multiply meaningful, most explicitly as an allusion to the wartime curfew (and the resultant risks of belatedness) but also to the underground *maquis* and to the primal scene of Lucas Steiner's underground eavesdropping. If, as Gaston Bachelard suggests, cellars also signify the unconscious, then Truffaut's portrayal of a Jew in the basement can certainly be read as an attempt to gain access to collective French repressed memories of World War II.

Repressed memories of wartime anti-Semitism (and knowledge of its persistence today) remain the stumbling block to French attempts to come to terms with the Occupation. Truffaut's film takes pains to say that the issue is not German anti-Semitism but French collaboration. He takes on the issue with a lot of his characteristically compassionate humor. After all, it is not coincidental that the hidden Jew has the beautiful "star" as his front. His theater setting suggests Nazism's sinister theatricality, as well as the duplicity and role-playing that the period spawned. And yet Daxiat is far from unsympathetic. He escapes across Europe at the end through a melodramatic flaming *X* that alludes to a similar scene in Lubitsch's *To Be or Not to Be,* while evoking the continuing *X* of censorship or denial.

Ultimately, in 1981, given Truffaut's temperament as an optimist and his professedly apolitical perspective, the ending of his film resolves nothing. There is a scene in Vonnegut's *Slaughterhouse Five* in which Billy Pilgrim fantasizes seeing a World War II movie in reverse: the bombs lift off the ground and fly back into the planes, and all of history unravels backward to "two perfect people named

Adam and Eve."[44] Similarly, Truffaut's wish is that history might be a dream from which you can awaken, or a play that will be over so you can catch the last metro home. Lucas Steiner would rather be deaf than hear the anti-Semitic propaganda on the radio. Truffaut's own expression of irrepressible optimism (or denial) takes the form of a refusal of the epic or the tragic. In "Introducing Pamela," the inner film of *La Nuit américaine,* a stunt man acts in the car crash that kills Pamela. The car careens over a cliff and bursts into flames, and the clearly bewigged stunt man who plays the role of Pamela can be seen rolling free of the car before it tumbles. Then follows a remarkable sequence in which the actors watch the rushes and the reel is played silently, and backward: the flames abruptly extinguish themselves, the car flies up the cliff and drives normally (but backward) out of the frame. In the framing film, after Alexandre is "really" killed in an accident, his colleagues bring him back to life as they watch the actor in the rushes. This fantasy can be traced back to Truffaut's debuts as a filmmaker. *Les Mistons* (1957) includes two such scenes. Children play at shooting each other, and then their actions are reversed thanks to footage played backward. Later, after the protagonist couple (Bernadette Lafont and Gérard Blain) have been separated by the young man's death, a poignant flashback replays their kiss. In both cases the film executes a kind of wishful deus ex machina that repairs tragedy.

This fantasy no doubt elucidates why Truffaut consistently maintained that cinema was an improvement over life.[45] The reel (real) can be wound backward, neither to discover history nor to resolve its problems, but to unravel them. The cinema director has the power to replay the past and make it come out right. If cinema can reverse death in *Les Mistons* and *La Nuit américaine, Le Dernier Métro* is where we watch it undo evil. If we miss the last metro, we can run the reel backward and catch it belatedly. The fantasy rectifies historical tragedies as well as individual ones: Truffaut rewinds the reel to travel back before the disaster, before speech, before the fall.

6. Durasian (Pre)Occupations

Elle avait dit : Parce que, elle, c'est avec sa douleur qu'elle comprendra l'histoire.
Il avait demandé encore:
– Et s'il n'y a pas de douleur?
– Alors tout sera oublié.
– Duras, *L'Amant de la Chine du Nord*

The *War* [*La Douleur*] is one of the most important things in my life," says Duras in her 1985 collection, referring both to the French title of her book and to her painful experience of war.[1] Like Truffaut, Duras is haunted by the Occupation, and yet after *Hiroshima mon amour* she remained silent about it for a quarter of a century. And while she affirms that the Nazi concentration camps are the "fundamental horror of our time,"[2] she did not explore their significance in a major work (even in *Hiroshima*) until the 1980s.[3] For Truffaut those memories lie hidden in the cellar of French consciousness and history. Duras says hers were buried at the back of an old closet, in the form of handwritten notebooks whose contents she claims to have forgotten. Like *Le Dernier Métro,* the stories in *La Douleur* recreate the emotional ambience of the Occupation period in a book whose status as autobiography should nevertheless not be taken for granted, as Jacques Vergès apparently did when he asked Duras to testify at the Klaus Barbie trial, and as the volume's English translation does, with its title, *The War: A Memoir.* Instead, we must use as a lodestar the book's dominant theme and French title—pain [*La Douleur*]—as we navigate between at least two genres and within a split temporal orientation (the opening story's diary format and the retrospective "memoir" of the English translation's subtitle). Even more crucially, we must negotiate between the pain in the French title and an understanding that pain is precisely what cannot be put into words: it veers incessantly toward silence and the visual.

Most readers who have followed Duras's career sense a deep continuity in her *oeuvre:* she seems to be trying again and again, in films and in books, to recount a story that cannot be told, and the obsessive, hallucinatory nature of that story as it recurs in multiple transformations provides a thread that ties all her works together. Hélène Cixous captured that overwhelming sense of unity when she suggested the presence of a Durasian "fundamental fantasy [*fantasme fondamental*]."[4] Many critics since Cixous have either assumed or analyzed that fantasy from various angles. A common focus in many such discussions is the pattern of traumatic loss and compulsive repetition already encountered in *Hiroshima mon amour*. In a recent study of Duras's fiction through the 1970s, for example, Carol Hofmann argues that the Durasian repetition compulsion derives from repressed mourning. Relying on the work of Freud and Melanie Klein, Hofmann describes the dreamlike, near-cataleptic state in which Durasian characters often prefer to live. Of particular usefulness to my examination of *La Douleur* will be her view that Durasian characters suffer from an obstinate and unconscious "refusal illness [*maladie de refus*]": they reject happiness and choose instead to fixate on one or several traumatic experiences from the past, forgoing mastery in order to preserve the pain of loss by arresting the mourning process before it can be resolved.[5]

It seems evident as well that the Durasian fantasy and the memory of the trauma that it obscures, if only imperfectly, even when embodied in a written text, is marked by an intensely visual or pictorial imagination. Both Madeleine Borgomano and Elisabeth Lyon have examined modalities of that imagination in Duras's novels, linking them to the cinema as itself figurative or fantasmatic. Borgomano traces a chain of regression in Durasian characters starting with *Un Barrage contre le Pacifique* (*The Sea Wall*, 1950) that makes of the cinema a metaphor for physical love, which is in turn connected to early childhood fusion with the mother.[6] And in her meticulous study entitled "The Cinema of Lol V. Stein," Lyon describes the fantasy that Lol alternately represses and replays obsessively in her head: the scene of the ball at S. Thalla, where she lost her fiancé and her mind. Ultimately she is obsessed with "shap[ing] the story into a fantasy of looking" in order to fulfill her "desire to see loss," that scene taking the form of "Lol's desire to see herself not being there." The fantasy is thus both an image of Lol's irreparable loss and an impossible figuration of her own death, the death of the subject viewed by the subject.[7] Both Lyon's approach and Borgomano's depend upon psychoanalytic theories of the cinema that see the cinematic apparatus inducing in the spectator a dreamlike, regressive state, an approach consistent with psychoanalytic descriptions of fantasy. LaPlanche and Pontalis, for example, see fantasies as pictorialized screenplays: "Phantasies are still scripts (*scénarios*) of organized scenes which are capable of dramatisation, usually in visual form."[8]

This visual emphasis in fantasy and the cinema tends (ironically, for a writer) to marginalize language, often replacing it with an emphasis on music or silence and with pure spectacle. From the rhythms of the sea and the colors of the sunset reflected on a child's face in *Moderato cantabile* (1958) through the description of the ball at S. Thalla, Duras has paid hallucinatory attention to *mise en scène*. *L'Amant* (1984) takes as its point of departure the memory of a scene in a snapshot that was never taken. In *Un Barrage contre le Pacifique* the mother of the young girl who is Duras's autobiographical persona plays piano accompaniment for silent films at the Eden Cinema. Given the difficulty of articulating pain and Duras's affinity for nonverbal forms of expression, it is not surprising that her first representation of the French war—in the Nevers sequences of *Hiroshima mon amour*—is silent, narrated from the outside. The French woman examines her own role as spectator as she claims, "I saw everything," when what she has seen is a documentary film in a museum. Similarly, as Lol V. Stein watches or imagines the lovemaking between Jacques Hold and Tatiana Karl, she too stages a drama (that is, she restages a trauma) of spectatorship.[9] And in *La Douleur* both a torturer and her victim imagine themselves at the cinema.

It would seem, in fact, that the unity of Duras's *oeuvre*—the recurrent obsessions, the repressions, even the imagery—is more than a *fantasy*. It indicates the presence of a *fantasmatic,* in the sense that LaPlanche and Pontalis give to the term:

It is the subject's life as a whole which is seen to be shaped and ordered by what might be called, in order to stress this structuring action, 'a phantasmatic' (*une fantasmatique*). This should not be conceived of merely as a thematic—not even as one characterised by distinctly specific traits for each subject—for it has its own dynamic, in that the phantasy structures seek to express themselves, to find a way out into consciousness and action, and they are constantly drawing in new material.[10]

This definition aptly and more fully defines what I take Cixous to mean by Duras's "fundamental fantasy." In other words it is not a component or feature of the Durasian imaginary but rather its generative and structuring principle, and as such it should be as much in evidence in her historical as in her nonhistorical texts and should even provide clues about the continuities between the two.

We are now in a position to consider this chapter's central question, namely, what is the place of the Durasian fantasmatic configuration in her historical texts? How does she historicize the obsessions that are so widely recognized as playing a central role in her purely fictional works? Or, from the reverse angle, how is her historiographic project (in *Hiroshima mon amour* and *La Douleur,* principally) shaped by the obsessively fantasized scenes sketched above (which will be examined more fully below)? I argued in part 1 that subjectivity is shaped by history. This occurs through spectatorship, as the French woman learns, with the help of her Japanese lover, to see the collective catastrophe of Hiroshima and Nevers. Or it occurs through language, as Claude Simon's protagonist despairs of ever understanding what has happened to him in the rout of 1940. Here, in the texts of the 1980s, I want to emphasize the reverse: that history is shaped by subjectivity. In *La Douleur* and other recent passages where she mentions the war, Duras's insistent fantasmatic is the armature on which her historiography is constructed. As in the case of Truffaut, then, but in another mode, fantasmatic narratives structure the unconscious and thereby also the representation of history.

Even before she became a filmmaker in her own right, Duras's myth of herself, like Truffaut's, has been associated with the silent cinema, *le muet*, which, in turn, is frequently tied to the maternal. Like Truffaut's, Duras's recent representations of the Occupation (like the rest of her fiction) are haunted by a primal scene of maternal exclusion and abandonment. That scene is most explicitly described in *L'Amant*, where the inaccessibility of childhood memories is intimately linked to the closed door of her mother's room:

In the books I've written about my childhood I can't remember, suddenly, what I left out, what I said. I think I wrote about our love for our mother, but I don't know if I wrote about how we hated her too, or about our love for one another, and our terrible hatred too, in that common family history of ruin and death which was ours whatever happened, in love or in hate, and which I still can't understand however hard I try, which is still beyond my reach, hidden in the very depths of my flesh, blind as a newborn child. It's the area on whose brink silence begins. What happens there is silence, the slow travail of my whole life. I'm still there, watching those possessed children, as far away from the mystery now as I was then. I've never written, though I thought I wrote, never loved, though I thought I loved, never done anything but wait outside the closed door. (25)

This story of the child excluded from the parental secret (with both the secret and the exclusion taking the form of a silence bordering on madness) constitutes the autobiographical mythos from which Duras writes her memories of war. Indeed, as in the case of Truffaut, Duras's belated war memoirs make it necessary to look back through the earlier work to glimpse the now visible threads linking the writing of history to a prehistorical primal scene.

To the above quotation, let us juxtapose another passage from *L'Amant*, the only spot in that book where the war is mentioned in general terms:

I see the war as I see my childhood. I see wartime and the reign of my elder brother as one. Partly, no doubt, because it was during the war that my younger brother died: his heart, as I've said, had given out, given up. As for my elder brother, I don't think I ever saw him during the war. By that time it didn't matter to me whether he was alive or dead. I see the war as like him, spreading everywhere, breaking in everywhere, stealing, imprisoning, always there, merged and mingled with everything, present in the body, in the mind, awake and asleep, all the time, a prey to the intoxicating passion of occupying that delightful territory, a child's body, the bodies of those less strong, of conquered peoples. Because evil is there, at the gates, against the skin. (62–63)

This disturbing paragraph demonstrates the difficulty of reading social meaning in Duras's texts even where a historical signifier is explicitly evoked. Her language weaves together images of war and colonialism (the colonial situation in Indochina, where Duras grew up) with a family portrait, so that it is impossible to separate the strands. The family, "that common family history of ruin and death," is both the literal context and the rhetorical framework for the young sister's experience of the war. Both passages demonstrate an obsession with borders and thresholds—*seuil, porte, peau*—which are alternately as impenetrable as doors and as easily violated as newborn skin. The hated elder brother's evil is contagious; it multiplies and spreads in a violation of boundaries readable as both an intimate and a military "Occupation." This elder brother or Occupation is the evil at the gates (of the nation) and against the skin (of the body). In contrast, the adored younger brother incarnates the sacrificial victim. Just as she characterizes her familial love and hate relationships, she will portray both the horror and the fascination of torture in *La Douleur*. And just as she experiences exclusion from the maternal scene, she will represent the war as a drama of birth and loss.

It is necessary at this point to take another brief look at *Hiroshima mon amour* in order to read that first war story as itself multilayered. It will then be possible to read forward to *La Douleur*, where the war reemerges as a major theme after a twenty-five-year hiatus. But first, and more perversely, I want to read *Hiroshima* backward as an adaptation of *Moderato cantabile*,[11] a novel in which the war makes no appearance at all. Reading from film to book will make it possible to understand the role of the war both as itself and as sign of the recurrent Durasian fantasy.

It will be remembered that Resnais described the film as "a love story—in my head it was something like *Moderato cantabile*—but from which atomic anguish would not be absent."[12] Duras, for her part, reiterated this curious intermingling of fiction and history in her statement that it is "Impossible to talk about Hiroshima. All one can do is talk about the impossibility of talking about Hiroshima."[13] Both in the film's genesis and in the final product, the horrors of the war and the anguish of the love story were in parallel montage, ambiguously and indirectly interrelated.

Hiroshima and *Moderato* have no doubt escaped more than passing comparison because the war is absent from the novel, while it is foregrounded in the film. Yet the two plots are inescapably similar. Each has a framing story in which a man helps a woman in her quest to understand and assimilate a violent death she has witnessed. In the novel, Anne Desbaresdes accompanies her small son to his weekly piano lesson. His scales are interrupted by the piercing sound of a scream from the café below. Arriving on the scene, Anne sees a man lying delirious beside the corpse of the woman he has just murdered, and she watches until he is led away by police. Fixated on the scene she has witnessed, Anne returns repeatedly to the café, engages Chauvin, a foundry worker, in conversation, and the two (re)construct the other couple's story, imagining that through an excess of passion the woman had begged her lover to kill her. In *Hiroshima* the French actress and her Japanese lover sit together in a café, where she reconstructs another story, that of her own love for a German soldier during the Occupation and his murder at the Liberation. She tells how she lay beside him on the quay until he died and how afterward she experienced a period of delirium.

Each death is perceived as an originary and mysterious trauma. Time began at that moment. It is a fantasmatically visualized scene, or, to use Lifton's formula once again, it is a "pictorialization of [the individual's] central conflict in relationship to the disaster."[14] But what disaster? In both stories the erotic relationship in the framing story reenacts or represents one that is remembered or invented, much in the manner of the psychoanalytic transference. The present relationship, perceived as illicit, stimulates the narration of a similar episode from the past. Boundaries of marriage, nation, race, or class are transgressed in each text, recreating what the French woman in Hiroshima terms the "taste of an impossible love" (73). There is also a strong masochistic component in each woman's desire. "You destroy me. You're so good for me," says the French woman. "Deform me, make me ugly" (25). And Anne identifies with a woman who wanted her lover to kill her. Or she wants the woman to have desired that death. Both stories avoid closure: it is impossible to know for sure whether the telling has been a "cure" or simply one instance in a series of neurotic repetitions.

It could be said, then, that in both works the story of the past retrieved and repeated also describes what links the film to the book: the film "remembers" and repeats the novel.[15] But the multiple representations are not the product of the usual metonymy of memory and adaptation. Rather, the affair between the Japanese man and the French woman, like the relationship between Anne and Chauvin, represents the traumatic memory metaphorically. The same can be said of the links between the two texts. Thus, in reading *Hiroshima* through *Moderato* it is productive to explore aspects of the novel that are less visible in the film but that can be brought into focus by the comparison. Slips in the text of *Hiroshima mon amour* reveal the shadow presence of *Moderato cantabile*. One such instance occurs in the French woman's flashback, as she explains to the Japanese man how she slowly emerged from madness: "I remember. I see the ink. I see the daylight. I see my life. Your death. My life that goes on. Your death that goes on" (63). The moment is a paradigm of the scene (seen) of writing: in the midst of a drama of *seeing*, the image shows the young woman lifting a bottle of ink and then pouring it in amazement, as if to suggest that future *writing* would be grounded in that episode of madness striving toward ritually symbolic repetition. Another revealing lapsus occurs when Duras describes the sounds of the sea outside the French woman's window in Nevers (script appendixes, 92). Since the real Nevers depicted in the film is nowhere near the sea, it is legitimate to situate that word in the context of other Duras works, beginning with *Un Barrage contre le Pacifique*, where the sea [*mer*] is connected to the mother [*mère*].

The significance of the sea and the mother in Nevers can be grasped through the transgressive "impossible" love story that is a crucial element in the recurrent fantasy. The emphasis in *Moderato* is on Chauvin and Anne as their developing relationship symbolically reenacts the café murder. But in fact there is evidence of a third, earlier scene that oriented Anne's obsession with the murder. Anne's perception of the murdered woman's scream is connected to an earlier, forgotten scream: as she tells Chauvin, "I think I must have screamed something like that once, yes, when I had the child." Chauvin continues inventing the story of the other couple (which has also become their own story): "They met by chance in a café, perhaps even here, they both used to come here. And they began to talk to each other about this and that. But I don't know. Was it very painful when you had your child?" To which Anne replies, "I screamed . . . You have no idea." Chauvin knows that Anne's attempt to retrieve that cry is important, for when he wants to provoke her, he contests it: "You have never screamed. Never." Thus there are already not one but two repetitions. Not two but three passions are interwoven into a metaphoric chain: the murder, the transgressive interaction between Anne and Chauvin that recreates it, and Anne's experience of childbirth. Anne's adoration for her child has a hallucinatory intensity. She wonders, whether she has invented him, and when he puts his small hand in hers, "Anne Desbaresdes almost [cried out], 'Oh, my love!'"[16]

Chauvin's claim that Anne "never screamed. Never" brings to mind the Japanese man's statement that the French woman "saw nothing in Hiroshima. Nothing," and indeed the two stories unfold in close parallel. Although the French woman of *Hiroshima* does have children, they are absent from her thoughts and from the film. Nevertheless, examining her story through the earlier book brings maternity into focus in another way. Among the most-discussed shots in the film is the first intrusion of the Nevers memory. In the morning, while the French woman watches the hand of the sleeping Japanese man, there is a momentary flashback to another hand, that of the dying German lover in Nevers. A later flashback in the long café sequence establishes another context for this fleeting scene. Following the French woman's remembered vigil over her dying German lover, there is a shot of the young woman, shorn and disgraced, running home into the arms of her mother. A second cut immediately leaps ahead fourteen years to show her in an identical position in the arms of her Japanese lover. As the French woman runs to her mother, here again there is a scream that mediates between two memories. That scream, an inhuman or primal moan, is in fact the only sound that emanates from within the Nevers memory; the rest of the soundtrack comes from the framing story in the Hiroshima café. Thus, in the film as well there are three traumatic events, two repetitions, two metaphoric substitutions. The French woman relives in Hiroshima not only the loss of her German soldier but also the lost maternal embrace, the origin of both history and its narration.

Given this configuration of overlapping losses that *Hiroshima* remembers from *Moderato,* we can understand the café murder and the Occupation flashback functioning simultaneously both as actual "historical" scenes and as screen memories veiling a still earlier trauma. The French woman's regression takes her back before her own maternity, so that unlike in *Moderato,* the emphasis is not on the protagonist's child but on *herself as child.* Thus the French woman asks the Japanese man to hold the glass for her as she drinks, as if she were a little girl. And there is more; even this maternal story is doubled: After her shame in Nevers, it is her mother who sends her away, but there is a suggestion that the memory is even more primal, of the earlier separation of the ego (forever incomplete in girls, according to Freud), when the child is bound to the mother as the original "impossible love." Through its substitutions and juxtapositions, the film thus hides the shadow of an earlier renunciation of the mother. The injunction to replace her with a heterosexual relationship is carried out literally in the montage. The Nevers memory is mute because its meaning precedes language, precedes the Fall. It is associated with the imaginary (Lacan) or with the semiotic (Kristeva), in short, with the mother in the Eden Cinema.[17] This interpreta-

7. *Hiroshima mon amour.* The French woman in the arms of her Japanese lover.

tion renders more plausible the French woman's claim that her loss has been "forgotten," has never before been told or even conscious. It also opens access to the pre-Occupation preoccupations that are the ground for Duras's representations of war.

"Impossible to talk about Hiroshima"—thus there are *two* events it is impossible to talk about. The traumatic losses of wartime and the preverbal loss of the mother come to represent each other through the typically Durasian emphasis on silence and madness and mediated by a scream of pain [*un cri de douleur*]. Tragic love and apocalyptic destruction are at once unforgettable and unrepresentable. As for the hysteric (who also acts out a repressed trauma), then, such memories enter representation metaphorically through reenactment, displaced from image to image, and from novel to film.

And so preoccupation with the maternal, as it shapes the war story, in turn links *Hiroshima* to *La Douleur*. In "La Douleur," the volume's opening story, the narrator—Duras herself, she claims—recounts her "agony" as she awaits the return of her husband, Robert L. (Robert Antelme), from a concentration camp, where he has been a political prisoner, betrayed by a collaborator. When he does return, emaciated and near death, she dedicates herself to nursing him back to health. As she watches for his return (and watches the people watching the crowds of waiting women), and then as she surreptitiously watches him begin painfully and ravenously to eat, she is yet another Durasian spectator figure. Like the French woman at the Hiroshima museum watching the other tourists weep, she is learning vicariously to see. She fantasizes her own death through his, in the way that Elisabeth Lyon describes Lol V. Stein's desire to "shape the story into a fantasy of looking" in order to see loss. In another echo of *Hiroshima* and *Moderato cantabile,* as she imagines his possible death she visualizes herself lying beside him as he dies.

Although it is his wife who awaits him, the story of Robert L.'s return from captivity is inscribed in a discourse of wounded maternity. The dead time of waiting is filled in with vignettes of women, who themselves come to represent Robert L.'s imagined nonreturn. A young man is arrested and taken away before the eyes of his horrified mother. Madame Bordes's apartment is full of tears; like France, she is "disfigured with crying" (31). Madame Katz mends and folds her daughter's meager wardrobe in preparation for her return from a concentration camp, where, it turns out, the daughter in fact died six months earlier. These women embody the epic of maternal waiting and mourning. "Madame Katz is challenging God" (45).

Here the Durasian fantasmatic takes on both a historical and a mythical dimension. All the personifications of waiting, mourning, and lamentation figure through their disfiguring tears what I take to be the underlying matrix-narrative of Duras's representations of the pain of war: the *mater dolorosa.* This is a drama in three moments: death and mourning, then resurrection, and finally renunciation. Just as through her mourning or compassion Mary duplicates or represents, with the sign of her own tears, the unrepresentable suffering of her son, the Durasian narrator experiences Robert L.'s imagined death in her own body, so that his return is in effect a resurrection. Similarly, the French woman in *Hiroshima* resurrects her dead German lover by reenacting the story, until at the end she says, "I bequeath you to oblivion." And again, after nurturing Robert L. back to life, the narrator divorces him, leaving him to his sacrificial meaning, "that grace peculiar to him but made up equally of the despair of all" (68). The rest is life after death, postmortem, postwar. In this way, the Durasian psychological drama of repression, remembering, and repetition intersects with Duras's biography and with France's historical narrative of war, recovery, and denial or mythmaking.

The *mater dolorosa* scene and story emerged in Europe during the thirteenth-century plague, and Marina Warner believes that it served to express this historical period of unimaginable mass suffering. Then—from a Franciscan brother's poem, through musical versions by Palestrina, Haydn, Pergolesi, and others—the Marian biography finally became official dogma in 1950, in the aftermath of another collective horror.[18] In wartime the all-caring and sacred image of Mary can serve as a reminder of "mother in the midst of terror," as one war poet put it.[19] Or, as Julia Kristeva suggests, in times of crisis "man overcomes the unthinkable of death by postulating maternal love in its place."[20]

The most striking instance of the motif in "La Douleur" occurs when the narrator identifies with another imagined waiting woman: "I think of the German mother of the little sixteen-year-old soldier who lay dying on August 17, 1944, alone on a heap of stones on the quai des Arts." And again: "I can't help thinking of the old gray-haired woman who'll be suffering and waiting [*qui attendra, dolente*] for news of the son who died so alone, at sixteen, on the quai des Arts" (46). This soldier is, of course, a recognizable variant of the German lover in *Hiroshima mon amour,* with the significant substitution of the German *mater dolorosa* for the young French girl. In fact, there are traces of a further substitution: the description of the "old gray-haired woman," surely too ancient to be the mother of a boy of sixteen, displays features of Duras's own mother, described in fiction and interview as old, gray-haired, and perpetually mourning.

Just as Marian iconography derives from myths (such as that of Isis and Osiris) merging loss of child and lover, in Duras's writing about the war all objects of waiting, love, and loss take on the aspect of a child. For example, fellow Resister Morland, whom she identifies as François Mitterrand, is described as her child as soon as she is called upon to protect him. Similarly, Robert L. takes his place in a chain that links the loss of her adored young brother to the later death of her own child during the war: "When I lost my younger brother and my baby I lost pain too. It was without an object, so to speak: it was built on the past" (63). Waiting for Robert L. reenacts or resurrects that pain. This dissolution of borders between birth and death, horror and love, can perhaps be traced back through an essay Duras contributed to the feminist magazine *Sorcières* in 1976: entitled "The Horror of Such Love," the article describes Duras's own child as having been killed by birth itself.[21] Elsewhere this event assumes mythic proportions: "The closest thing I've seen to assassination is childbirth," she says. "The first sign of life is a howl of pain [*douleur*]."[22] Labor pain and mourning, two meanings of the word *douleur,* meet at a zero degree of horror. Where birth and death collapse into one event, the abandoned child and the abandoning mother converge (whence, perhaps, the recurrent figure of the Durasian beggar woman, who is both in one). These chains of metaphors are fused together into one myth or fantasy characterized by pervasive undifferentiation or in-difference that points to more than just the description of maternity in war narrative: it is the inscription of war *as* maternity.

La Douleur everywhere stages the dissolution of categories and the violation of boundaries. The narrator's hysterical identification with her absent husband's hallucinated sufferings abolishes the distance between herself and him: "I feel very close to the death I wished for. It's a matter of indifference to me; I don't even think about it's being a matter of indifference. My identity has gone. I'm just she who is afraid when she wakes. She who wills in his stead, for him" (62–63). Similarly, in *Hiroshima mon amour* the French woman remembers lying beside her dying lover, unable to find any difference between his body and her own. The characters strive toward allegory: Robert L. is not hungry; he represents hunger. Madame Bordes does not live *in* chaos; she embodies it. And the narrator is not indifferent. As she simultaneously longs for and fears fusion with another, she personifies in-differentiation. She is the site where meaning implodes.

In this light, it is again important that Duras has never actually written in any sustained fashion about her experience of the war itself. In *La Douleur* as in *Hiroshima mon amour,* it is not the war that concerns her, but rather the Liberation, that liminal historical moment when oppositions between public and private, enemy and friend, collaborator and resister cease to function. At such times there arises an urgent need to reestablish difference in order to stabilize social, political, and linguistic order along with individual identity. In the Nevers flashback sequences in *Hiroshima mon amour,* the French woman found herself in a "sacrificial crisis" (as René Girard defines it),[23] playing the role of surrogate victim in rituals of exclusion designed to reestablish stability. In *La Douleur* it is up to the writing itself to perform the ritual task of reimagining (reimaging) difference, of making meaning possible once again. It is no wonder that Duras declares, in her preface to one of the short pieces in the book, that "these texts . . . are sacred" (115). However, the book repeatedly reveals an urge to set up new boundaries and categories, and then, just as consistently, it refuses to allow these to stand. I believe that Duras does this for explicitly political reasons.

Unlike *Hiroshima mon amour,* Duras's war memoirs of the 1980s emphasize the role of de Gaulle in the immediately postwar transitional crisis. "La Douleur" in particular assumes an outspokenly ideological as well as historiographic stance. In her capacity as a member of a (communist) Resistance intelligence network, the story's narrator interviews French war prisoners arriving at the Gare d'Orsay. She characterizes the repatriation officers presiding over the scene as follows:

Uniforms all over the station. [. . .] We wonder where these people have sprung from, and these clothes, impeccable after six years of occupation, these leather shoes, these hands, this tone of voice, scathing and always scornful whether it expresses anger, condescension, or affability. D. [her companion, presumably Dionys Mascolo] says, "Take a good look at them. Don't forget." I ask where all this has come from, why it's suddenly here among us, and above all who it is. D. says, "The Right. That's what it's like. What you see here is the Gaullist staff taking up its positions. The Right found a niche in Gaullism even in the war. You'll see—they'll be against any resistance movement that isn't directly Gaullist. They'll occupy France. They think they constitute thinking France, the France of authority. They're going to plague the country for a long while, we'll have to get used to dealing with them." (13–14)

Elsewhere the text identifies other features of the victorious Gaullist strategy:

On April 3 he [de Gaulle] uttered these criminal words: "The days of weeping are over. The days of glory have returned." We shall never forgive. [. . .] De Gaulle doesn't talk about the concentration camps, it's blatant the way he doesn't talk about them, the way he's clearly reluctant to credit the people's suffering with a share in the victory for fear of lessening his own role and the influence that derives from it. (32–33)

In these two brief passages, Duras offers a thumbnail sketch both of the emerging postwar authority of Gaullist discourse and of the leftist opposition to it. She considers the official myth of the Resistance, particularly its willed ignorance of the plight of the deportees and the Jews and its erasure of the communists, to be a form of political censorship.

The bitter and ominous tone of these passages highlights the mechanisms of post-Liberation discourse formation (on both sides) in the process of erasing old differences and establishing new ones. The communist Resistance, whose position Duras takes above, spuriously assimilates Gaullism and Nazism as two forms of "occupation." The passages just cited constitute a postwar "we" ("We wonder where these people have sprung from"; "we'll have to get used to dealing with them"; "We shall never forgive") and a new "they" ("They'll occupy France. They think they constitute thinking France, the France of authority. They're going to plague the country for a long while, we'll have to get used to dealing with them"). According to Henry Rousso, among others, this is exactly the effect de Gaulle deliberately set out to create at the Liberation. What Rousso calls the "Gaullist resistancialist myth" institutionalized de Gaulle's vision of a strong country united behind a monolithic Resistance. It erased the role of the communists to such an extent that *unified* soon became a code word for *anticom-*

munist, and it swept the memory of the deportees and the Jews under a rug of national jubilation. What is more, Rousso asserts that "the vision he [de Gaulle] proposed sprang solely from his imagination." Nevertheless, this founding myth was eagerly received by the general public and continued to dominate the postwar Gaullist period.

Interestingly in the context of the understanding of the New Novel and the New Wave that I have proposed, Rousso proposes that the Liberation functioned as a kind of screen memory, masking loss and internal conflict and effectively preventing the nation from mourning its traumas. Instead, collective amnesia, ratified by the imposition of official amnesty, foreclosed resolution and rendered meaningful commemoration impossible. "Memory of the war would therefore develop largely outside this official framework [of the Gaullist resistancialist myth], which had gained acceptance only at the cost of distorting realities."[24] Literature and film provided arenas where conflicting memories could be worked out, but most often under a self-imposed (when not official) censorship.

Rousso's description of the Liberation and its attendant mythologies corresponds closely to the Durasian fantasmatic. As Carol Hofmann points out, Duras habitually captures her fictional characters just as their traumatic memories are beginning to resurface and we (and they) can begin to see the turmoil behind the screen of apparent tranquility. Their story—that is, the story of the French woman in Hiroshima, Lol V. Stein, the Vice Consul, the elderly woman who narrates *L'Amant* and *L'Amant de la Chine du Nord,* and many others—consists in the slow and painful unblocking of memory. The publication of *La Douleur* captured the nation at just such a moment: the crumbling of the Gaullist injunction to forget, followed by the far-reaching reassessment of the Occupation that began in the mid-1980s. Considered as a whole, the book's fragmentation into many stories and multiple points of view (of collaborator, Resistance torturer, Jew, bystander, deportee) deconstructs the resistancialist myth more effectively even than Duras's occasional explicit diatribes against it, cited above. In this the book can be compared to *Le Dernier Métro* and *Le Chagrin et la pitié.* Her writing pierces the smooth screen memory to make underlying contradictions apparent. She shows the vulnerable and understandable side of an arch-collaborator as vividly as she sketches the dark motives of a Resistance worker. Like the Barbie trial, with its accusations of crimes against humanity, Duras's final story about the terrors of a Jewish child in hiding bring the Holocaust back into the picture. Realizing the nature of the continuities between Duras's texts that contain historical material and those that do not, we can see to what extent the Durasian fantasmatic itself all along constituted the historical dimension of her texts, even those with no historical references at all. Occupying Germans, Gaullists, and older brother converge. Familial and political discourses intersect.

If the opening story of *La Douleur* seems to legitimize new categories (a new "we" and "they," a new "Occupation"), the book as a whole takes care to leave boundaries unstable. By means of her stories' juxtapositions, Duras refuses to resolve contradictions, to transcend conflict, to establish a new stasis. Instead, the book preserves and highlights its own disorder and ambiguity. Duras is painfully aware that as difficult as the sacrificial crisis or liminal moment may be, reestablishing difference poses serious dangers as well. Just as there is a risk of creating a new enemy (or doomed love affair), one occupation can replace another. Juxtaposition of "La Douleur" with another story in the volume makes the danger clearer. Set one week after the Liberation, "Albert des Capitales" portrays the participation of a young woman named Thérèse in the anarchic Purge as she directs the torture of a collaborator. The name Albert applies to several sketchily drawn characters: an informer, one of his torturers, and a name (of his boss?) found in the traitor's datebook and adopted by Thérèse's group to refer to their victim. The signifier *Albert* thus points both to the victim and to the knowledge he withholds; it is at once the means of torture, its object, and its excuse. The Capitals is a café, the scene of the crime become the name of the criminal. Rather than identifying anyone, then, proper names render everyone identical. With this device, the differences that support language collapse into a few emblematic but utterly nonreferential signs.

The pretext for torturing "Albert" is to force him to divulge the color of his identity card, thereby establishing some visible signifier that would distinguish collaborators from resisters. This impulse persists today, as the Barbie trial and the continuing furor over the Touvier and Bousquet "affairs" attest and as the popularity of Duras's book confirms. But as the narrator orders the interrogation and torture, the stability of meaning is only momentary, undermined by the very process that would construct it. The task of reestablishing difference takes place under the ominous sign of reversal. Now it is the collaborator who waits: "He's afraid. Afraid of us. Of us who were afraid. Of those who had been afraid he was in great fear" (128). "He's become someone without anything in common with other men. And with every minute the difference grows bigger and more established" (132). It appears for a moment that the ritual of torture will fulfill what Elaine Scarry maintains is its function of producing knowledge or meaning and of (re)establishing boundaries and categories. But the chorus of watching women begins to chant the withdrawal of their solidarity with the ceremony. At this point birth imagery reappears. This time it is the victim who will give birth . . . to words: "But if the blows stop, he won't talk. Everyone's waiting with bated breath for this delivery [*cet accouchement*]. . . . It'll soon be the end now. . . . Thérèse cries out" (139). But in fact no one cares about the color of the man's identity card. This information was already known, and besides, it literally "makes no difference." Renewed stability of boundaries is stillborn.

Both short texts end with the narrator's tears. First, in "La Douleur," there are the tears of the *mater dolorosa* ("At the name, Robert L., I weep. I still weep. I shall weep all my life" [67]). In "Albert des Capitales" Thérèse weeps after the ordeal is over, when the other women mock her, at the failure of violence to reestablish what Scarry calls a "fiction of power."[25] Even the perpetrator is powerless before torture's status as pure spectacle, so it is no wonder that the narrator-torturer remarks, "Now I'm here, in this dark room, shut in with . . . this betrayer of Jews and members of the Resistance. I'm at the cinema" (125). The French woman experienced a similar helplessness before the images of the Hiroshima bomb victims: ". . . what else can a tourist do, really, but cry?" (18). Both women remain outside the closed door of knowledge. In the dark room of the cinema the primal scene is imaginary and inaccessible, "screened" in two senses of the word.

All these tears flow from multiple visions of the war and incompatible voices (of an ego, of a historical perspective) fiercely held in hostile coexistence. Duras's maternal metaphors and her tears of frustrated powerlessness perpetually reinscribe instabilities, rather than their resolution. The Durasian "fundamental fantasy," then, in the historical as in the other texts, has to do with forging an association between pain and a willful refusal to forget. The French woman in Hiroshima knows that memory is maintained by "indifference. And also the fear of indifference." (33). The young autobiographical persona of *L'Amant de la Chine du Nord* says that "it's the pain [*douleur*] that will make her understand the story [or history]." When her Chinese lover asks what will happen if there is no pain, she responds, "Then it will all be forgotten."[26]

It is not surprising that "Albert des Capitales" interested Jacques Vergès, who apparently chose to read Duras's "Thérèse is me [Thérèse c'est moi]" literally and not as a Flaubertian comment on fiction. He served his own purposes well when he removed the one story from its context in the volume. But it is the juxtapositions and contradictions in *La Douleur* that constitute its historiographic voice. The reversal of the narrator's position between "La Douleur" and "Albert des Capitales" suggests that if war produces dissolution of culture, civilization, and meaning, Duras sees the risks one runs in attempting to resurrect them. Instead, she slides again into private history, but now that slippage itself carries the message of a refusal to stabilize categories or erect confident discourses of victory that would create a credible new enemy. Her language even suggests that there is no difference between the familial and the historiographic (for, as she states in *L'Amant*, "I see wartime and the reign of my elder brother as one" [62]). This is where Duras's writings are not only *un*cathartic, as Julia Kristeva has pointed out,[27] but patently *anti*cathartic.

The uncomfortable cohabitation of two temporal perspectives is also part of this project. *La Douleur* is written in the form of an intimate diary and in this resembles other recent war memoirs. For example, Alice Kaplan points out that the diary format of Lucie Aubrac's 1984 Resistance memoir "resuscitate[s] history, [makes] the past into a current event."[28] It seems to me as well that whether Duras's claim to have found papers written in 1944–45 is true or contrived, her diary form and the staging of a temporal lapse between composition and publication suggest an effort to bring the present forcibly and abruptly into the past. Either way, however, *La Douleur* belongs to the 1980s. While the diary format of "La Douleur," its raw anger (about Gaullism), and its fresh pain (of awaiting Robert L.'s return) have a compelling immediacy, the book as a whole bears readable signs of a retrospective glance. For example, when Thérèse, participating in a scene of torture, imagines herself at the cinema, it is plausible to read this statement through the hindsight of scores of World War II movies. It is unlikely, too, that Duras's courageous description of atrocities committed by Resistance members dates from 1945. Rather, the book as a whole shows the distance born of maturity and of the reversals and disillusionments following the Algerian war period, the discrediting of Soviet communism and the French Communist Party, and perhaps the election of Mitterrand and subsequent disappointments. Even the tears have different meanings in different historical moments, especially if one bears in mind de Gaulle's statement, so bitterly reported by Duras, that "the days of weeping are over. The days of glory have returned." Tears shed in 1945 and published in 1985 represent delayed mourning, and the reasons for that delay are both personal ("pain needs room," says the narrator [7]) and political. Duras felt that both her grief and her speech were censored by the discursive horizons of the Gaullist postwar rhetoric of victory. In the meantime, *Moderato cantabile, Le Ravissement de Lol V. Stein, Le Vice Consul,* and many other texts kept the pain alive, embalmed in their fantasmatic configurations. And "it's the pain that will make [us] understand the story [or history]." The "return" of Robert L. thus represents both the release of a war prisoner in 1945 and his return to consciousness and speech forty years later.

7. Looks That Kill: Louis Malle's Portraits of Collaboration

The posture which inaugurates knowledge is defined by a backward turn. – Christian Metz

In a statement accompanying the published script of *Au revoir les enfants*, Louis Malle says that his film was

inspired by the most tragic [*dramatique*] memory of my childhood. In 1944, I was eleven years old and boarding at a Catholic school near Fontainebleau. A new boy joined us at the beginning of the year. A brilliant student, he intrigued me. He was different; his background was mysterious. He didn't talk much the first few weeks. Little by little we became friends, when, one morning, our small world collapsed.

That morning of 1944 changed my life. It may have triggered my becoming a filmmaker.[1]

Yet Malle did not so much as allude to the incident in any of his films until 1987, forty-three years (and twenty-eight films) afterward, at the age of fifty-four. "I should have made it the subject of my first film," he remarks, "but I preferred to wait." My own questions here will be: Why did he too wait so long? How does the "tragic memory" depicted in *Au revoir les enfants* explain Malle's vocation as a filmmaker? What in his life or in the historical, political, or social milieu of the 1980s finally made it possible or necessary for him to create this film and to shape the event narratively and visually as he does? And what is the truth value of the memory depicted? That is, what exactly is the experience that is being represented, given Malle's insistence that the movie does not depict the memory the way it happened at all and, in particular, that the crucial scene is not autobiographical but rather pure invention?[2] I want to examine Malle's film, and one scene in particular, as a very literal example of the process of pictorialization of disaster described by Lifton and to theorize the relation of image making to Malle's representations of personal identity and responsibility in history.

The anecdote of *Au revoir les enfants* is deceptively straightforward and realis-

186

tic. The action takes place over a few weeks in the winter of 1944 at a Catholic boarding school. The head priest, Père Jean (who is active in the Resistance), hides three Jewish boys in the school under assumed names. Julien Quentin, Malle's autobiographical persona, befriends one of the new boys, Jean "Bonnet" (Kippelstein), who also rivals him as top student in the class. Julien applies his academic acumen to deciphering the enigma of Jean's identity. Meanwhile, war intrudes on the isolated school in the form of air raids, a kitchen helper's dismissal for black market activities, the lawless behavior of Vichy police thugs harassing an elderly Jewish gentleman in a restaurant, and more pervasively in the rationing of heat and food and in the boys' conversations, which incorporate overheard and half-understood remarks about Pétain, *les collabos*, the militia, the Russian Front, the STO, the Allies' advance, and so on. On the fatal day, the regional Gestapo chief descends on the school to arrest Jean Kippelstein and the two other Jewish boys, along with Père Jean. Meanwhile, the school proctor, also a Resistance member, escapes across the roof. The final frames—a prolonged shot of the empty doorway through which Jean and the others have just disappeared followed by a closeup of Julien Quentin's face registering shocked sorrow—are accompanied by an adult first-person voiceover telling us that all three boys perished at Auschwitz. The voice, presumably that of the filmmaker himself, adds: "Over forty years have passed, but I will remember every second of that January morning until the day I die."

At first this seems a simple tale of resistance and heroic defeat. The headmaster courageously harbors the three boys. Julien's brother graduates from playing annoying pranks on German soldiers (he gives misleading directions so that they will lose their way in the town) to a tentative decision to join the underground *maquis*. The boys themselves stoically "resist" wartime conditions of deprivation and family separation. Julien's friendship with Jean grows apace with his progressive understanding of his friend's perilous situation. The film's narrative line is sustained by a detective plot, mirrored internally by the two boys' shared reading of Sherlock Holmes. Julien deciphers clues: an overheard midnight prayer; a family photograph hidden in a locker; an erased but faintly legible name in a schoolbook; his friend's evasion of certain questions about his birthplace, the whereabouts of his parents, his dietary habits. When Julien finally pieces together the puzzle of his friend's Jewish identity, he refuses to understand it. "What's a kike?" he asks his brother, who answers that it is someone who does not eat pork. "You're putting me on. . . . What exactly do people blame them for?" (39). The spectator, from a vantage point that is both more adult and historically retrospective, has understood from the beginning but nonetheless identifies with the unintended but sinister irony of the young boy's questions. Julien's conscious attitudes and deliberate actions, as they naively deconstruct the very notion of racial and religious difference by rendering it ludicrous or meaningless, constitute an act of resistance.[3]

A closer look reveals, however, that the film is haunted by small as well as flagrant acts of collaboration and of foolish risk taking that betrays. The extent to which collaboration is the ambiguous subterranean trauma of *Au revoir les enfants* can be discerned in certain echoes from Malle's 1974 portrait of a collaborator, *Lacombe Lucien*. The earlier film, scripted by Patrick Modiano following Malle's outline, follows a sullen and doltish teenage boy's descent into brutality and recounts the conflict between his activities on behalf of the local Gestapo and his growing attachment to a Jewish tailor and his daughter, France. When the German police arrive to arrest France (having already taken away her father), Lucien kills the German, and he and France live a brief but idyllic life as fugitives until the war ends. A final subtitle informs us of Lucien's postwar trial and execution for collaboration.

Both films take place in 1944 and portray an adolescent boy, present in virtually every scene, who befriends and acts as would-be protector of a Jew. Both show history to be largely the sum of events and actions that would have been minor in other circumstances. Collaboration is portrayed (entirely in the early film, episodically in the later one) as occurring when characters commit small thoughtless acts that might have proved inconsequential in normal times but result here in tragedy. For example, an inebriated Lacombe gossips about a schoolteacher who is then captured and tortured by the Gestapo. In *Au revoir les enfants,* Père Jean refuses communion to a Jewish boy, thereby revealing the limits of his Christian charity and his religious training.[4] He similarly protects his tuition-paying, middle-class charges by dismissing Joseph, the kitchen helper, using him as a scapegoat for collective misbehavior. Destitute and resentful of the injustice done to him, Joseph will turn informer. In fact, Lucien and Joseph are variants of a single character from Malle's childhood: the initial draft of the earlier film's scenario opened with Lucien, summarily dismissed from his job as a domestic in a Catholic school, turning to the *milice*. Ultimately, Lucien's character became more enigmatic when his motives for collaborating were deleted from the script,[5] but that context reappears in Joseph's denunciations to the Gestapo in *Au revoir les enfants*. Most central to the later film's plot and significance, however, Jean Bonnet/Kippelstein's arrest follows directly from an inadvertent gesture on the part of Julien himself. In both films a final voice-of-God conclusion announces the subsequent death of a protagonist as a direct result of the events just witnessed.

Malle conceived the project of *Lacombe Lucien* on the basis of his research into the psychology of the traitor. He decided to incarnate that interest as a collaborator only after considering a string of subjects: the Mexican Halcones (police stooges who infiltrated student rebel groups in 1968); a young French accountant-turned-torturer Malle had interviewed in Algeria; Algerian Harkis, who aided the French army during the Algerian struggle for independence; and Lieutenant Calley of the U.S. Army, in prison at the time for the torture of Vietnamese villagers.[6] Even before its precise historical context was determined, then, the genesis of *Lacombe Lucien* foregrounded Malle's fascination with collaboration in the more general sense and with unquestioning obedience to authority as forms of human behavior. Even in the absence of concrete motives, Lucien's actions can be explained psychologically. They result from character weaknesses, in particular a craving for adult identity and authority, and from situations that lead Lucien inexorably down what we might call the path of least resistance.

The film's ambivalence about Lucien, its sympathetic or at least nonjudgmental portrayal of a person engaged in detestable behavior, is reflected in the scandal it unleashed. The press at first unanimously hailed the film as a masterpiece, only to execute an abrupt about-face a month later and condemn it. All sides found fault with the representation of the collaborator as unremittingly stupid and proletarian. The Right criticized it for painting French fascism's adherents as a band of marginals devoid of ideological commitment and driven by a latent brutality only waiting for the opportunity to express itself. Lucien is not even an antihero: he becomes what he is by chance; his collaboration is unknowing and almost inadvertent. He simply follows the drift, drawn along by events he does not understand. The Left criticized Malle for making a film about a collaborator at all, for exculpating a scoundrel (that is, for implicitly making a case for compassion or even amnesty), and for portraying the *Résistants* as murdering marauders.[7] The controversy revealed a deep unwillingness, at every point along the political spectrum, to demystify the Resistance or to delve into the psychic or even the political logic of collaboration. One scene shows Lucien idly chatting with a tortured Resistance prisoner chained to a radiator. Angered because the man calls him "tu"—that is, treats him like a child—Lucien tapes his mouth shut. I like to read this scene, particularly its slice of masking tape, which constitutes yet another *carré blanc,* as emblematic of the censorship still in place in 1974 with regard to representations of the Occupation.

And yet *Lacombe Lucien* itself helped to disrupt taboos as well. The film and the controversy surrounding it are widely seen as a prominent instance or even a launch pad for what soon became known as the *mode rétro.* More than a simple

8. *Lacombe Lucien*. The *carré blanc* is still in place.

fashion or fad, though it was those as well, that mode continues today and helps to explain the appearance of many films, novels, and memoirs, including those examined here. It involves a "backward turn"[8] in the form of both a nostalgic style and an intellectual trend to reexamine the "dark years" of the Occupation. Many commentators have noted that Malle and Modiano picked their moment well, for as we have seen, the mood in post-1968 France was for self-examination. The political eclipse and then the death of de Gaulle, the death of Pompidou, and the election of Valérie Giscard d'Estaing made it possible to question the Gaullist hagiography of the Resistance, what Rousso called "resistancialism." Because *Lacombe Lucien* makes moves characteristic of such demystification, Malle and Modiano were suspected by many of rightist sympathies.[9] As enumerated by Alan Morris, strategies used to dismantle the reigning ideologies included casting doubts on the motives and unity of the Resistance; implicitly or explicitly rehabilitating individual collaborators or collaboration as a whole; and portraying events or choices made by individuals as the result of chance. Morris points out that these strategies had been evident in writing about the Occupation since the end of the war but only became acceptable after 1968. By foregrounding the collaborator as protagonist, by its less than glowing portrayal of the Resistance, and by giving chance a crucial role in shaping events, *Lacombe Lucien* contributed to the emergence of a countermyth. The resistancialist credo would have it that most French people (with the exception of a few collaborationist bad guys) were innocent. The countermyth that emerged in the early 1970s represented a pendulum swing in the other direction: everyone (except a small number of Resistance heroes) was to some degree guilty.[10]

As far as exploring psychological dimensions of collaboration, *Lacombe Lucien* goes a step beyond Sartre's 1939 portrait of the budding fascist in "L'Enfance d'un chef,"[11] whose protagonist, it will be remembered, was also named Lucien. Malle's portrayal is less Manichean. He injects notes of pathos and tragedy into the collaborator's itinerary, and he makes his Lucien more troubling. Falling in love with a woman whose name—France—is certainly allegorical, Lacombe identifies himself with, and even as, a victim.[12] Sartre's Lucien was more intellectual and cosmopolitan, and he, like Lucifer, whose name Lucien perhaps recalls, chose evil more lucidly. And while his development is nonetheless believable, Lucien Fleurier is not a sympathetic character, and Sartre makes no excuses for him.

The critical response to *Lacombe Lucien* obliges us to revise the truism that Marcel Ophuls's *Le Chagrin et la pitié* unmasked once and for all the Gaullist myth of the Resistance and opened the way for responsible reexamination of the Occupation. In truth, the floodgates of memory, especially memories of collaboration, were more like a revolving door, opening in stages. Ophuls's film marks a double scandal, first because of what it attempted to reveal and then because it took the French government ten years to accord it the screening it deserved in France. For although the film was released in 1971, it was banned from French television until the Mitterrand ministry of culture (and the new program director at TF1, André Harris, who had co-produced *Le Chagrin et la pitié*) finally broadcast it, amidst renewed controversy, in 1981.[13] Its delayed release and the magnitude of its effect measure the strength of the resistance to it, for what Ophuls's documentary challenged was the tremendous investment in the official Gaullist construction of history, according to which national unity in resisting the occupier was marred by only a handful of traitors, cowards, and fools.[14] Even more persistent was the belief that collaborators and resisters were themselves two clearly defined and completely distinct groups. *Le Chagrin et la pitié* shatters such Manichean views of the Occupation and delineates instead a complex array of degrees and forms of collaboration and resistance. To justify the suppression of Ophuls's film in 1971, the then director of French radio and television (the ORTF), Jean-Jacques de Bresson, argued that "this film destroys myths that the French still need."[15] That need is still in evidence, and *Le Chagrin et la pitié, Lacombe Lucien, Le Dernier Métro, La Douleur,* and *Au revoir les enfants* all constitute incremental, anguished, and still incomplete attempts to come to terms with the past and contribute to the evolution of public perspectives and discourse.

Moreover, the stakes remain high even today, for if *Le Chagrin et la pitié* showed the French public that Germans and a few French lackeys were not the only villains of the Occupation, Ophuls's more recent film, *Hotel Terminus: The Life and Times of Klaus Barbie* (1988), traces the responsibility for Barbie (and tracks Barbie himself) from one protective cover to the next and from Germany and France to Latin America by way of the United States. Ophuls's film, like so many stories about the Holocaust, including *Au revoir les enfants,* is a monstrous postmodern detective story in which there is a detective (Julien in Malle's film and Ophuls himself in *Hotel Terminus*) but from which the crime, the criminal, and even the trial are missing. Furthermore, while there is no real "solution" at the end of either film, the criminal's guilt was manifest from the start, and what is spellbinding is how many others (individuals, governments) became accessories to his crimes by helping him to escape. Curiously, Barbie's itinerary, traced by Ophuls, also provides a map of Malle's own travels in search of a nationality for his collaborator: from France to Latin America and Algeria to the United States and back to France. So it is no simple cinematic tribute, but rather an ironic commentary, that in *Au revoir les enfants,* when Julien and Jean and the others are treated to a movie, the schoolmaster's choice is Charlie Chaplin's *The Immigrant,* in which the spectator watches with the schoolboys the scene where the Little Tramp arrives in view of the Statue of Liberty.

Now evident in the succession of Ophuls's relentless documentaries are the stages in an epic scandal that threatens to include an ever-increasing number of participants in the spiraling taint of Nazism and the contagion of the guilt deriving from it. For when categories break down, as the distinctions between resistance and collaboration do in *Le Chagrin et la pitié,* who is to say what the definition of a collaborator is? When the prophylactic spell of the Gaullist narrative is broken, anyone might be guilty, even those whose only role was to witness the events. Complacent distance is no longer possible. The critical controversy surrounding *Lacombe Lucien,* the intervening censorship and re-release of *Le Chagrin et la pitié,* as well as the numerous other films and novels and documents disseminated in the interval and since, no doubt contributed to the greater complexity of the psychological portraits and the subtlety of the representation of collaboration in *Au revoir les enfants.*

If we look carefully at the differences between Malle's two films, we can measure his evolution—and the progress of the *mode rétro*—from 1974 to 1987. Perhaps because of its abstract and philosophical genesis, *Lacombe Lucien* executes a variety of maneuvers that systematically distance the protagonist and protect the audience from too direct involvement with Lucien. Despite his boyish charm and his status as protagonist, he remains remote from his typical audience because of his class situation and his apparently unthinking and instinctive responses. Although he is present in every scene, his visual point of view is never that of the film. He is opaque: his thoughts are enigmatic, and as spectators, we watch *him,* not *with him.* He and, by extension, collaboration remain in the sphere of spectacle. At the same time, he is not unappealing as an awkward and desiring adolescent, and the interest of the film lies in the scandal, presented as tragic in its inexorability, of his stumbling descent into brutality.

Awareness of the contagious nature of guilt about collaboration and an attempt to take responsibility for it account for many differences between *Lacombe Lucien* and *Au revoir les enfants,* differences that can be discerned in the structure and techniques of narration. The extradiegetic statements that conclude the films have very different impacts. The autobiographical voice that emerges at the end of *Au revoir les enfants* speaks from a consciousness split between character and narrator. The remembering adult remains scandalized and contaminated by his childhood experiences, haunted by a conflict he came to understand only much later. This self-reflective and retro-spective dimension (the "backward turn") is totally absent, on the other hand, from *Lacombe Lucien,* which is a prospective story with an anonymous "voice-of-God" narrator who announces (in subtitles) the sequel to the story but not its effect on the present.

There are significant differences in the portrayal of collaboration, as well. *Au revoir* foregrounds the death of the victim of collaborationist policies, whereas *Lacombe Lucien* sketches a portrait of the collaborator as victim of his own latent brutality, of the Purge, and of history itself. And in *Au revoir* collaboration is not conceived as inherent in the character of the protagonist. It is not even a slippery slope of incidental or unknowing small choices. Even Joseph, the kitchen helper (a Lacombe with motives revealed, as I have shown), makes a deliberate decision to seek revenge by denouncing the school. Then, significantly, he accuses Julien Quentin, who had joined with him in black market exchanges of jam for postage stamps, of a guilt equal to his own. The two films also deploy different answers to the question, Collaboration with what? Lucien is accomplice to torture of individuals in the Resistance; at stake in *Au revoir les enfants* are acts of complicity with genocide.

These shifts delineate the changed context in which the later film was made. It might be understandable (though of course inexcusable) that the Holocaust, being the most repugnant and thus most repressed French crime of the Occupation, has taken the longest time to surface. The enormous public resistance to facing it might have prevented its resurgence even now had not the trial of Klaus

Barbie (and the later Bousquet and Touvier cases) raised the issue of statutes of limitation and made it necessary to prosecute on the basis of crimes against humanity. The French public, especially members of the Resistance, would clearly have preferred that Barbie be tried for the murder of Jean Moulin.[16]

The most disturbing and complex moment in *Au revoir* involves Julien himself in a decisive moment of collaboration. What is troubling and courageous in Malle's portrayal here is that collaboration is not an *essence* but an *act*. More significantly for Malle and for us, it is an act of *looking*. For Julien Quentin, the traumatic memory of that morning in January 1944 begins with the Gestapo's arrival at his school to arrest his friend. But the way the scene is played out implicates Julien as more than a passive bystander or witness: it implicates him *as* a spectator. The *mise en abyme* device is familiar. Like *Hiroshima mon amour*, but with significant differences, as I will show, *Au revoir les enfants* is what Nick Browne calls a "specular text" in that "the significant relations have to do with seeing—both in the ways the characters 'see' each other and the way those relations are shown to the spectator."[17] As it unfolds, the configuration of filmmaker, characters, and spectators in and outside the film becomes a mode of access to the historical trauma and its impact on the present.

When the Germans arrive at the school the boys in their classroom are in the midst of a lesson, watching their teacher pin tiny colored flags into a map of Europe while he gives an update on the progress of the Allies. He has just stepped away from the map and begun a geometry lesson when a Gestapo officer, Doktor Muller, marches into the classroom, accuses the Fathers of hiding Jews in the school, and demands to know which student is Jean Kippelstein. The boys freeze and lower their eyes. After a stunned moment of silence the teacher states that there is no one by that name in the school. Muller then steps impatiently to the map and begins angrily to pull out the colored pins, flinging them to the ground. During this instant while Muller's back is to the class, Julien turns furtively to reassure himself that his friend Jean is all right. His glance is intercepted by Muller, who strides directly to Jean's desk. Under Muller's triumphant stare, Jean puts away his writing materials, slowly and with dignity retrieves his cape from its peg, and begins to shake the hands of his classmates, bidding them good-bye one by one. As he reaches for Julien's hand, he is dragged from the room.

As if there were any doubt about the gravity or the choreography of the gesture, it occurs a second time, in a slightly different context, with Julien playing a different but related role. A few moments after the scene just described, the boys are all gathering their belongings, the school having been peremptorily and punitively closed. From the classroom Julien has gone to prepare his own knapsack and thence to the infirmary, where he will help a sick classmate pack his things. Meanwhile, the Gestapo officers search the school for the two other Jewish boys. With the proctor's help, one of the remaining Jewish boys, Négus, takes refuge in the infirmary, posing as a patient under the covers of a sickbed. When the two officers burst into the room, Julien looks on as a nurse betrays the boy wordlessly, with a meaningful glance in the direction of the bed. Julien Quentin clearly understands, and we see him understanding, that he was not simply a witness to Jean's arrest. It was his own act, however inadvertent, that gave his friend away, just as fatally as the nun's deliberate denunciation of Négus. Motivation makes no difference whatsoever in the outcome. Despite Jean's reassurance—"Don't sweat it. They would have caught up with me in any case" (71)—the fact remains that Julien is not innocent. Nor, for that matter, is the public, in France or in the United States, including the filmmaker himself. The portrayal of Julien's and the nurse's acts as a glance rather than some other gesture shortens the distance between active betrayal and the role of a witness or spectator who fails or is unable to intervene.

Thus is collaboration figured as a specular drama, a moment of active looking that causes the death of another.[18] This intercepted glance provides a rhetorical or geometrical (triangular) figure for the structure and even a definition of betrayal. Given the Catholic school setting and the film's incessant use of religious motifs, it is not out of place to call this look a Judas kiss. The juxtaposition of the two scenes cleverly and accurately conveys the dynamic of denunciation and counterdenunciation that characterized the anarchic final months of the Occupation. Julien witnesses an act of collaboration in the infirmary scene. In the classroom scene he had played the collaborator's role himself. These are truly looks that kill.

I submit that this moment of Julien's glance—his backward turn—constitutes the primal scene, or, in Lifton's words, the "residual image," the "pictorialization of [the individual's] central conflict in relationship to the disaster" that haunts the narrator in the final voiceover, presumably Malle himself. The distance between intention and outcome is pictorialized as a difference between looking *at* (betraying) and looking *with* (protecting). Viewing the Chaplin film together, their profiles framed side by side in extreme closeup, Jean and Julien are enchanted by a cinematic image that provides for them, in the words André Bazin used to describe Chaplin, "unlimited imagination in the face of danger."[19] As the group enjoys the film, successive frames demonstrate, by means of the familiar *mise en abyme,* the magical power of the cinema to bridge religious, class, and sexual distances, abolish hierarchies, and forge an ideal community. Joseph the kitchen helper shares a moment of laughter with the Fathers; competition and enmity among the boys is set aside; François summons up the courage to offer the pretty music teacher a chaste kiss on the cheek. It is an idyllic moment—the script specifies that it is a "moment of forgetfulness"—reminiscent of Truffaut's rosy view of the cinematic Eden, and we can borrow Bazin's words as cited above to describe Malle's optimism about the function of cinema in general and perhaps his hopes for this specific film vis-à-vis a French public still reluctant to confront the dangers of memory. Within a politicized thematic of looking in a "specular text," Malle seems to suggest, watching a film can itself constitute a political choice. In 1944, because of Chaplin's politics and his reputedly Jewish origins,[20] *The Immigrant* would have provided an obvious contrast with the anti-Semitic propaganda films that may have been screened in other schools. It is also poignantly ironic, especially in the light of Jean Bonnet's transfixed attention to the screen, that when the ship of immigrants arrives in New York, within view of the Statue of Liberty, the Little Tramp is not permitted to debark. The film is as close as the boy comes to survival.

In glancing at Jean and thereby identifying him as a Jew, Julien inadvertently performs the fundamental anti-Semitic act as it is defined by Sartre in *Réflexions sur la question juive,* written in 1944 and published in 1946. Sartre's essay is permeated with a vocabulary of visibility and looking. In times of persecution, Sartre notes, the Jew seeks invisibility, for it is the anti-Semite's fear and hatred that constitutes the Jew as such. So powerful are the anti-Semite's hatred and the gaze that embodies it, and so clearly does that hatred preexist the social identity of the Jew, Sartre argues, that it is the anti-Semite who creates the Jew, and if the Jew did not exist, the anti-Semite would have to invent him.[21]

Although he is not generally recognized as a film theorist per se, Sartre prefigures much contemporary thinking on film; in particular, he has made his mark as a theorist of the gaze. He was, in fact, intensely interested in the cinema and wrote eleven screenplays, most of them based on his own writing for the theater. Gertrud Koch has noted the affinity between Sartre's texts for the cinema and his philosophical essays on "the master/slave dialectic of the gaze."[22] Especially remarkable in our context here are Sartre's works of the wartime and immediate postwar period (including and providing a context for *Réflexions sur la question juive*), in which he is preoccupied with the dynamics of subjectivity as it is shaped by the look.

Extending his discussion of phenomenology in *Being and Nothingness* (1943), Sartre addressed his attention to the impact on subjectivity of being seen, of what he calls "the act of being-looked-at," as origin of identity and the sense of shame. The discovery that the Other, who appears as an object for us, has a consciousness and the power to look back mediates our understanding of ourselves. I see myself because somebody sees me, or as Sartre puts it, "I am conscious of myself escaping myself."[23] Just as I naturally tend to see the Other as an object in the world, the existence of the Other-as-subject is a threat to my own subjectivity. The result is a reciprocal, zero-sum struggle, with each objectifying the other in order to preserve the self. Because "the Other is the one who excludes me by being himself, the one whom I exclude by being myself," each participant engages in this struggle aiming to preserve a state in which "self-consciousness is identical with itself by means of the exclusion of every Other." Sartre thus considers Hegel's view of the master-slave dialectic too optimistic, because "between the Other-as-object and Me-as-subject there is no common measure" (236–38).

But at the same time he notes Hegel's brilliance in understanding that both the subject and the object (of the look) depend on each other in their being and therefore neither can doubt the other without doubting the self. Thus, as contemporary (especially feminist) film theory has demonstrated, the gaze constitutes the looker as well as the looked at. For both, identity is produced by the gaze. In this configuration, power is defined as the ability to affirm one subjectivity and the dominance of one identity—"my" gaze—over the Other. In "Orphée noir," his introduction to a 1948 anthology of works by African and Caribbean poets, Sartre applies this understanding of the gaze and subjectivity to the dynamics of colonialism and racism. He locates the origin of liberation movements in the refusal to be reduced to an object by another's gaze. "For three thousand years," Sartre proclaims, "the white man has enjoyed the privilege of seeing without being seen; he was only a look." Now, however, revolt against European domination can be perceived in the fact that "today, these black men are looking at us, and our gaze comes back to our own eyes." Sartre describes the power of that revolt as it is readable in the poetry, and he expresses to his readers his "hope that you—like me—will feel the shock of being seen."[24] Finally, perhaps the most succinct expression of Sartre's understanding of the struggle for possession of the gaze is to be found in *Huis clos* (1944; *No Exit*), where being objectified by the look of the Other while remaining deprived of the power to determine (see) oneself serves as a definition of Hell.

In short, Sartre's thinking about anti-Semitism is part and parcel of his understanding of the look as a social force with the power to make and unmake subjectivity. And with Malle's emphasis on eyes and the power of the look to define the Other, it is as if *Au revoir les enfants* were a fictional dramatization of Sartre's argument. The Gestapo chief's stare defines and condemns Jean Bonnet/Kippelstein. Although Jean attempts to maintain his own subjectivity by returning Muller's stare and by shaking hands with his classmates, he is ultimately defeated by the political realities of early 1944. Muller has already won the zero-sum struggle: he has the power to determine both sides of the transaction, both subject and object of the gaze, both anti-Semite and Jew. His gaze and then his words establish categories and differences. After Jean is taken away, Muller explains to the other boys: "This boy is not a Frenchman. This boy is a Jew" (69). By choreographing the fatal scene in such a way that Julien's glance mediates Muller's, Malle portrays Julien as participant or collaborator in the Nazi's defining gaze.

But perhaps I am unfair. After all, Julien clearly is not an anti-Semite. Quite the contrary. His fatal gesture is motivated not by betrayal but by the opposite desire to reassure himself that his friend is safe. And in any case, how guilty can a twelve year old be? And of what exactly? It becomes important to note that in contrast with the narrator's backward quest revealed at the end, and until the Gestapo arrives, *Au revoir les enfants* is much less concerned with Nazism than with adolescent sexual curiosity. Julien is both a naive Sherlock Holmes discovering the murderous mysteries of Nazism and an adolescent boy in search of sexual secrets. The scene immediately preceding Muller's arrival at the school shows Jean and Julien in the dormitory late at night, reading together by the light of a pocket lamp. Julien reads aloud an erotic passage from *The Arabian Nights:* "And with a quick motion she threw off her veils and disrobed completely to show herself in her native nakedness. . . . Truly, she combined the lascivious movements of Arab girls with the heat of the Ethiopians, the startled candor of the Franks with the consummate science of the Indians, the coquetry of the women of Yemen" (67). And so on. The boys nod off to sleep, and there is an abrupt cut to the fatal classroom scene. Malle's editing shows that it is precisely when and because history intervenes that sexual investigation is displaced. This displacement makes the confession scenes peculiarly ironic. Being pressed to admit to euphemistically evoked sexual "bad thoughts" (25) seems especially ludicrous within the atmosphere of mortal danger and real evil that prevails and that is the substance of the film's overall confessional project.

Given the juxtaposition of erotic and political curiosity—and the inherent voyeurism of the camera eye, which can make all taboo subjects interchangeable—it would have been all too easy to let one become a metaphor for the other, but Malle did not choose this path. Instead, the film shows how each shapes the other: circumstances dictate that for Julien (as for Lucien Lacombe, for that matter) sexual and political awakening are intermeshed, and there is a corresponding loss of innocence in both domains. The best visualization of this is again to be found in Jean and Julien's furtive nocturnal reading of *The Arabian Nights*. As is evident in the passage quoted above, that book serves both as an improvised sex manual for adolescents and as a lesson in (spurious) racial differentiation. So it is that when, to his acute embarrassment and fear, Julien is or-

dered by the Gestapo officer to drop his pants, it is not sexual but racial difference (and survival) that are being determined. *The Arabian Nights* is also, of
course, a tale of captivity and a storyteller's attempt to outwit death, and so perhaps Julien communicates his hope for his friend's survival by giving the book to
Jean before he departs. Ultimately, the sense of responsibility for the lost
friend's fate resides with the adult Julien will become (his continuity with the final voiceover) and is invested in the act of storytelling and filmmaking.

The intertwined quests for political and sexual knowledge are also foregrounded in Julien's conversations with his older brother. François is interested
in girls, though, while Julien is still passionately caught in the coils of the family
romance. The film opens in a train station on the scene of mother and son's tear-
ful farewells. Julien's declaration to his mother that he would rather stay in Paris
with her, pleading that his father need not know, recalls the incestuous relationship between mother and son in Malle's 1971 *Souffle au coeur* (*Murmur of the
Heart*). Both of these films (and others, such as *Pretty Baby*), like Truffaut's *Les
Quatre Cents Coups,* are punctuated by the child's suspicions or discovery of maternal unfaithfulness. In *Au revoir les enfants* Malle appropriates and superim-
poses the Freudian family romance motif on the equally triangular intercepted
gaze of collaboration, producing an overdetermined figure of guilty memory. It
is this composite of guilty secrets, both sexual and political, that forms the target
of the adult filmmaker-detective's backward glance.

And it is in this sense that the crucial moment of *Au revoir les enfants* can be
read as a primal scene and begin to be understood as a fictional construct. In his
case study of the Wolf-Man, Freud investigates how his patient's sense of self
was constituted by an act of traumatic and inadvertent looking, and he narrates
this psychoanalytic project as if it were a detective story. In an attempt to understand the irresistible appeal of detective narratives, Geraldine Pederson-Krag
compares Freud as narrator of his case study to readers of detective stories, and
she isolates elements common to both genres that describe just as well the memory quest of *Au revoir les enfants.* Both the psychoanalytic primal scene and the
detective story include a secret scene of wrongdoing, an anxious but curious
child detective, a submerged memory of a witnessed scene that is only partially
understood, and the child's uncertainty whether he has simply witnessed or actually been a participant in the scene.[25] Geoffrey Hartman too stresses that detective fiction shares with the psychoanalysts' deciphering of sexual memories a
witnessed wrongdoing—what he calls a "heart of darkness scene" or a "scene of
suffering"—that is understood to enfold some primal mystery. As readers or
writers of such fiction, according to Hartman, we are motivated by a "reality-
hunger, our desire to know the worst and the best."[26] Julien is hungry to learn

the realities of sexuality, and he suspects some of the murderous realities of the Occupation. But sexuality and death are also secrets that are most often repressed during childhood, and sometimes later as well.

The convergent quests for sexual and political knowledge in *Au revoir les enfants* make it possible for Malle (like Jean Vigo before him in *Zéro de conduite* [1933; *Zero for Conduct*] and Truffaut in *Les Quatre Cents Coups*) to use a school as a microcosm of the society at large. When the normal sexual curiosity of adolescence coincides with traumatic historical events, the memory of each is colored by the other, and both domains of adult experience, incomprehensible to the child, may trigger anxiety. This possibility sheds light from a different angle on one of the features of *mode rétro* fiction. Alan Morris identifies in the work of writers in the postwar generation—those who were children during the war or born afterwards—a "theme of a missing heritage." Referring to them as literal or metaphysical "orphans," Morris speculates that they write in order to uncover a missing piece of the past, the story the parents failed (or refused) to tell about themselves.[27] If this is so, and Morris makes a convincing case in his examination of fiction by Pascal Jardin, Marie Chaix, Evelyne Le Garrec and Patrick Modiano, it is not surprising that such a quest for parental secrets, even when these are not sexual but political (as one finds in the stories of children of collaborators), is also a question about one's own origin and identity and thus might find apt expression in primal scene motifs. Diane Kurys's *Coup de foudre* (1983; *Entre nous*) can be seen as another filmic example of how the stories of the parents' marriage and of the war and its aftermath become inextricably interwoven. For the postwar generation, at least until events of the late sixties finally released a flood of previously silenced stories, the war was the parents' guilty secret.

Moreover, like curiosity, guilt is contagious. It travels from parents to children and from spectacle to spectator. Just as Freud understood in his analysis of the Wolf-Man's primal scene, Malle demonstrates in *Au revoir les enfants* that looking is an act that shapes the spectator's consciousness in a way no other figuration of guilt could achieve. Alfred Hitchcock knew this when he made *Rear Window,* in which the voyeuristic activities of a character (and, by implication, of the spectator who identifies with them) involve him in a crime. In the fatal classroom scene of *Au revoir les enfants* the gazes of character (Julien), camera, and spectator converge to indicate the Jew for the Nazi. This sort of suture shot establishes the spectator's direct participation in the act (though as involuntarily as Julien's), all the more so because the spectator has been induced, both narratively and visually, to identify with Julien. The spectator's capacity for guilt is further increased through the dramatic irony of hindsight. Thus Malle's film not only *portrays* a mechanism of involuntary complicity but also *enacts* it. The operations of cinematic suture orient the spectator's consciousness, so that Malle's primal scene becomes the spectator's as well.[28]

Sartre's work has been useful as an aid for appreciating the power dynamics of the gaze that can be reciprocated, the gaze that challenges subjectivity by introducing the possibility of the self-as-object. The configuration he describes in *Being and Nothingness*, *Réflexions sur la question juive*, *Orphée noir*, and *Huis clos* has helped us to understand the significance of the intradiegetic glance of *Au revoir les enfants*. But the scenario attains the status of a primal scene for character and spectator alike when the look takes place under cover. The child outside the parents' bedroom door peeks without being seen, and he is traumatized, and his identity and identification are shaped, not by a challenging reciprocated stare but by the scene itself. He is both excluded from it—an abandoned outsider before the parental couple—and guilty—of watching, of not intervening to protect the mother, whom he interprets as a victim of aggression. This is the dynamic of the cinematic spectator's look as it has been studied through a psychoanalytic perspective by Christian Metz and Jean-Louis Baudry, for example, and by feminist critics such as E. Ann Kaplan, Laura Mulvey, and Kaja Silverman, who are concerned with how watching a spectacle constructs psychological and social (including gender) identity.

Basing their investigation on Lacan's analysis of the mirror stage, the point at which the very young child identifies with its image in the mirror and begins to construct a separate ego, these theorists turn their attention to how film can induce the spectator to identify with the image, and thus how the image can position and shape spectators' consciousness. As mentioned earlier, Baudry describes two kinds of identification. Identification with a character in the fiction is secondary. The primary identification is with the camera; it is an identification of and with the self as the possessor of the gaze. As Baudry puts it, there are

two levels of identification. The first, attached to the image itself, derives from the character portrayed as a center of secondary identifications, carrying an identity which constantly must be seized and reestablished. The second level permits the appearance of the first and places it 'in action'—this is the transcendental subject whose place is taken by the camera which constitutes and rules the objects in this 'world.' Thus the spectator identifies less with what is represented, the spectacle itself, than with what stages the spectacle, makes it seen, obliging him to see what it sees; this is exactly the function taken over by the camera as a sort of relay.[29]

And Metz, building on Baudry, specifies that "the spectator identifies with himself, with himself as pure act of perception (as wakefulness, alertness): as the condition of possibility of the perceived."[30]

Because it is a form of *"unauthorized* [that is, unreciprocated] scopophilia," cinema evokes primal-scene configurations more readily than does, say, the theater. The spectacle (the historical trauma) is "radically ignorant of its spectator."[31] Like all cinematic spectators, we are distanced from the scene both spatially and, in historical films, temporally. Yet as in the case of *Hiroshima mon amour,* this distance is overcome and the spectator's implication in events is assured when abyssal configurations—spectators watching characters watching a movie—reinforce the suturing operation by bringing about a convergence of the two forms of identification. Similarly, when Julien Quentin, Jean Kippelstein, and the others enjoy the Chaplin film, it is impossible for the spectator to be carried away by the fiction to the extent of avoiding identifying (with) him- or herself as spectator. The complexity of references adds to the spectator's pleasure in the sequence, but it also adds to the poignancy of its implications.

Insights drawn from Lacan and film theories of suture and the gaze as they explain the formation of the ego through looking might be combined with Malle's fictional construct in order to imagine *Au revoir les enfants* as a sort of rear-view mirror [*rétroviseur*]. This is the *mode rétro* at its most literal. In *Au revoir les enfants* a backward glance in time (memory) is figured as a backward glance in space (in the classroom). As in the primal scene, the scenario is informed, both for Julien and the spectator, by an ambiguity that might take the form of an implicit question, namely, Is this horror something I (or my parents) *saw* (as an innocent bystander, a powerless witness), or is it something I did? This is the postwar question par excellence. If, as Christian Metz proposes, "the posture which inaugurates knowledge is defined by a backward turn," what sort of knowledge does this backward turn inaugurate for me, and what should I do about it? How can this historical or personal trauma be converted into knowledge? It is not surprising that the need to figure out the parental secret is a theme of the *mode rétro,* which in fact transforms the primal scene into a trope of individual and collective memory and identity.

Through its relays linking Julien, Malle, and the cinematic spectator, the figure of the fatal intercepted glance thus ensnares the profession of filmmaking as well, and the traumatic memory "pictorialized" as a guilty glance offers an insight into Malle's vocation as a filmmaker. In Malle's film, historical memory is not simply a displacement or reworking of the family romance. Rather, the film provides a broadened notion of the primal scene in which the act of looking, with its potential for evil, is heavily bound up with racism and with filmmaking.[32] Recent writings on primal-scene theory question the archaeological and referential model of psychoanalysis and emphasize instead the displacement whereby the child witness to the primal scene or "secret wrongdoing" unconsciously constructs guilty memories in which he assumes the guilt of the fathers.[33] War and sex are two domains from which parents attempt to exclude or protect the child, and consequently, the child is forced to invent them.

In Malle's film, it has become impossible even to identify with fathers, who are absent. There are several sets of fathers in *Au revoir les enfants:* Julien's real father is conspicuously absent. The school Fathers mean well, but their authority is ultimately ineffectual and illusory. Even God fails to step in, as when the children recite the Our Father while the Jewish children are being rounded up and taken away.[34] Finally, of course, it is the intervention of the Nazi authorities themselves (with the word *Halt,* the *nom* or *non du père*) that marks the end of childhood. It is not "au revoir *les enfants,*" then, but "au revoir *l'enfance,*" goodbye to childhood. The child-detective is left with the bag, and with the question of where real agency is located, who is guilty. As is well known, children tend to believe in the magical power of thoughts and wishes and easily feel guilty for sins they have not committed. The story is not a confession of responsibility for a past wrongdoing; rather, the specific act is invented to account for a pervasive (and collective) sense of guilt.

In his figuration of guilt as a furtive glance backward, Malle, even more explicitly than Duras or Truffaut a few years earlier, paints a portrait of a generation and reveals the particular images in which its memories are cast. In 1944 Julien, like Malle and others of his generation (such as Truffaut, who was born the same year), is too old to be oblivious and too young to be responsible. That Julien's awakenings to the primal mysteries of sexuality and history coincide suggests the necessity of reexamining the connections between Nazism and eroticism as these have been theorized by, among others, Michel Foucault and Susan Sontag, who analyze the appeal of Nazism through adult understandings of sexuality and power.[35] Hayden White has shown how narrative history is "emplotted" according to the generic conventions of storytelling—tragedy, comedy, farce, irony.[36] Malle's films and his career as a filmmaker—like *Le Dernier Métro* and the memoirs by Duras—suggest that we may also need to investigate the ways historical memories are mediated by psychic mechanisms and developmental narratives, with their attendant guilts and censors, desires and displacements.

Despite the similarities, though, significant contrasts separate *Au revoir les enfants* from *Le Dernier Métro* and *La Douleur* (and *Hiroshima mon amour*). In his effort to represent the collective past, Malle gives us neither Truffaut's cheery denial nor Duras's obsessive reenactment. Malle's is, in fact, the first work studied here to represent simple reminiscence. By that I mean that clear distances are established between the traumatic events and the filmmaker and the spectator living now, and the emotions and ideological positions of the past are distinct from, but continuous with, those of the present.

This distance is visible in the film's treatment of Julien. First, significantly, he is a child, and a rather naive one at that (his sexual and political innocence are repeatedly underscored). This innocence may serve in part as the adult narrator's retrospective self-protective justification, to be sure, but the child's responsibility is shown as well. In the penultimate scene, Julien encounters Joseph in the courtyard in the company of one of the Gestapo agents. The former kitchen helper is dressed to the nines and lighting expensive cigarettes with a silver lighter. Julien slowly catches on to what Joseph's game has been, and he is too shocked to speak. Joseph takes the opportunity to disculpate himself and incriminate others: "It's not such a big deal. Those are just Jews." And in any case, his denunciation of the school was his revenge for the unjust punishment he received: "Don't act so pious! It's all your fault. If I hadn't done business with you guys, I wouldn't have been fired. [. . .] I'm telling you. That's war for you, old boy" (74). This is a complex scene. Although we reject the logic of his act, it is impossible to deny that he was indeed used as a scapegoat. Clearly, we do not identify with Joseph, but neither are we completely off the hook. By means of the same sort of relays we saw in *Le Dernier Métro,* character, filmmaker, and spectator become implicated in, but still remain at an ironic distance from, Joseph's crime and Julien's naiveté.

Nowhere is the distance between present and past (and between Malle's film and the works studied earlier) more evident than in the final voiceover. In the works by Truffaut and Duras, the adult and the child are one, frozen in time at the moment of trauma. The child within the adult and the repressions and compulsions that link the two drive the story and give it its convoluted form. Truffaut, ultimately unable to lead the traumatic events of the past to any meaningful resolution, gives us an ending amounting to a sleight of hand, a conclusion that suggests the whole tale might be a piece of acting or pretending, or a bad dream. Duras claims that she found her journal in a closet and recognized the handwriting, but she makes this claim in short prefaces to the pieces of *La Douleur,* paragraphs appearing on separate pages and in different (italic) typeface. In both (as in *Hiroshima mon amour* and even *La Route des Flandres* as well), the operative mode is temporal rupture, and while the story is gripping and the characters are believable, the source of narration remains troublingly unlocatable. "I found this diary [. . . .] I have no recollection of having written it," Duras asserts.[37] Present self and past trauma, adult and child are so fused, and so locked into compulsive repetition, that meaningful continuities, chronology, or even temporal movement are ultimately impossible to trace, and the future, when evoked at all, promises only more of the same.

In contrast, the split between character and retrospective narrator in *Au revoir les enfants* locates the subject and object of history: the voiceover issues from a different place and speaks from a different time. This time is precisely situated ("Over forty years have passed") and chronologically linked not only to the past ("but I will remember every second of that January morning") but even to the future ("until the day I die"). Amy Lawrence proposes that "when there is a temporal disjunction between the offscreen self of the narrator and the figure we see, it is caused by trauma."[38] At the same time, the fact that the temporal disjunction is embodied in two separate characters—a child in the past and an adult in the present—indicates the capacity to distinguish between past and present selves. And when the adult autobiographical voice gets the last word, there is a certain anchoring in the present that distinguishes Malle's film from earlier works that left their characters stuck in the past. This is the sort of memory—freed of regression and compulsive reenactment—that emerges *after* a psychoanalytic cure, *after* the mourning work is completed.[39]

Perhaps all of this is why *Au revoir les enfants* is the most accessible of all the works studied here. Even compared with *Lacombe Lucien,* here the narration is no longer tortured and the characters are neither undecidable, morally ambiguous, nor allegorical. The narrator is straightforwardly autobiographical, not hidden or multiple or anonymous. Guilt, regret, and loss still dominate the mood, but it is significant that in *Au revoir les enfants* the accusation comes from outside the protagonist and it is spoken aloud (by Joseph). Accuser, child, and narrator are three distinct but related characters, facets, perhaps, of a single historical consciousness able to recognize gradations of complicity. Most significantly, there is no gap or hole or leap that signals repression or censorship and renders expression indirect or "incomprehensible."

In addition to returning to unconvoluted narration and character, *Au revoir les enfants* harks back to earlier films via allusion, but allusion with a difference. Unlike in *Les Quatre Cents Coups* and *Zéro de conduite,* here Malle has not excised the wartime context from his story of a boys school and social microcosm; rather, he has given it central importance. Unlike *Lacombe Lucien* and *Les Quatre Cents Coups, Au revoir les enfants* does not end in a freeze-frame. Almost but not quite: Julien is not frozen in time. He simply stands immobile, his eyes filling with tears, as he, along with the spectator, stares at the empty doorway through which Jean Kippelstein has just been dragged away. Time and responsibility continue to the present. Without sacrificing formal complexity, and still treating those troubling issues of memory, the relation between present and past, between self and society, and between identity and the image (and the interconnections among these) that mark its continuity with the heyday of the Nouvelle Vague and even its relation to *Le Dernier Métro,* this film clearly is not a return to the simple, unselfconscious *cinéma de papa* of the pre–New Wave period, but signals the beginnings of a post–New Wave sensibility emerging in the eighties.

Ultimately, it matters less what Julien knows in 1944 than what Malle knows in 1987, and what we know with him. If the backward glance, both spatial and temporal, is the condition for knowledge, we can say with Mary Ann Doane that "the spectator becomes the unified ground of knowledge, of the knowable," and that "the look of the spectator is the originary moment."[40] The distance between the adult Malle voiceover and the child Julien allows the transmission of trauma into knowledge. A new historical subject can be constituted here: one who can remember without either repressing or reenacting. This is perhaps a stage in the project of achieving individual and national suture, in both the medical and the cinematic sense. It becomes possible to stitch the wound while simultaneously locating the narrator and the spectator in history.

Conclusion: The New Novel, The New Wave, and National Identity

Those who do not remember the past are condemned to relive it. – Santayana, epigraph to *Lacombe Lucien*

Who am I? If this once I were to rely on a proverb, then perhaps everything would amount to knowing whom I 'haunt.' – André Breton

Godard's *Tout va bien* ends with a song:

Il y a du soleil sur la France
Et le reste n'a pas d'importance. . . .
[There is sunshine over France
And the rest is not important. . . .

Intercut with snatches of the song can be heard quotations from the film itself—a union leader, a factory worker—and from the earlier sequence of a 1968-style street demonstration, with voices shouting: "Fascistes! Flics! Patrons! Assassins!" Among these quotations are interspersed isolated statements by a man and then a woman, the same narrators who began the film with a dialogue about the prerequisites of filmmaking—money, a love story, "she and he," and "a story." This time the voices intone shorthand remarks like "Me, you, France, 1972" and "Let each of us be his or her own historian." This soundtrack is accompanied by a very long tracking shot in extreme closeup along a brick wall that fills the entire screen. The sequence is obviously complex and didactic. It begs to be compared with the earlier hypermarket tracking sequence that brought into conflict students, a book hawker, and the police as background to Jane Fonda taking notes for her article on alienated consumerism. The tracking shot that closes the film is also characterized by a visual and auditory collage effect and a general choppiness, due to a hand-held camera, that are reminiscent of the earliest Nouvelle Vague films.

I believe that these final shots recount the sequel of May 1968. What distinguishes them from the earlier hypermarket sequence is what is lacking: conflict.

207

Only fleeting fragmentary and disconnected quotations of conflict remain, like memories—"fascists, cops, bosses, murderers." The significance of the brick wall lies in what is not shown. The bricks are blank, clean; they are devoid, notably, of graffiti. With the wall scrubbed clean, once again we are confronted with an image of the Gaullist government's ability to suppress dissent and regain political and discursive control, as it did in the elections of June 1968. That control involved erasure of the traces of revolt. A clean wall and the sun over France ("et le reste n'a pas d'importance") are acid images, almost unreadable, of frustration and disillusionment.[1] The last frame shows the printed word *Terminé,* subtitled "It's over," referring both to the film and to the events of 1968 themselves.

Marcel Ophuls's *Le Chagrin et la pitié* also ends with a song. It occurs in the context of an American newsclip from 1945 showing an apprehensive Maurice Chevalier addressing American and British audiences from his Paris apartment. Speaking in English in his famous heavy French accent, he is refuting a rumor that he made a tour of Germany during the war. He explains that he only went to Germany to cheer up French prisoners in a POW camp, the very camp, he insists, where he himself had been imprisoned in 1914. Then he announces that he will entertain his postwar audience with a song he used to sing before the war, during other visits abroad. And he sings a few bars unaccompanied, until the soundtrack takes over with the fully orchestrated recording of Chevalier:

> Let the whole world sigh or cry.
> I'll be high, in the sky
> Up on top of a rainbow, sweeping the clouds away.
> I don't care what's down below.
> Let it rain, let it snow.
> I'm on top of a rainbow, sweeping the clouds away.

With the song as accompaniment, the credits begin to unfold against newsreel footage of Charles de Gaulle's apotheosis: the victory parade down the Champs Elysées on 26 August 1944. The final credits are shown against a freeze-frame shot from the newsreel that shows de Gaulle extending his hand in greeting toward the hand of a soldier in the crowd. The hands do not quite meet.

Le Chagrin et la pitié was filmed just after 1968, and Ophuls has repeatedly stated in conversations and interviews that the moment was uniquely propitious. After May 1968 the French public was momentarily willing, if belatedly, to take a collective backward look at the war, perhaps for the first time, he explains, but shortly thereafter the floodgates of memory snapped shut again. That moment occurred in part because in 1969 France was once again reflecting

9. *Le Chagrin et la pitié*. Charles de Gaulle's apotheosis: the victory parade on the Champs Elysées, 26 August 1944.

on subjects related to the central issue of *Le Chagrin*, which Ophuls says is about "courage and cowardice in a period of crisis."[2] Ophuls's film was released in April 1971, but it was banned from French television for just over a decade, until October 1981. Approval of its televising was one of the first acts of the new Mitterrand government's ministry of culture. When it was finally aired, it was widely watched and discussed, and whether or not it should have been shown—whether or not old wounds should be reopened—was hotly debated. A habit of sweeping the clouds of ambivalent national memories behind a screen of sunshine and rainbows does not die easily. But it began to die in the eighties.

These two filmed finales are part of a pervasive effect that is discernible, in one form or another, in all the texts we have examined here, in many others of the Nouvelle Vague and the Nouveau Roman, and especially in their aggregate. I want to call that effect *belatedness*. Ophuls's film is itself twice belated. The ending of *Le Chagrin et la pitié* depicts one critical moment of passage in French national identity (the Liberation of 1944); the film was made in the wake of another (1968) and finally disseminated in the context of a third (1981 and the socialist electoral victory). *Tout va bien,* whose title, roughly translated as "everything's okay," conveys the same irony as its concluding song,[3] was released the year after *Le Chagrin*. Godard's film remembers 1968 a few years after the events but also, by means of its song (and perhaps the hurled insult, "fascistes!"), can be understood to remember 1968 *through Le Chagrin* and World War II. The wartime reminiscences Ophuls captured in his film are evoked on the streets of 1968 as well: another popular slogan of May—"We are all German Jews"—similarly implies a comparison of two historical situations, present and past. That slogan is most closely associated with Daniel Cohn-Bendit, the University of Nanterre student who emerged as a leader and symbol of the revolts. As the son of German Jewish immigrants, Cohn-Bendit himself also served to evoke the unfinished business of World War II.[4] Cohn-Bendit reports that after the events of May he was to be expelled from France partly for having accused the French minister for youth of talking like a member of the Hitler Youth.[5] As when *Hiroshima mon amour* was excluded from the Cannes Film Festival during the Algerian conflict, it was again made clear that memories of one crisis that resurface in the midst of another crisis need to be strictly controlled.

I have adapted the term *belatedness* from Freud's term *nachträglichkeit* [deferred action], which he used to refer to the reworking of early traumatic events that is made possible by later stages of psychic development. In their discussion of *nachträglichkeit*, or *l'après-coup* in French, Laplanche and Pontalis stress that it is "only the occurrence of the second scene [that] can endow the first one with pathogenic force."[6] In other words, for the individual (or the collective, as I have been arguing throughout), understanding the mechanisms of the primal scene, mourning, repression, and repetition compulsions depends on ulterior reworking or reinterpretation (or even revision) of these in the context of later crises, as sense is progressively made of the past and its effect on the present. The impetus behind the *mode rétro,* including even such controversial phenomena as "negationism" (as Henry Rousso and others have dubbed the argument that the Holocaust was an Allied propaganda ploy), reveals the belated necessity of negotiating the relative consequences of memory and continued denial. This impulse to superimpose differently traumatic historical moments can also be exploited by individuals like Jacques Vergès, whose defense of Klaus Barbie was built on, and thoroughly muddied by, a reinterpretation of Barbie's war crimes in the light of subsequent atrocities, notably during colonial wars, perpetrated by the French military.

Belatedness is the flip side of repetition, and the events of French history lend themselves particularly well to selective forgetting and tardy remembering as well as to the kinds of comparison implicit in belated or deferred interpretation. For example, as many historians have pointed out, the errors of 1940 were committed by the heroes of 1914–18. Marc Bloch, it will be remembered, attributed the "strange" (or uncanny) defeat of 1940 to just this sort of belatedness. Pétain himself was an uncanny figure: a hero in 1914, he was resurrected in 1940 to snatch symbolic victory from the jaws of military defeat. And de Gaulle's star repeatedly rose in periods of crisis: a hero in one war, he was called back in 1958 to resolve another, and having coped with one near civil war in 1958, he returned to avert another in 1968. Multiple revolutions. Repeated debacles and defeats, similar in surprising details or facing the same enemy. Five republics. It is no wonder that the 1989 bicentennial of the Revolution unleashed a frenzy of reenactment and restaging, of reassessments (should the king have been condemned to death?) and committees for the rehabilitation of key figures (e.g., Robespierre). Or to take another example, in Michel Drach's film *Les Violons du bal* (1974) the story of a young man escaping police during the riots of 1968 is braided together with that of the narrator's parents escaping the Occupied Zone. The *passeurs* who facilitate the two escapes are even played by the same actor. And although a producer tells the protagonist in the framing story (a filmmaker trying to make a film about World War II) that memory and history will not sell, it is the past that is filmed in vivid color, while the present, in black and white, seems more remote. Perhaps it is this layering of memory in the national imagination that has compelled so many storytellers to construct complex fictions with multiple and inextricably interwoven stories, false paths that cancel each other out, and unsatisfying conclusions. Except in cases of crimes against humanity, reinterpretation of the past in the courts is arrested by statutes of limitation. The national psyche, however, respects no expiration dates, and the construction of memory imposes an ongoing project. Works of art both provoke and reflect this process of juxtaposing disparate moments and superimposing crises. Its capacity to produce willful entanglements of different moments makes art an important site where national identity is both reflected and forged.

Belatedness can be at work in a novel or a film even when history is not its thematic content. Most obviously in the texts studied here, their overriding emphasis on memory means that their stories always come afterward—after a fall, either mythic or civic, psychic or military, historical or imaginary. The texts do not always represent, but they do re-present in one way or another: flashbacks, primal scenes, hysterical discourses, ironies, repetitiousness, and the uncanny are the ways the texts "suffer from reminiscences" (Freud). These cognitive and psychic mechanisms function as principles of structuration. What is more, the texts remember each other in a circulation of meanings that cuts deeper than simple intertextuality. The texts and the events themselves are apprehended not simply as coming *after* but as being understood *through and by means of* previous

10. One national identity crisis is represented, through allusion, as a belated reenactment of a previous crisis. Poster by the Atelier Populaire de l'ex-École des Arts, 14 July 1968.

ones. Thus, from individual novels and in his *oeuvre* as a whole, Claude Simon compiles a dense superimposition of historical moments from the Revolution through the present instance of writing. And reading him (or seeing *Hiroshima mon amour*) in the context of the Algerian revolution brings together two moments separated by twenty years. Pure intransitive belatedness is both the structure and the content of *Marienbad*. Louis Malle belatedly remembers the Occupation in the early 1970s and then again in the mid-eighties. Then in 1990 he makes *Milou en mai* (*May Fools*), about May 1968. And in 1991 Bertrand Tavernier films *La Guerre sans nom* about the Algerian conflict.[7] While that film's title ironically trumpets the persisting taboo about mentioning the conflict, its format, which is identical to that of *Le Chagrin et la pitié* (four hours of interviews with residents of a single town—Grenoble—about their activities, attitudes, and memories regarding the Algerian war), and its dedication to Marcel Ophuls signal that the later war is still being rethought within the conceptual grid provided by the earlier one. The belated return of World War II memories in the 1980s, already examined in the work of Truffaut, Duras, and Malle, is particularly startling, because apparently gratuitous, in a pair of films by Claude Lelouch. *Un Homme et une femme* (1966) is a love story of a couple on the fast track moving forward: he (Jean-Louis Trintignant) is a racing-car driver, she (Anouk Aimée) an ambitious script girl. Twenty years later, in *Un Homme et une femme: Vingt ans déjà,* he has entered middle age and settled down to a job test-driving racing cars, and she has risen to become a producer, making a film that looks backward on World War II.

Selective recollection and willful forgetting of one crisis in the context of the next is not new, any more than the Nouvelle Vague and the Nouveau Roman were the first to challenge their predecessors. But these cultural movements do have their own characteristic forms and contents and their own discourse, as described in this study. This discourse can best be described as literally postwar. World War II is never far below the surface, and its unresolved issues shape both postwar events and texts, and within the texts, both anecdote and form. Even a writer like Patrick Modiano, born in 1947, finds that writing necessarily entails belated examination of that war, and so, shortly before he authored the script for *Lacombe Lucien,* he wrote *Les Boulevards de ceinture,* in which a postwar, first-person narrator undertakes a quest for knowledge about his father's collaborationist activities, which seem incriminating even unto the next generation.[8]

The advancing age of the artists is no doubt a factor in the increasing urgency with which their texts execute a backward turn. So is the lag of two decades between events and their telling, which can frequently be found in other historical fiction, as in the case of Elie Wiesel, who kept a twenty-year silence before he began to testify in his writing to the horrors he had witnessed. But there is more. The particular character of postwar French belatedness can be defined by an alternating rhythm of recollection and deliberate collective forgetfulness. The texts recall both history and each other in cycles. Between crises, there are periods of deliberate sensory failure, of willful amnesia, both personal and collective, sometimes even official. In the fictions, erasures, censorship (and self-censorship), blank spaces, deafness and silences are the objective correlatives of this amnesia, its characteristic structuring devices, whatever the content may be.

If the discourse of the Nouveau Roman and the Nouvelle Vague is postwar, it also belongs very peculiarly to the Gaullist years. The towering figure of de Gaulle dominates the cultural mythology of the period, both literally and figuratively. The rhetorical power of Gaullist oratory to manipulate images and construct histories cannot be overestimated, and it is frequently alluded to in the works studied here. In the name of national unity, de Gaulle's speeches during the Occupation and after the Liberation established the official representation of the war, including erasure of the communists' role in the Resistance and of the misery of returning deportees, as Duras, still angry about it in 1985, recounts in *La Douleur*. Beginning around 1958 and continuing for several years, censorship was official and vigilant, as I have shown. Again after 1968, what could be said and thought about the revolts was circumscribed by means of what Foucault called "systems of exclusion."[9]

No single individual, not even Charles de Gaulle, could have accomplished this single-handedly, of course, and the phenomenon is much more diffuse than any brief description could convey. For such discursive horizons to be naturalized to the extent that they were required widespread assent. Moreover, they did not spring from the void; nor did they disappear all at once. But if the Nouveau Roman and the Nouvelle Vague are to be understood as counterdiscursive representational practice, as I have argued, then they are part of, because counter to, a specific representational regime. That is, they are fictions of the Gaullist era. In particular, the specific difficulties involved in looking backward during those years find their counterpart in a near obsession with memory. This helps to explain why the film noir genre, imported from Hollywood, has had such a compelling appeal in France and why it inspired Godard and Truffaut to rework its elements in films like *A bout de souffle* and *Tirez sur le pianiste* (1960; *Shoot the Piano Player*). The basic film noir story involves an alienated and suspicious hero in flight from his past. Within the visual and narrative conventions of the genre, Louis Malle was attempting to historicize the givens of film noir in the second half of *Lacombe Lucien,* where Lucien and France are on the run from Nazi authorities.

That leaves us with the question, Now that the Gaullist period has been more or less supplanted, are the New Novel and New Wave finally over? Have they been replaced by a *mode rétro* that overrides attention to form and signals a return to something "before"? Yes and no. The problem of periodizing regimes and locating the end of the postwar period will probably be debated by historians for a long time to come, but a few concluding observations can be made here. Celia Britton suggests that as the New Novelists attained individual fame and secured an appreciative public in France and abroad, they could afford to move away from an aggressively theoretical stance, and they no longer needed to define themselves as a group with common goals and concerns. As a collective, she argues, the New Novel has ceased to exist.[10] More recent works by the writers and filmmakers studied here certainly do display discontinuities with the past, although even these discontinuities seem to be held in common. Most visible of these discontinuities is their turn, examined in the preceding chapters, to personal introspection, to description of an identifiable self, and to explicit historiography. This has been accompanied by apparently more straightforward narration and the less evasive but still veiled presence of a scriptor in the text. The young woman protagonist of Duras's recurrent story of family drama, sexual initiation, and loss is finally called "Je" in *L'Amant*. And Malle says "Je" at the end of *Au revoir les enfants*. In the case of Simon, whose *La Route des Flandres* was composed of language that seemed to issue from nowhere (where and when did Georges write it, if he did write it?), *Les Géorgiques* (1981) goes back over the historical periods that have always interested the author—the Revolutionary Convention, the Spanish Civil War, World War II—while this time including traces of a writing subject. His *L'Acacia* (1989) is an autobiographical account of his parents' youth, his father's death, and his own childhood. And in *Le Miroir qui revient* (1984), the first volume of a projected trilogy of autobiographical "Romanesques," Robbe-Grillet, for his part, admits, "I have never spoken of anything but myself."[11]

On the other hand, the continuities between the early and the more recent works are many. I have shown to what extent the historiographic mode of Duras, Truffaut, and Malle is self-consciously mediated and deliberately fictionalized. Robbe-Grillet, for his part, repeatedly pulls the rug out from under any imputed autobiographical pact with his readers by making such statements as "The above passage must be a complete fiction" (17). In no case should recent works by New Novelists and New Wave filmmakers be seen as a return to a pre-experimental phase of fiction, to a traditional novelistic model or a *cinéma de papa* against which the earlier works defined their newness. After all, Duras wrote the script for *Hiroshima mon amour*, by no means traditional or straightforward in form, before turning away from historical topics for a quarter of a century. Even during what Rousso characterizes as periods of repression and denial, Claude Simon only left historical topics for a short while.[12] And Lelouch's *Un Homme et une femme: Vingt ans déjà*, mentioned above, self-consciously incorporates its historical motifs into a film-within-a-film or *mise en abyme* configuration that is the hallmark of New Novel and New Wave production. Pascal Ory's observation that much of the *rétro* fashion involves the consumption of nostalgia in the form of "pastiches d'ancien"[13] suggests that there is no incompatibility between the will to be postmodern, including postwar modern, and a concern with the past.[14] It is even possible that for the artists of the New Novel and the New Wave the nostalgic mode fulfills the same function today that it did in 1958–62: looking backward might once again constitute a way of avoiding, managing, or allegorizing issues of the present that for some reason remain inexpressible. Most importantly, as I have argued throughout, the New Novel and the New Wave have never left history behind, and they continue to be defined by a discourse whose context gives it meaning.

The question is more complicated still, as can be seen most readily in another volume of fiction by Robbe-Grillet, *Un Régicide*.[15] That novel encompasses the entire period discussed here: it was finished in 1949 and published, belatedly, in 1978, as Robbe-Grillet explains in his preface. Constructed on a rhythm of remembering, forgetting, and repetition, the novel recounts once again ("une fois de plus" is its refrain) a story of a crime that may or may not have occurred. The possibly guilty protagonist suffers from intrusive "memories, but of what he did not know" (134). That the novel's double historical provenance is not an aberration is suggested by the fact that it finds echoes elsewhere: Duras claims she found the manuscripts of *La Douleur* in a closet in her home and that she does not remember writing them. She must have written the notebooks before 1945, she claims, but she only published them in 1985. These books by Robbe-Grillet and Duras both face in two directions (once again, Henri Langlois in a freeze-frame), and they address two contexts. In both, the self is split between a third and a first person, and both writers published their memoirs in two volumes. In this sense they are actually *about* discontinuities and the effort to be new, oppositional, and suspicious. They also suggest the New Novel's and the New Wave's largely unsuccessful attempts to disengage the present from the past. That the very first sentence in Robbe-Grillet's career as a novelist is "Une fois de plus" only compounds the disorientation, rendering it willful and systemic. In both cases, temporal dislocation of the manuscript itself creates a figure of belatedness.

Un Régicide also embodies the oppositional stance that these artists still strive to maintain. The theme of regicide is, of course, weighty with implications both for cultural history (precursors who have to be displaced) and for historiography (writing as an attack on dominant discourses). It aims to upset regimes both political and representational. The theme made its appearance with the earliest of the New Novels, Robbe-Grillet's *Les Gommes* (1953; *The Erasers*), and it has been a constant with Robbe-Grillet as well as Simon, whose historiographic fictions repeatedly stage the execution of Louis XVI as the founding event in a chain of violent deaths. The freeze-frame and regicide (including the death of the father, the orphaning of the self and the nation) might serve as master-motifs of the period, each accompanied by an ambivalence commensurate with its far-reaching implications. If we recall that in *La Route des Flandres* the crux of the narrator's quest was the killing at the crossroads of the novel's father figure, Captain de Reixach, we might adopt Pierre Nora's term *lieu de mémoire* or, even more appropriately, his description of these as *lieux-carrefours*[16] to refer to this preoccupation with regicide as it constitutes a recurrent and privileged site of collective identity. Killing the king is a never-ending project, as the protesters of May 1968 knew when they self-consciously represented their struggle through images of the Revolution (see illustration 10). Jacques Vergès was clearly playing on the same public reflexes of guilt and ambivalent memory when he juxtaposed the Barbie trial with a mock referendum on the execution of Louis XVI. A further juxtaposition is instructive as well: factions of the French public were engaging in this belated squeamishness about the king's execution in tandem with another ongoing debate about another father figure, asking whether, after the Liberation, Pétain should have been executed rather than spared. This superimposition of monarchy, republic, and the Etat français makes it seem as if several versions of national identity were still vying for legitimacy. Which have been truly superseded? Which represents the "real" France? Alain Duhamel speculates that France's dark preoccupation with history derives in part from a nostalgia for "past splendor" and "eroded grandeur," an "obsession du déclin" on the part of a nation that is no longer at the center of its own universe. But Duhamel goes on to catalog the worries that cast doubts today on French identity—the loss of empire, the economy, the new Europe (including the renewed vigor of a united Germany), immigration, urban development, the new information technologies, and so on—and he suggests that however painful contemplation of the past may seem, history may prove less troubling than France's fear of its future.[17] It is no wonder that fiction reveals a concern about lost fathers, regicide, orphans, and lost heritages. Nor should it be surprising that a contestatory artist such as Robbe-Grillet would now put *socialism* between quotation marks and suspect it of establishing a new order that is as nefarious as the old. It might be said that regicide signifies a desire to be oppositional, to outwit recuperation, to champion disorder against any orthodoxy.

Robbe-Grillet's *Le Miroir qui revient* contains a primal scene. That scene does not uncover the secrets of the sinister and fascinating Henri de Corinthe, who makes mysterious nocturnal visits to the family home. It does not afford a glimpse of his parents' Anglophobia or their anti-Semitism or their Pétainism (though all these are described elsewhere in the volume) or even their sex life. Through a translucent red curtain that separates the midnight darkness of his bedroom from the adjoining dining room, the young boy can peek out at his mother. And he watches her *reading*. What she reads is "her massive daily dose of papers ranging from *La Liberté* to *L'Action française*." In parentheses, he adds: "My parents were extreme right-wing anarchists." Outside the closed parental parentheses, on the narrator's side of the red curtain, the scene the reading mother does not see involves the boy's "solitary pleasures, which already had a strong sadistic tendency" (10).

This scenario proposes several curious reversals. First, it inverts the Freudian primal scene by putting the sexual "secret" on the side of the spectator, so that it is no secret. Here, though, it is the mother's reading (significantly, of political material) that is furtively viewed by the small voyeur. The book thus also reverses Robbe-Grillet's habit of spying on often bizarre or cruel sexual acts and keeping silent about politics. But the positioning of the two scenes is unstable, and they can easily be reversed once again. After all, his mother has only to return the look. In this primal scene, as in his *oeuvre* as a whole, whatever is taboo is subject, albeit sometimes belatedly, to Robbe-Grillet's gleeful investigation. Whatever is in place is what he wants to dismantle. This is why he claims to dislike order of any kind.

If primal scenes are the retrospective ground upon which later representations are elaborated—both in personal fictions and in public historiography—this primal scene of reading is emblematic of a continuing will to construct counterdiscourses. In *Le Miroir qui revient*, Robbe-Grillet remarks: "I write to destroy, by describing them exactly, the nocturnal monsters that threaten to invade my waking life" (11). This statement can be read to construe writing as a personal quest or talking cure. Given the overall subject matter of the book—memories of a family's involvement in a collective past—it can also be appreciated as an attempt to exorcise the more daunting monsters of national identity. Robbe-Grillet (with others) has shown that he will continue to tell the story of trying to tell the story. In that sense the Nouveau Roman will not be over before he is gone. This is because Robbe-Grillet, for one, will never let anyone, including himself, have the last word.

Notes

INTRODUCTION

1. Georges P. Langlois and Glenn Myrent, *Henri Langlois: Premier Citoyen du cinéma* (Paris: Denoël, 1986), 99–100.

2. For example, Georg Lukács, *The Historical Novel* (Lincoln: U of Nebraska P, 1962), conceives of the historical novel entirely in terms of realism, that is, as a form that renders "an artistically faithful image of a concrete historical epoch" by means of "the specifically historical, that is, derivation of the individuality of characters from the historical peculiarity of their age" (19). But what of the novel that has no individually defined characters? If we were to amend Lukács to read "the specifically historical, that is, derivation of the individuality of *textual forms* from the historical peculiarity of their age," we would be moving closer to my project here.

3. Linda Hutcheon, *The Politics of Postmodernism* (London: Routledge, 1989), 47.

4. Among the sympathetic critics have been Roland Barthes ("Littérature objective," *Critique* 10 [1954]: 581–91, reprinted in *Cahiers internationaux de symbolisme* 9–10 [1965–66]); Gérard Genette (*Figures II* [Paris: Seuil, 1969]); Jean Ricardou (*Problèmes du nouveau roman* [Paris: Seuil, 1967], *Pour une théorie du nouveau roman* [Paris: Seuil, 1971], and *Le Nouveau Roman* [Paris: Seuil, 1973]); Stephen Heath (*The Nouveau Roman: A Study in the Practice of Writing* [London: Elek, 1972]); John Sturrock (*The French New Novel: Claude Simon, Michel Butor, Alain Robbe-Grillet* [London: Oxford UP, 1969]); and Leon S. Roudiez (*French Fiction Today: A New Direction* [New Brunswick: Rutgers UP, 1972]). For harsher evaluations, see Pierre de Boisdeffre, *La Cafetière est sur la table* (Paris: Table Ronde, 1967); and Jean-Bertrand Barrère, *La Cure d'amaigrissement du roman* (Paris: Albin Michel, 1964). Less polemical were Jean Bloch-Michel, *Le Présent de l'indicatif: Essai sur le nouveau roman* (Paris: Gallimard, 1963); and Lucien Goldmann, "Nouveau Roman et réalité," in *Pour une sociologie du roman* (Paris: Gallimard, 1964), 279–333. See also Jacques Leenhardt, *Lecture politique du roman: La Jalousie d'Alain Robbe-Grillet* (Paris: Minuit, 1973).

5. Roy Armes, *French Cinema* (New York: Oxford UP, 1985), 169–70, 180.

6. Claude Simon, *Discours de Stockholm* (Paris: Minuit, 1986), 30.

7. Simon was not the first New Novelist to present this double line of argumentation informed by this misunderstanding. See, for example, Alain Robbe-Grillet, *Pour un nou-*

veau roman (Paris: Gallimard, 1963). The tension is particularly flagrant in *Que peut la littérature?* (Paris: Union générale d'éditions, 1965), the transcript of a debate at the Mutualité that pitted the New Novel against existentialism. Jean Ricardou subsequently pursued the same angle in *Problèmes du nouveau roman* and *Pour une théorie du nouveau roman*.

8. Nathalie Sarraute, "The Age of Suspicion," in *Tropisms and the Age of Suspicion,* trans. Maria Jolas (London: John Calder, 1963), 95.

9. Alain Resnais, Chris Marker, and Agnès Varda have alternately been called the Left Bank filmmakers and assimilated to an enlarged conception of the Nouvelle Vague.

10. François Truffaut, "Une Certaine Tendance du cinéma français," in *Le Plaisir des yeux* (Paris: Cahiers du Cinéma, 1987), 192–206. Truffaut was following in the direction that Alexandre Astruc had sketched out in his 1948 call for a "caméra-stylo." Astruc's essay appears in translation as "The Birth of a New Avant-Garde: La Caméra-Stylo," in *The New Wave: Critical Landmarks,* ed. Peter Graham (New York: Doubleday, 1968).

11. Jean-Paul Sartre, preface to *Portrait d'un inconnu,* by Nathalie Sarraute, 3d ed. (Paris: Gallimard, 1956). Available in English as *Portrait of a Man Unknown,* trans. Marie Jolas (New York: Braziller, 1958).

12. Françoise Giroud soon collected the series of articles she had written for *L'Express* and published them as *La Nouvelle Vague: Portraits de la jeunesse* (Paris: Gallimard, 1958). See also Georgia Gurrieri, "From New Waves to the New Wave" (paper presented at the Colloquium for Twentieth Century French Studies, University of Iowa, Iowa City, April 1990). In her longer study of the vogue for the new in the 1950s, Gurrieri is one of the few critics to juxtapose the New Novel and the New Wave filmmakers ("New Waves: Literature and Cinema in Postwar Paris" [Ph.D. diss., University of Iowa, 1991]). The term *Nouveau Roman* first appears in Maurice Nadeau, "Nouvelles Formules pour le roman," *Critique,* fall 1957, 707–22.

13. "Cent soixante-deux nouveaux cinéastes français," *Cahiers du cinéma,* December 1962, 61–84.

14. Briefly assimilated with the New Novelists under the rubric of experimental or avant-garde fiction, Faye, Sollers, and others by 1960 had become identified with their own review, *Tel quel.* This was mostly a younger generation of writers who shared the New Novelists' goal of revolutionizing fiction by writing self-consciously. The *Tel quel* writers were initially more concerned with ideology and considered themselves more radical. For a discussion of the stormy relations between the two groups, see Celia Britton, *The Nouveau Roman: Fiction, Theory, and Politics* (New York: St. Martin's, 1992), 86–117.

15. Duras and Resnais's *Hiroshima mon amour* and Truffaut's *Les Quatre Cents Coups* were recognized at the Cannes Film Festival in 1959. The Prix Jean Vigo was awarded in 1959 to Chabrol's *Le Beau Serge* and in 1960 to Godard's *A bout de souffle.* Malle's *Les Amants* and Chabrol's *Les Cousins* were crowned at the Venice (1958) and Berlin (1959) film festivals, respectively. Literary prizes were awarded to Butor's *La Modification* (Prix

Renaudot, 1957) and his *L'Emploi du temps* (Prix Fénéon, 1957), Claude Ollier's *La Mise en scène* (Prix Médicis, 1958), and Simon's *La Route des Flandres* (Prix de l'Express, 1960).

16. Paul Monaco, "The New Wave and Existentialism" (paper delivered at the Colloquium for Twentieth Century French Studies, University of Iowa, Iowa City, April 1990). In his chapter "The First Crest of the New Wave," in *Ribbons in Time: Movies and Society since 1945* (Bloomington: Indiana UP, 1987), 33–61, Monaco links the early New Wave films with broad cultural developments of the period. Susan Hayward identifies 1958 as the divide between the modern and the postmodern. She divides the New Wave into two moments and locates these in the early and late 1960s, respectively, suggesting in passing a correlation with periods of social unrest. During these phases, New Wave and avant-garde converged, but Hayward sees the New Wave as becoming mainstream thereafter (see *French National Cinema* [London: Routledge, 1993], 206–10).

17. See Hervé Hamon and Patrick Rotman, *Les Porteurs de valises: La Résistance française à la guerre d'Algérie* (Paris: Albin Michel, 1979); the text of the "Déclaration sur le droit à l'insoumission dans la guerre d'Algérie," with a list of signatories, is printed on pp. 393–96. New Novelists and New Wave filmmakers whose names appear in the list are Michel Butor, Marguerite Duras, Claude Ollier, Alain Resnais, Alain Robbe-Grillet, Nathalie Sarraute, Claude Simon, and François Truffaut, along with the New Novelists' publisher at the Editions de Minuit, Jérôme Lindon.

18. The Union des écrivains included filmmakers (although there were other groups of film industry workers), thus underlining my point about a common *écriture*.

19. Jean Ricardou chaired the colloquium with Françoise von Rossum-Guyon and edited the proceedings, published as *Nouveau Roman: Hier, aujourd'hui*, 2 vols. (Paris: Union générale d'éditions, 1972).

20. See David Caute, *Communism and the French Intellectuals* (New York: Macmillan, 1964); and Herbert R. Lottman, *The Left Bank: Writers, Artists, and Politics from the Popular Front to the Cold War* (Boston: Houghton Mifflin, 1982).

21. Henry Rousso, *The Vichy Syndrome: History and Memory in France since 1944*, trans. Arthur Goldhammer (Cambridge: Harvard UP, 1991).

22. Alain Resnais, "Un Cinéaste stoïcien: Interview d'Alain Resnais," *L'Esprit* 6 (June 1960): 934–36; *Tu n'as rien vu à Hiroshima* (Bruxelles: Institut de Sociologie, Université Libre de Bruxelles, 1962), 113.

23. Barthes, "Littérature objective."

24. For example, Simon's novels often describe visual phenomena using cinematic vocabulary, and Simon describes his process of "montage" in "Interview with Claude Simon," by Claud DuVerlie, *Sub-stance* 8 (winter 1974): 3–20.

25. Proceedings published in *Cahiers internationaux de symbolisme* 9–10 (1965–66).

26. Marc Elys, "Une Certaine Elite," *Obliques* 16–17 (1978): 42.

27. Whether the young Godard and Truffaut flirted with the Right is a matter of de-

bate: the *politique des auteurs,* publication of a few articles in right-wing journals, and their early, seemingly apolitical stance are sometimes cited as evidence of this.

28. Caute, *Communism and the French Intellectuals,* 318–35; Lottman, *Left Bank,* 264–88. See Britton, *Nouveau Roman,* 12–47, for a discussion of Sartre's affinities with and distance from socialist realism and the New Novelists' reliance on and quarrels with him.

29. Jean-Paul Sartre, *"What Is Literature?" and Other Essays,* trans. John MacCombie (Cambridge: Harvard UP, 1988), 34–40.

30. Serge Guilbaut, *How New York Stole the Idea of Modern Art: Abstract Expressionism, Freedom, and the Cold War,* trans. Arthur Goldhammer (Chicago: U of Chicago P, 1983), 2.

31. Pierre Sorlin, *European Cinemas, European Societies, 1939–1990* (London: Routledge, 1991), 143–44.

32. Jérôme Lindon, "Littérature dégagée," *New Morality* 2, nos.2–3 (1962): 112.

33. Mas'ud Zavarzadeh, *Seeing Films Politically* (Albany: State U of New York P, 1991).

34. Alain Robbe-Grillet, *Ghosts in the Mirror,* trans. Jo Levy (New York: Grove Weidenfeld, 1988), 6; originally published as *Le Miroir qui revient* (Paris: Minuit, 1984).

35. Richard Terdiman, *Discourse/Counter-Discourse: The Theory and Practice of Symbolic Resistance in Nineteenth-Century France* (Ithaca: Cornell UP, 1985), 13, 15–16, emphasis in the original.

36. M. M. Bakhtin, "Discourse in the Novel," in *The Dialogic Imagination,* ed. Michael Holquist, trans. Caryl Emerson and Michael Holquist (Austin: U of Texas P, 1981), 284.

37. This is how Roland Barthes describes the referential illusion of classical historical discourse in "Le Discours de l'histoire," *Informations sur les sciences sociales* 6, nos.2–3 (1967): 65–75.

1. MYTHS OF TEXTUAL AUTONOMY

1. Claude Brémond, Evelyne Sullerot, and Simone Berton, "Les Héros des films dits 'de la Nouvelle Vague,'" *Communications* 1 (1961): 142–76. The study was part of a larger project commissioned by UNESCO and directed by Edgar Morin. Note the similarities between this description of the films and Françoise Giroud's survey, mentioned in my introduction, of the generation itself, in *La Nouvelle Vague.*

2. *Hiroshima mon amour,* trans. Richard Seaver (New York: Grove, 1961). The original script was published in Paris by Gallimard in 1960. Page references to Duras's script, preface, and filming notes refer to the English-language edition. Although I rely on the published scripts for quotations, it is important to remember, first, that the film is a collective enterprise, notably produced by the collaborative efforts of Duras and Resnais, and second, that my argument depends on the fact that it is a *film,* that is, that it is primarily an experience of seeing and hearing, rather than reading, a text.

3. René Guyonnet, *L'Express,* 17 March 1960.

4. It must be noted that *Casablanca* is set in the present, and so its portrayal of the role of the individual in history does not involve themes of memory (although the film does contain flashbacks to an idyllic prewar period). It does depend on a discourse of history, however, and by the time it is cited in *Hiroshima mon amour* it is part of a discourse that the latter film contests.

5. Frédéric de Towarnicki, *Spectacles* 1 (October 1960), reprinted as "Naissance d'un classique" in *L'Avant-scène cinéma* 61–62 (July–September 1966): 9.

6. Alain Robbe-Grillet, *L'Année dernière à Marienbad, ciné-roman* (Paris: Minuit, 1961), published in English as *Last Year at Marienbad,* trans. Richard Howard (New York: Grove, 1962), 8. Page numbers refer to the English-language edition.

7. Hayden White, *Metahistory: The Historical Imagination in Nineteenth-Century Europe* (Baltimore: Johns Hopkins UP, 1973), 37.

8. Roland Barthes, *Le Degré zéro de l'écriture* (Paris: Seuil, 1953), 25–31.

9. Georges Poulet, *Studies in Human Time,* trans. Elliott Coleman (Baltimore: Johns Hopkins UP, 1956), 36.

10. Paul De Man, *Blindness and Insight: Essays in the Rhetoric of Contemporary Criticism* (New York: Oxford UP, 1971), 152. De Man's own complicity with Nazism later rendered this very statement ironic. Questions of belatedness and guilt are dealt with in the conclusion.

11. Marcel Proust, *A la recherche du temps perdu,* 3 vols. (Paris: Gallimard, 1954), published in English as *Remembrance of Things Past;* here see vol. 3, trans. C. K. Scott Moncrieff, Terence Kilmartin, and Andreas Mayor (New York: Vintage, 1981), 924.

12. "I wanted to create the equivalent of a reading, to give the spectator as much freedom of imagination as a reader of novels has," Resnais says in "Un Cinéaste stoïcien," 936. In the same interview, Resnais calls his films examples of a "cinéma romanesque" (934). Edgar Morin claims that Resnais wants to "reconnect [the cinema with] literature" and calls him the "first novelist of the screen" (*Tu n'as rien vu à Hiroshima,* 113). Roger Boussinot, in his *L'Encyclopédie du cinéma* (Paris: Bordas, 1980), takes a dimmer view of collaboration with novelists, claiming that the association has hampered Resnais. In particular, he states that *Hiroshima* was a good film in spite of Duras's "texte logorrhéique." While one wonders what the film would be without its scenario, his remark helps explain the film's novelty and the discomfort it caused.

13. Marguerite Duras, "Resnais travaille comme un romancier . . . ," *L'Avant-scène cinéma* 61–62 (July–September 1966): 8.

14. The phrase is from Ihab Hassan, *The Dismemberment of Orpheus: Toward a Postmodern Literature* (New York: Oxford UP, 1971). Walter A. Strauss links Orphic imagery to themes of memory in *Descent and Return: The Orphic Theme in Modern Literature* (Cambridge: Harvard UP, 1971).

15. Maurice Blanchot, *L'Espace littéraire* (Paris: Gallimard, 1955), 234.

16. Roland Barthes, "Rhetoric of the Image," in *Image—Music—Text,* trans Stephen Heath (New York: Hill & Wang, 1977), 44, emphasis in the original, originally published as "Rhétorique de l'image" in *Communications* 3 (1962): 40–51. Barthes laid the groundwork for this essay in "The Photographic Message," *Image—Music—Text,* 15–31, originally "Le Message photographique," *Communications* 1 (1961): 127–38.

17. Christian Metz, "Le Cinéma, langue ou langage?" in *Essais sur la signification au cinéma* (Bruxelles: Klincksieck, 1968), 79, emphasis in the original.

18. Christian Metz, "A propos de l'impression de réalité au cinéma," in *Essais,* 18.

19. Claude Simon, quoted in "Questions aux romanciers," *Cahiers du cinéma* 185 (December 1966): 103 (special issue, "Film et roman: Problèmes du récit").

20. Michel de Certeau, "L'Opération historique," in *Faire de l'histoire: Nouveaux problèmes,* ed. Jacques Le Goff and Pierre Nora (Paris: Gallimard, 1974), 17.

21. Pierre Nora, "Le Retour de l'événement," in *Faire de l'histoire,* 210–28.

22. For example, Marcel Ophuls, public discussion at the University of Minnesota, Minneapolis, spring 1972.

23. Hayden White, *Tropics of Discourse: Essays in Cultural Criticism* (Baltimore: Johns Hopkins UP, 1978), 106.

24. Jean Chesneaux, *Du passé faisons table rase? A propos de l'histoire et des historiens* (Paris: Maspéro, 1976), 53, 19.

25. Marc Bloch, *The Historian's Craft,* trans. Peter Putnam (New York: Vintage, 1953), 46. Bloch himself fought in both world wars, was a leader of the Resistance in Lyon, and was tortured and killed by the Germans in 1944.

26. Jacques Le Goff and Pierre Nora, "Présentation," *Faire de l'histoire,* xiii.

27. Jacques Lacan, *Le Séminaire I: Les Ecrits techniques de Freud* (Paris: Seuil, 1975), 195; see also p.201 and idem, *Ecrits* (Paris: Seuil, 1966), 46.

28. Jacques Lacan, *Le Séminaire IX: Les Quatre Concepts fondamentaux de la psychanalyse* (Paris: Seuil, 1973), 28.

29. Lacan, *Séminaire I,* 19–20.

30. For example, *Ecrits,* 16, 575.

31. de Certeau, "L'Opération historique," 33, emphasis in the original.

32. Philip Rosen, "Securing the Historical: Historiography and the Classical Cinema," in *Cinema Histories, Cinema Practices,* ed. Patricia Mellencamp and Philip Rosen (Frederick MD: American Film Institute, 1984), 17–34.

33. I take the term *cinematic apparatus* to mean the material machinery of the cinema and the articulation of that machinery with such of its necessary effects as subject positioning and signification or the shaping of meaning. Its hardware and its software, if you will. See Philip Rosen, ed., *Narrative, Apparatus, Ideology: A Film Theory Reader* (New York: Columbia UP, 1986), 281–83.

34. Maureen Turim, *Flashbacks in Film: Memory and History* (New York: Routledge,

1989), 17, 103–5, 210–16. Her discussion includes analysis of the flashback structure of *Hiroshima mon amour.* Sorlin, *European Cinemas, European Societies,* also locates in about 1960 a shift in the filmic representation of history. While Turim examines the development of modernism from within, Sorlin is interested in the sociological factors, such as the widespread presence of televisions in family homes, that had an impact on the evolution of cinematic historiography. Like Nora (see "Le Retour de l'événement"), he speculates, for instance, that the televised images to be found in news programming created the possibility of varying versions of a single event.

35. Thomas Elsaesser, *New German Cinema: A History* (New Brunswick: Rutgers UP, 1989).

36. Anton Kaes, "Holocaust and the End of History: Postmodern Historiography in Cinema," in *Probing the Limits of Representation: Nazism and the "Final Solution,"* ed. Saul Friedlander (Cambridge: Harvard UP, 1992), 206–22.

37. Jean-Louis Baudry, "The Apparatus: Metapsychological Approaches to the Impression of Reality in Cinema," in Rosen, *Narrative, Apparatus, Ideology,* 299–318; Christian Metz, "The Fiction Film and Its Spectator: A Metapsychological Study," in *The Imaginary Signifier: Psychoanalysis and the Cinema,* trans. Celia Britton, Annwyl Williams, Ben Brewster, and Alfred Guzzetti (Bloomington: Indiana UP, 1977), 99–147.

38. Jacques Lacan, "Le Stade du miroir comme formateur de la fonction du Je," *Ecrits,* 93–100.

39. Numerous film scholars have written on the subject. See Jean-Louis Baudry, "Ideological Effects of the Basic Cinematographic Apparatus," in Rosen, *Narrative, Apparatus, Ideology,* 286–98; Christian Metz, "The Imaginary Signifier," *The Imaginary Signifier,* 1–87; Mary Ann Doane, "Misrecognition and Identity," in *Explorations in Film Theory: Selected Essays from "Ciné-Tracts,"* ed. Ron Burnett (Bloomington: Indiana UP, 1991), 15–25; Graeme Turner, *Film as Social Practice* (London: Routledge, 1988), 94–127. For the implications of such identification for the female ego, see esp. Laura Mulvey, "Visual Pleasure and Narrative Cinema" and "Afterthoughts on 'Visual Pleasure and Narrative Cinema' inspired by *Duel in the Sun,*" in *Feminism and Film Theory,* ed. Constance Penley (London and New York: BFI Publishing and Routledge, 1988), 57–79.

40. See, for example, Linda Williams, "Hiroshima and Marienbad: Metaphor and Metonymy," *Screen* 17 (spring 1976): 35.

41. Alain Resnais, "Entretien avec Alain Resnais," *Tu n'as rien vu à Hiroshima,* 215.

42. Christian Metz, "Le Significant imaginaire," *Communications* 23 (1975): 34.

43. Robert Jay Lifton, *Death in Life: Survivors of Hiroshima* (New York: Basic Books, 1967), 10.

44. The contagion may even extend to the desire to study this and other works of art.

45. Sigmund Freud, *The Interpretation of Dreams* (London: George Allen, 1913), 365.

46. Marcel Proust, *A la recherche du temps perdu,* 2:87, 1:46.

47. "The unconscious is also spectacle, perhaps the primal spectacle" (Alain Resnais, in "Jouer avec le temps" [interview with Resnais], *L'Arc* 31 [1967]: 96).

48. For a discussion of repetition compulsion and the death drive in *Hiroshima mon amour*, see Sharon Willis, *Marguerite Duras: Writing on the Body* (Urbana: U of Illinois P, 1987), 33–62. Willis's analyses confirm and intersect with mine, though she asks different questions. For another discussion of the repetition compulsion in Duras, see Joan Copjec, "*India Song/Son nom de Venise dans Calcutta désert*: The Compulsion to Repeat," in Penley, *Feminism and Film Theory*, 229–43.

49. Sigmund Freud, "Recollection, Repetition, and Working Through," in *Collected Papers*, vol. 2 (London: Hogarth, 1950), 369–71.

50. Sigmund Freud, *Beyond the Pleasure Principle*, trans. James Strachey (New York: Norton, 1961), 12.

51. Elisabeth Lyon, "The Cinema of Lol V. Stein," in Penley, *Feminism and Film Theory*, 261–62, emphasis in the original.

52. Freud, *Beyond the Pleasure Principle*, 10.

53. Freud, *Beyond the Pleasure Principle*, 6, 27.

54. The term *autobiographical pact* is Philippe Lejeune's; see his *L'Autobiographie en France* (Paris: PUF, 1971).

55. Lacan describes recollection itself as an activity of reading and rewriting "that cryptogram which is what the subject possesses in his/her consciousness" (*Séminaire I*, 20).

56. Bruno Vercier, "Le Mythe du premier souvenir: Pierre Loti, Michel Leiris," *Revue d'histoire littéraire de la France* 75, no. 6 (1975): 1029–45.

57. Vercier, "Le Mythe," 1039.

58. Marguerite Duras, *Le Ravissement de Lol V. Stein* (Paris: Gallimard, 1964), 138.

59. Describing the evolution of the modern novel, Nathalie Sarraute writes that "characters, having lost the two-fold support that the novelist's and the reader's faith afforded them, and which permitted them to stand upright with the burden of the entire story resting on their broad shoulders, may now be seen to vacillate and fall apart." Contrasted with Balzac's characters, the character in the modern novel has lost "that most precious of all possessions, his personality—which belonged to him alone—and frequently, even, his name" ("The Age of Suspicion," 84).

The modern characters Sarraute describes, like the protagonists of *Hiroshima*, can be understood to function like first- and second-person pronouns as explained by linguist Emile Benveniste: "Instances of the use of *I* do not constitute a class of reference since there is no 'object' definable as *I* to which these instances can refer in identical fashion. Each *I* has its own reference and corresponds each time to a unique being who is set up as such. What then is the reality to which *I* or *you* refers? It is solely a 'reality of discourse'" (*Problems in General Linguistics*, trans. Mary Elizabeth Meek [Coral Gables: U of Miami P, 1971], 218).

60. Sören Kierkegaard, *Repetition: An Essay in Experimental Psychology* (Princeton: Princeton UP, 1941).

61. Hassan, *Dismemberment of Orpheus,* 198.

62. Edward Saïd, *Beginnings: Intention and Method* (Baltimore: Johns Hopkins UP, 1975), 280.

63. René Girard, *Violence and the Sacred,* trans. Patrick Gregory (Baltimore: Johns Hopkins UP, 1977).

64. Girard seems unsure of the role of women in his sacrificial paradigm. He declares that "women are never, or rarely, selected as sacrificial victims" but then refers to "some half-suppressed desire to place the blame for all forms of violence on women." Finally, describing the Dionysian cult, he says, "We can therefore postulate a mythological substitution of women for men in regard to violence" (*Violence,* 12, 36, 139). Since I am suggesting that the shorn woman is a sacrificial substitute, an illustration can be made by reversing the roles. To my knowledge, no French men were publicly humiliated for sleeping with German women, although there were some women among the occupying forces in France. If there were such punishments, they certainly have not attained the status of mythical or imaginary image. On the contrary, such behavior by subjugated men might have been punished by the occupying power but would most certainly have been considered revenge against the enemy, precisely because women are considered marginal and the property of men in a given society. The same asymmetrical treatment of the sexes in terms of revenge can be seen in the history of race relations in the United States and in colonial situations (see Calvin C. Hernton, *Sex and Racism in America* [New York: Grove, 1966]; and Frantz Fanon, *Peau noire, masques blancs* [Paris: Seuil, 1975]).

65. Girard, *Violence and the Sacred,* 95–96. See also Sigmund Freud, "The Antithetical Sense of Primal Words," *Collected Papers,* vol.4 (London: Hogarth, 1950), 184–91.

66. Bruno Bettelheim, *Surviving and Other Essays* (New York: Knopf, 1979), 27.

67. Resnais, "Jouer avec le temps," 94.

68. Duras's biographer recounts that Françoise Sagan and Simone de Beauvoir were initially considered as scenarists (Frédérique Lebelley, *Duras ou le poids d'une plume* [Paris: Grasset, 1994], 183).

69. For details concerning the filming, production, and distribution of *Hiroshima mon amour,* see, in addition to the interviews with Resnais already mentioned, Edgar Morin, "Aspects sociologiques de la genèse du film," in *Tu n'as rien vu à Hiroshima,* 25–29. It should be noted that this analysis applies to the French context only; the role of the Japanese man in the film and the history of the film's reception in Japan and elsewhere will of necessity be another story.

70. Bruce Morrissette, "Post-Modern Generative Fiction: Novel and Film," *Critical Inquiry* 2, no.2 (1975): 259–60, reprinted in idem, *Novel and Film: Essays in Two Genres* (Chicago: U of Chicago P, 1985), 1–11.

71. Gérard Genette, *Figures III* (Paris: Seuil, 1972), 245.

72. Edgar Morin, "Conditions d'apparition de la 'Nouvelle Vague," *Communications* 1 (1961): 139–41.

73. Lucien Dällenbach, *The Mirror in the Text*, trans Jeremy Whiteley with Emma Hughes (Chicago: U of Chicago P, 1989). Dällenbach rescues the term *mise en abyme* from reductive and derisive usage, and his is an important contribution to the systematic study of the device. But although Dällenbach acknowledges the possibility of *mise en abyme*'s moving outward from the text, ultimately he sees movement in both directions resulting in infinite regress, and none of his three "species" of *mise en abyme* takes the possibility of external duplication into account (beyond mirroring the artist figure). In fact his overall definition of the *mise en abyme* as "any aspect enclosed within a work that shows a similarity with the work that contains it" (8) explicitly establishes the closure of the text itself as telos.

2. PROBLEMS OF PLOTTING

1. Claude Simon, *The Flanders Road*, trans. Richard Howard (London: John Calder, 1985), originally published as *La Route des Flandres* (Paris: Minuit, 1960). Page numbers cited in the text refer to the English-language edition.

2. Numerous critics have commented on the play of contrary forces in Simon's fiction. Thus Celia Britton's *Claude Simon: Writing the Visible* (Cambridge: Cambridge UP, 1987) examines "how Simon's writing is held in the tension of two contrary movements: a basically representational discourse which attempts to translate sense impressions, especially visual ones, into language, and secondly, working against this, an orientation towards the autonomous generative impulses within language itself" (162); and Lucien Dällenbach, in his *Claude Simon* (Paris: Seuil, 1988), characterizes Simon's writings as "mimesis doublée d'une poiesis" (43).

3. Simon, "Interview with Claude Simon," 10. Simon was discussing two "operations"—invention and the organization of elements—in the design of his novels.

4. Simon, *La Corde raide* (Paris: Sagittaire, 1947), 178.

5. Maurice Merleau-Ponty, "Cinq Notes sur Claude Simon," *Médiations: Revue des expressions contemporaines* 4 (winter 1961): 6.

6. Simon, *La Corde raide*, 174–75.

7. Ludovic Janvier, *Une Parole exigeante: Le Nouveau Roman* (Paris: Minuit, 1964), 91; Barrère, *La Cure d'amaigrissement*, 73. The vocabulary is Simon's, and the preoccupation spans his entire *oeuvre*. See Simon's *L'Herbe* (Paris: Minuit, 1958), 35, and *Les Géorgiques* (Paris: Minuit, 1981), 446, for further examples.

8. Michel Butor, "Le Roman comme recherche," in *Répertoire* (Paris: Minuit, 1960), 7–11.

9. Claude Simon, "Interview avec Claude Simon," by Bettina L. Knapp, *Kentucky Romance Quarterly* 16, no.2 (1969): 189.

10. Jean Ricardou, "'Claude Simon,' textuellement," in *Claude Simon: Colloque de Cerisy*, ed. Jean Ricardou (Paris: Union générale d'éditions, 1975), 8.

11. Stendhal, *La Chartreuse de Parme* (Paris: Garnier, 1961), 35–49.

12. Jean Ricardou sees "l'anarchie du discours" as one level of collapse among many in Simon's novel ("Un Ordre dans la débâcle," *Problèmes du nouveau roman,* 44–55). The novel itself implies causal connections.

13. Claude Simon, "La Fiction mot à mot," in Ricardou, *Nouveau roman: Hier, aujourd'hui,* 2:86–87.

14. Claude Simon, "Les Secrets d'un romancier," interview by Hubert Juin, *Les Lettres françaises,* 6 October 1960. See also Madeleine Chapsal, *Quinze écrivains: Entretiens* (Paris: R. Julliard, [1963]).

15. Claude Simon, *Orion aveugle* (Geneva: Skira, 1970), preface. See also idem, "Claude Simon: The Crossing of the Image," interview by Claud Duverlie, *diacritics,* December 1977, 47–58.

16. Simon, "La Fiction mot à mot," 87–88. A segment of *Les Corps conducteurs* (1971) first appeared under the title "Propriétés des rectangles" in *Tel quel* 14 (1971): 3–16.

17. Claude Simon, in Chapsal, *Quinze écrivains,* 165–66.

18. It is possible to reconstruct a chronology of events, both historical and invented, referred to in the novel. The earliest layer concerns the Convention of 1792–95, during which the de Reixach ancestor votes the death penalty for the king. That same ancestor, become a general, participates in Napoleon's Spanish campaign of 1808–13 and then returns, defeated, and kills himself. His descendant de Reixach marries Corinne in 1936. She is eighteen, much younger than he is. Between their marriage and the invasion of 1940, Iglésia, de Reixach's jockey, is perhaps Corinne's lover: scenes of horse racing and sex recounted by Iglésia or imagined by Georges in prison took place during this period (if they took place at all). The winter of 1940 sees de Reixach a cavalry captain, with Iglésia as his orderly. Georges is stationed with them when de Reixach receives a letter from Sabine, Georges's mother, and learns they are cousins. In May the French army is defeated at the Meuse. De Reixach is killed or commits suicide. Iglésia and Georges try to escape to safety, but they circle back, encountering the same dead horse four times. Finally they are captured. In the train on the way to prison camp Georges meets up with Blum, an old friend. Georges, Blum, and Iglésia spend their time in prison camp telling stories, many involving Corinne. Georges attempts escape and fails. Blum dies. After the Liberation, Georges returns from the war, gives up his studies, and becomes a farmer. In May of 1946 he visits Corinne in Toulouse. She has remarried. Several months later they spend a night together in a hotel. Early in the morning Corinne gets angry and leaves. *La Route des*

Flandres is published in 1960. The origin of the text is problematic, especially since the most logical scriptor figure, Georges, has abandoned his learning and rejected his father and all he represents, including writing. Unlike in the later *Géorgiques,* in which some of the same events are recounted, there is no writing figure within the novel, and it is impossible to tell from where the text emanates.

19. Albert Camus, "The Myth of Sisyphus," in *The Myth of Sisyphus and Other Essays,* trans. Justin O'Brien (New York: Knopf, 1955), 10–11.

20. See, for example, Françoise Van Rossum-Guyon, "De Claude Simon à Proust: Un Exemple d'intertextualité," *Les Lettres nouvelles,* September–October 1972, 107–37; and Domingo Pérez Minik, "Los caballos de Claude Simon en *La Ruta de Flandes,*" in *La novela estranjera en España* (Madrid: J. Betancor, 1973), 44–50.

21. For a full discussion of the connotations of the word *chevaucher,* see Lucien Dällenbach, "Mise en abyme et redoublement spéculaire chez Claude Simon," in Ricardou, *Claude Simon: Colloque de Cerisy,* 158–61.

22. Simon, *Orion aveugle,* preface. Simon's short preface is handwritten and unpaginated. Many of the ideas and phrases from the preface recur in Simon, "La Fiction mot à mot," 73–97.

23. Simon, "La Fiction mot à mot," 88–89.

24. Ricardou, *Le Nouveau Roman,* 89. In all probability Ricardou devised his diagram from Simon's novel, although he does not mention *La Route des Flandres* in this connection. The figure's reappearance demonstrates the close connection between fiction and theory in the New Novel.

25. Care must be taken with words like *prefigure* and *repeat.* Sometimes what precedes at the level of the narration (i.e., in the text) follows at the level of the fiction (the story), or vice versa. Since history and historiography move in opposite temporal directions, as chapter 1 shows, any consideration of temporal priority has to specify whether it is dealing with textual or historical chronology.

26. Corinne denies having had an affair with Iglésia, and Iglésia remains silent, a silence that authorizes Georges's inventions. Stories are most often told by characters who have no direct information on the subject under discussion. In terms of the novel's epistemology, then, it is important to note that narratives derive not from knowledge but rather from the *lack* of knowledge, in other words, from desire.

27. Otto Rank, *The Double: A Psychoanalytic Study,* trans. Harry Tucker Jr. (Chapel Hill: U of North Carolina P, 1971). Freud speculates that fiction is a domain where one can imagine one's own death as a spectator ("Thoughts for the Times on War and Death" [1915], *Collected Papers,* 4:304–5). Jean LaPlanche writes that "in the unconscious, death would always be the death of the other" (*Life and Death in Psychoanalysis,* trans. Jeffrey Mehlman [Baltimore: Johns Hopkins UP, 1976], 6).

28. Simon, "La Fiction mot à mot," 89.

29. Serge Doubrovsky, "Notes on the Genesis of an *Ecriture*," in *Claude Simon*, ed. Celia Britton (London: Longman, 1993), 166–68.

30. Peter Brooks, "Freud's Masterplot," *Yale French Studies* 55–56 (1977): 295, reprinted in idem, *Reading for the Plot: Design and Intention in Narrative* (New York: Vintage, 1985), 90–112.

31. Sigmund Freud, "The Uncanny" (1919), *Collected Papers*, 4:368–407.

32. Simon has repeatedly claimed that nothing happens by chance in his novels, a contention that seems to invite the uncanny. In other words, he seems to believe that a Mallarméan toss of the dice (a "coup de dés") can abolish chance, as in the following passage from the novel: "dans ce désordre de l'esprit, ce désarroi, ce désespoir: défait, désoriente, désarçonné, dépossédé de tout et peut-être déjà détaché, et peut-être déjà à demi détruit" (*La Route des Flandres*, 199).

33. Or, as Jacques Lacan claims about Poe's "Purloined Letter": "A letter always arrives at its destination" (*Ecrits*, 41).

34. Celia Britton amplifies the discussion of the father figure in Simon's work by investigating its autobiographical coloring. Noting that Simon lost his father as an infant, at the beginning of World War I, Britton speculates that Simon's obsession with violent death creates parallels "between himself and the father he never knew: for Simon, to live through the horror of 1940 is in a sense to *relive his father's death*" (Britton, *Claude Simon*, 2, emphasis in the original).

35. See Serge Doubrovsky, *La Place de la madeleine: Ecriture et fantasme chez Proust* (Paris: Mercure de France, 1974). The word *madeleine* does not appear in the novel, but the Proustian memory theme has been widely commented upon. If Doubrovsky is right about the madeleine in *A la recherche du temps perdu*, Georges accomplishes literally what Proust does metaphorically.

36. Marc Bloch, *Strange Defeat: A Statement of Evidence Written in 1940*, trans. Gerard Hopkins (London: Oxford UP, 1949).

37. Camus, "Myth of Sisyphus," 29.

38. Geoffrey Bruun, *The Rise of the French Imperium* (New York: Harper, 1959); Owen Connelly, *The Gentle Bonaparte: A Biography of Joseph, Napoleon's Elder Brother* (New York: Macmillan, 1968).

39. White, *Metahistory*.

40. Simon, "Secrets d'un romancier."

41. Jean-Paul Sartre, *Situations V: Colonialisme et néo-colonialisme* (Paris: Gallimard, 1964), 59, 103, 73–74.

42. Gordon Wright, *France in Modern Times: From The Enlightenment to the Present*, 2d ed. (Chicago: Rand McNally, 1960), 423.

43. Karl Marx, *The Eighteenth Brumaire of Louis Bonaparte* (New York: International, 1954), 5.

44. Freud, "The Uncanny," 398.

45. Claude Simon, untitled address to a colloquium whose proceedings were published in *Three Decades of the French New Novel,* ed. Lois Oppenheim (Urbana: U of Illinois P, 1986), 81–82.

46. But as Lacan has remarked, "Chasser l'inconscient [the unconscious, or for our purposes here, history, or language], il revient au galop."

47. Frank Kermode, *The Sense of an Ending: Studies in the Theory of Fiction* (New York: Oxford UP, 1967), 45–46.

48. Camus, "Myth of Sisyphus," 2.

3. FIGURING OUT

1. Robbe-Grillet, *Last Year at Marienbad,* 10.

2. Lucien Goldmann, "Les Deux Avant-gardes," in *Structures mentales et création culturelle* (Paris: Anthropos, 1970), 179–208.

3. Marker has commonly been associated with Resnais and Agnès Varda, the so-called Left Bank filmmakers, to distinguish them from the *Cahiers du cinéma* group.

4. Alain Robbe-Grillet, *For a New Novel: Essays on Fiction,* trans. Richard Howard (New York: Grove, 1965), 153, emphasis in the original.

5. Sigmund Freud, "Screen Memories," in *Collected Papers,* vol. 5, ed. James Strachey (London: Hogarth, 1950), 47–69.

6. Bruce Kawin, *Mindscreen: Bergman, Godard, and First-Person Film* (Princeton: Princeton UP, 1978), 82. For a feminist refutation of this hypothesis and its implications, see Lynn A. Higgins, "Screen/Memory: Rape and Its Alibis in *Last Year at Marienbad,*" in *Rape and Representation,* ed. Lynn A. Higgins and Brenda R. Silver (New York: Columbia UP, 1991), 303–21.

7. A few examples will give a sense of the variety of perspectives. Bruce Morrissette, *Les Romans de Robbe-Grillet* (Paris: Minuit, 1963), uses the principles of hypnosis to explain the characters' behavior. François Weyergans describes A's internal conflict between the pleasure and the reality principles in "Dans le dédale," *Cahiers du cinéma* 123 (1961): 22–28. Claude Ollier, in "Ce Soir à Marienbad," *Nouvelle revue française,* nos. 106 (October 1961): 711–19 and 107 (November 1961): 906–12, analyzes a similar struggle between reason (in the person of M) and irrational obsession (X). James Monaco decides that ultimately the film is "about storytelling. It is X's job to convince, A's job to resist: the primal relationship between storyteller and audience" (*Alain Resnais: The Role of Imagination* [New York: Oxford UP, 1978]). Jean-Edern Haller sees the film as a story about the desire for immortality, with M playing the role of Death ("Toute une vie à Marienbad," *Tel quel* 7 [1961]: 49–52). And so on. These and other critics stress that there are many possible interpretations. An exception is John Ward's *Alain Resnais, or the Theme of Time* (Garden

City NY: Doubleday, 1968). Ward declares that "what exactly took place the year before" was that "M kills A and X is left alone to mourn" (39).

8. Umberto Eco, *The Open Work,* trans. Anna Cancogni (Cambridge: Harvard UP, 1989).

9. Alain Resnais, in *Interviews with Film Directors,* ed. Andrew Sarris (New York: Avon Books, 1967), 436. The interview was originally published as "Entretien avec Resnais et Robbe-Grillet," by Andre S. Labarthe et Jacques Rivette, *Cahiers du cinéma* 123 (1961).

10. Olga Bernal, *Alain Robbe-Grillet ou le roman de l'absence* (Paris: Gallimard, 1964), 40.

11. Alain Robbe-Grillet, in "Entretien avec Resnais et Robbe-Grillet," 18.

12. Jeffey Kittay, "Alibi: On Handwriting, Rewriting, and Writing Rhythms and *Le Voyeur,*" *Romanic Review* 71, no.1 (1980): 57–74.

13. Bruce Morrissette, "Games and Game Structures in Robbe-Grillet," *Yale French Studies* 41 (1968): 159–67; "Entretien avec Resnais et Robbe-Grillet," 1.

14. By the nineteenth century the genre had been assimilated into traditional theater, where titles are supplied by authors, as in Musset's *On ne badine pas avec l'amour* and *Il faut qu'une porte soit ouverte ou fermée* (see Clarence D. Brenner, *Le Developpement du proverbe dramatique en France et sa vogue au XVIIIe siècle* [Berkeley: U of California P, 1937]).

15. A. J. Greimas, *Du Sens* (Paris: Seuil, 1970), 313.

16. François Truffaut, *Hitchcock* (New York: Simon & Schuster, 1984), 138–39.

17. Alain Robbe-Grillet, quoted in Andre Gardies, *Alain Robbe-Grillet* (Paris: Seghers, 1972), 118.

18. Alain Robbe-Grillet, in Sarris, *Interviews with Film Directors,* 451.

19. Sigmund Freud, "Fixation upon Traumas: The Unconscious," in *A General Introduction to Psychoanalysis,* trans. Joan Riviere (New York: Pocket Books, 1952), 291.

20. Lacan, *Ecrits,* 276–89.

21. Sigmund Freud, "Dreams," *A General Introduction to Psychoanalysis,* 146.

22. Leo Strauss, "Persecution and the Art of Writing," in *Persecution and the Art of Writing* (Glencoe IL: Free Press, 1952), 24. For the same mechanisms applied to taboo feminist content, see Judy Chicago, *Through the Flower: My Struggle as a Woman Artist* (Garden City NY: Anchor, 1977), 34–35, 40, 63–64, 145, 194, for example: "I was never interested in 'formal issues' as such. Rather, they were something that my content had to be hidden behind in order for my work to be taken seriously" (40); and "I had come out of a formalist background and had learned how to neutralize my subject matter" (63).

23. Robin Wood, *Hollywood from Vietnam to Reagan* (New York: Columbia UP, 1986), 69.

24. Sigmund Freud, *Dora: An Analysis of a Case of Hysteria* (New York: Collier, 1963), 31.

25. Freud, "Fixation upon Traumas," 291.

26. Lacan, *Ecrits*, 493–528.

27. See the epigraph to this chapter for an explanation from the U.S. Department of Defense.

28. Robbe-Grillet and Resnais first met to discuss the project during the winter of 1959–60. Filming took place from summer through winter 1960, first in Germany, then in Paris. Because Resnais was involved in antiwar activities, the French government did not permit *Marienbad* to be entered in the 1961 Cannes Film Festival. In August Resnais submitted it to the Venice Festival, where it won the Golden Lion award. The film finally premiered in Paris in September 1961.

29. Martin Harrison, "Government and Press in France during the Algerian War," *American Political Science Review* 63, no.2 (1964): 277. In view of American press censorship during the Gulf War of January–March 1991 (under the guise of preventing "another Vietnam"), it is enlightening to note that one of the reasons Harrison cites for the ferocity of censorship during France's Algerian conflict is the government's belief that France's war in Indochina had been lost by the press (273).

30. It should be recalled that the Editions de Minuit was founded during the Occupation and in support of the Resistance. See Hamon and Rotman, *Les Porteurs de valises,* for complete documentation on antiwar activities during the period of the war in Algeria and for accounts of individual instances of censorship. A particularly notorious incident was the case of Henri Alleg's *La Question* (Paris: Minuit, 1958), an account of the author's own detention and torture by the French army in Algiers in 1957.

31. In France, official preventive censorship of the arts began in wartime with the creation of the Commission nationale de censure in 1917 (see René Prédal, *La Société française, 1914–1945, à travers le cinéma* [Paris: Armand Colin, 1972], 52–53).

32. Anecdote reported in Lottman, *Left Bank,* 191.

33. Marcel Ophuls, "Avant propos," *Le Chagrin et la pitié* (Paris: Alain Moreau, 1980), 12. As noted earlier, the film was nonetheless banned from French television until 1981.

34. *L'Express,* 29 September 1960.

35. Henrik Ibsen, *The House of Rosmer,* trans. Brian J. Burton (Birmingham: C. Combridge, 1959). The play's ending corresponds to that of the play within *Marienbad:* a man and a woman leave together, for a new life, perhaps, but more probably for a double suicide. Note that the title *Rosmer* is a fragment of the original, *Rosmersholm,* after the manner of the truncated titles and proverbs already encountered.

36. Robbe-Grillet, quoted in Gardies, *Robbe-Grillet,* 111.

37. "Entretien avec Resnais et Robbe-Grillet," 3.

38. Robbe-Gillet, in Ricardou, *Nouveau Roman: Hier, aujourd'hui,* 1:172–73.

39. Alain Robbe-Grillet, "'What Interests Me Is Eroticism': An Interview with Germaine Brée," in *Homosexualities and French Literature: Cultural Contexts, Critical Texts,* ed. George Stambolian and Elaine Marks (Ithaca: Cornell UP, 1979), 93.

40. It is also the town where Lacan first presented the paper that he eventually published as "Le Stade du miroir comme formateur de la fonction de Je."

41. Fredric Jameson, *The Ideologies of Theory, Essays 1971–1986, I: Situations of Theory* (Minneapolis: U of Minnesota P, 1988), 169.

42. See *Le Canard enchaîné* beginning 21 September 1960. The portrayal of de Gaulle as king (Charles XI, Louis XIV, and even Ubu) precedes the appearance of the column, however.

43. Robin Morgan, *Going Too Far: The Personal Chronicle of a Feminist* (New York: Vintage, 1978), 169.

44. The dossier of the case was published by Simone de Beauvoir and Gisèle Halimi a few years later in *Djamila Boupacha* (Paris: Gallimard, 1962).

45. Hamon and Rotman, *Les Porteurs de valises,* 266.

46. "Un *Marienbad* historicisé," remarks Claude Ollier without explaining (*Souvenirs écran* [Paris: Gallimard, 1981], 148).

47. Jean Cayrol, *Muriel: Scénario et dialogues* (Paris: Seuil, 1963), 33, 21.

4. SIGNS OF THE TIMES

Section headings in this chapter are taken from 1968 Parisian graffiti and wall slogans; the locations are given in parentheses. They are cited from Julien Besançon, ed., *Les Murs ont la parole: Journal mural mai 68, Sorbonne Odéon Nanterre etc.* . . (Paris: Tchou, 1968), where the one from Censier can be found on 54; the first from Odéon, on 17; that from Condorcet, 128; that from Nanterre, 87; the second from Odéon, 168; and that from the Sorbonne, 159.

1. Joni Mitchell, "Free Man in Paris," from *Court and Spark,* Asylum Records 7E-1001, 1974. The song recounts a conflict between freedom and cooptation very similar to the one I trace in this chapter.

2. Patrick Combes, *La Littérature et le Mouvement de mai 68: Ecriture, mythes, critique, écrivains, 1968–1981* (Paris: Seghers, 1984).

3. For an excellent survey of explanations of the events of May 1968, see Philippe Bénéton and Jean Touchard, "Les Interprétations de la crise de mai–juin 1968," *Revue française de science politique,* June 1970, 503–42. The authors examine eight types of explanatory theories: communist conspiracy, the breakdown of the university, a youth rebellion, a spiritual revolt ("crise de civilisation"), class conflict, political crisis, and a chain of circumstantial events. See also Michel Winock, *La Fièvre hexagonale: Les Grandes Crises politiques, 1871–1968* (Paris: Calmann-Levy, 1986), 327–73.

4. Edward Saïd plays with the term *cover* in his book *Covering Islam: How the Media and the Experts Determine How We See the Rest of the World* (New York: Pantheon, 1981), in which he shows how journalism has "covered" the Arab world while covering it up. His

analysis suggests to me that the same dynamic is at work in the novels Combes studied (see Combes, *La Littérature et le mouvement de mai 68*).

5. Daniel Cohn-Bendit and Gabriel Cohn-Bendit, *Obsolete Communism: The Left Wing Alternative,* trans. Arnold Pomerans (New York: McGraw-Hill, 1968), 11–12.

6. Tom Wolfe, "Radical Chic," in *Radical Chic and Mau-mauing the Flak Catchers* (New York: Farrar, Straus & Giroux, 1970), 40.

7. For my understanding of the concept, I rely on J. Milton Yinger, who coined the term *counterculture* in 1960 and discusses its components and definitions in *Countercultures: The Promise and the Peril of a World Turned Upside Down* (New York: Free Press, 1982).

8. This is the sense of much of American "sixties bashing" in the press and elsewhere, even now. For example, much of the journalism surrounding the 1991 war in Iraq turned around the desire to avoid "another Vietnam" and the countercultural and antiwar movements associated with that period.

9. Keith A. Reader, *Intellectuals and the Left in France since 1968* (New York: St. Martin's, 1987), 13.

10. Greil Marcus, *Lipstick Traces: A Secret History of the Twentieth Century* (Cambridge: Harvard UP, 1989), demonstrates the affinities that link the situationists to punk (especially the Sex Pistols), to dada and surrealism, as well as to certain strains of medieval mysticism.

11. See *La Révolution surréaliste* (Paris: Jean-Michel Place, 1975).

12. It should be noted that in the United States in the same period Vance Packard and Herbert Marcuse were demystifying the innocence of the mass media and redefining their power (see Vance Packard, *The Hidden Persuaders* [New York: Pocket Books, 1957]; and Herbert Marcuse, *One Dimensional Man: Studies in the Ideology of Advanced Industrial Society* [Boston: Beacon, 1964]).

13. Guy Debord, *La Société du spectacle* (Paris: Buchet-Castel, 1967), recently made available in English as *The Society of the Spectacle,* trans. Donald Nicholson-Smith (New York: Zone Books, 1994).

14. And I will be most unsituationist in citing it: *Internationale situationiste, 1958–69* (Amsterdam: Van Gennep, 1970). One wonders, though, about the status of this copyright.

15. *Internationale situationiste* 1 (1958): 8; 3 (1959): 9; 7 (April 1962): 23; 3 (December 1959): 7. Debord puts forth his ideas on cinema in his script of *Contre le cinéma* (Aarhus: Bibliothèque d'Alexandrie, 1964).

16. Among those whose works derive from the situationists is Jean Baudrillard, who Keith A. Reader argues plagiarized situationist writings (Reader, *Intellectuals and the Left,* 131–35).

17. Roland Barthes, *L'Empire des signes* (Geneva: Skira, 1970), available in English as *Empire of Signs* (New York: Farrar, Straus & Giroux, 1983).

18. For further discussion of Barthes's approaches to Japan and China, see Lynn A. Higgins, "Barthes's Imaginary Voyages," *Studies in Twentieth Century Literature* 5, no.2 (1981): 157–74.

19. Roland Barthes, *S/Z* (Paris: Seuil, 1970), 10–11.

20. Louis Althusser, "Ideology and Ideological State Apparatuses (Notes toward an Investigation)," in *Lenin and Philosophy and Other Essays,* trans. Ben Brewster (London: New Left Books, 1971), 123–73.

21. Or, in Althusser's well-known phrasing, "Ideology represents the imaginary relationship of individuals to their real conditions of existence" ("Ideology," 153).

22. Numerous sources recount the events in detail. See Sylvia Harvey, *May 68 and Film Culture* (London: British Film Institute, 1980), 14–16; Langlois and Myrent, *Henri Langlois,* 318–57; and Richard Roud, *A Passion for Films: Henri Langlois and the Cinémathèque Française* (New York: Viking, 1983), 148–60. Roud, Harvey, and Myrent, among others, have defended Langlois's case. A few have been critical of his directorship. For example, Diana Johnstone provides evidence that under Langlois scores of films were damaged or lost. She argues that his management style and record keeping were deliberately idiosyncratic and disorganized in order to hide these losses ("Langlois's Bathtub: The Genesis Myth of the Cinémathèque Française," *Harper's,* July 1978, 74–81).

23. Roland Barthes, "From the Work to the Text," in *Textual Strategies: Perspectives in Post-Structuralist Criticism,* ed. Josué Harari (Ithaca: Cornell UP, 1979). Barthes's essay originally appeared in 1971. The nature of and the relationship between speech and writing had been a subject of debate at least since Derrida's *De la grammatologie,* published by Minuit in 1967.

24. Roland Barthes, "L'Ecriture de l'événement," *Communications* 12 (1968): 108–12. The entire issue was entitled "La Prise de la parole."

25. Although they are not the focus of this book, it seems unfair not to mention that the *Tel quel* writers were closely involved with many of these developments, and in fact Barthes, Ricardou, Derrida, and many others were writing in the pages of their journal at the time. A succinct summary of the style and the program of this group can be found in Reader, *Intellectuals and the Left,* 10. See also Danielle Marx-Scouras, "The Powers of Literature: The Tel Quel Years (1960–1982)," unpublished manuscript.

26. Duras speaks repeatedly about the repressive nature of the book. See, e.g., her *Les Yeux verts* (Paris: Cahiers du Cinéma, 1980), 132; and Duras and Xavière Gauthier, *Les Parleuses* (Paris: Minuit, 1974), 116.

27. Madeleine Borgomano, *L'Ecriture filmique de Marguerite Duras* (Paris: Albatross, 1985).

28. Jameson, *Ideologies of Theory*, 177–78.

29. Combes, *La Littérature et le mouvement de mai 68*, 49.

30. Kent E. Carroll, "Film and Revolution: Interview with the Dziga-Vertov Group," in *Focus on Godard*, ed. Royal S. Brown (Englewood Cliffs: Prentice-Hall, 1972), 50–64.

31. Mao Tse-tung, "The Question of 'Going Too Far,'" *Selected Works of Mao Tse-tung*, vol. 1 (Peking: Foreign Language Press, 1965), 28.

32. In light of post-1968 French interest in the Chinese Cultural Revolution and the Maoist features of *Tout va bien*, it is possible to reevaluate Godard's oft-mentioned debt to Brecht. Steve Cannon suggests that the extreme formalist inaccessibility of the earlier Dziga Vertov works in fact betrays the Brechtian project of creating estrangement effects in order to raise political and esthetic consciousness ("Godard, the *Groupe Dziga Vertov*, and the Myth of 'Counter-Cinema,'" *Nottingham French Studies* 32 [1993]: 1, 74–83). It is even possible, in an ironic turnaround, that Brecht himself may be indebted to traditional Chinese theater in his elaboration of distancing techniques, his emphasis on situation over character, and his highlighting of the historical and political dimensions of everyday life (see Wu Zuguang, Huang Zuolin, and Mei Shaowu, *Peking Opera and Mei Lanfang* [Beijing: New World, 1981], 24–25).

33. Cohn-Bendit and Cohn-Bendit, *Obsolete Communism*, 27. The old adage that those who respect the law and love sausage should never watch either being made also comes to mind.

34. Mao Tse-tung, "The Question of 'Going Too Far,'" 28.

35. It is important to note that *Tout va bien* is the last of the Dziga-Vertov films, made by Gorin and Godard after the larger collective began to fall apart. *Tout va bien* in fact marks a partial return to narrative filmmaking, perhaps as a reaction to the inaccessibility (and limited distribution) of the group's earlier efforts. Peter Wollen enumerates the characteristics of the Dziga-Vertov challenge to mainstream cinema—narrative intransitivity, estrangement, subversion of fiction and of pleasure—in his "Godard and Counter-Cinema: *Vent d'est*," in Rosen, *Narrative, Apparatus, Ideology*, 120–29. Steve Cannon ("Godard, the *Groupe Dziga Vertov*, and the Myth of 'Counter-Cinema'") takes issue with Wollen and doubts the effectiveness of these techniques, pointing to the films' tendency to undercut the revolutionary potential of counterdiscursive practices by deploying them in films that are overly theoretical and abstract. *Tout va bien* nevertheless maintains the goal of being, as Godard liked to put it, "a political film made politically," that is, of questioning dominant modes of social interaction both through thematic content and by foregrounding the materiality of filmic and narrative production.

36. At the end of 1972 Godard and Gorin made *Letter to Jane*, a companion film to *Tout va bien* born of the two filmmakers' disgust with Jane Fonda's trip to Hanoi earlier that year and in particular with a cover article in *L'Express* (31 July–6 August 1972, 57–60) featuring Fonda's account of her trip. They criticize her most harshly for putting herself in

the spotlight, speaking for and in the place of the Vietnamese, and appropriating their point of view without their consent, a gesture they see as repeating and prolonging a colonialist stance in relation to Vietnam. *Letter to Jane,* ostensibly a letter to Fonda consisting of Godard's monologue over a series of photographs taken from the *Express* article, ironically repeats the gesture, however, by silencing Jane Fonda and treating her as an object of discourse rather than an interlocutor by not allowing her to respond. The attempt to be more politically correct backfires when the gendered dimensions of power are taken into account (as Fonda argues they should be in *Tout va bien*). This episode demonstrates in miniature the evolution I am tracing in this chapter: that the egregious sexism of the so-called revolutionary politics of May 1968 paved the way for the emergence of the feminist movement.

37. Lebelley, *Duras ou le poids d'une plume,* 217.

38. Marguerite Duras, "An Interview with Marguerite Duras," by Susan Husserl-Kapit, *Signs: Journal of Women in Culture and Society* 1, no.2 (1975): 425.

39. Duras and Gauthier, *Les Parleuses,* 49.

40. For a pertinent discussion of Duras's politics of silence, see E. Ann Kaplan, "Silence as Female Resistance in Marguerite Duras's *Nathalie Granger* (1972)," in *Women and Film: Both Sides of the Camera* (New York: Methuen, 1983), 91–103.

41. Duras and Gauthier, *Les Parleuses,* 78.

42. Hélène Cixous and Catherine Clément, *La Jeune Née* (Paris: Union générale d'éditions, 1975), published in English as *The Newly-Born Woman,* trans. Betsy Wing (Minneapolis: U of Minnesota P, 1986).

43. Ibid., 37, emphasis in the original.

44. Marguerite Duras, *Nathalie Granger, suivie de la femme du Gange* (Paris: Gallimard, 1973), 90.

5. TRUFFAUT'S OTOHISTORIOGRAPHY

1. Marguerite Duras, *La Douleur* (Paris: POL, 1985), published in English as *The War: A Memoir,* trans. Barbara Bray (New York: Pantheon, 1986).

2. Robert Faurisson, *Mémoire en défense,* preface by Noam Chomsky (Paris: Vieille Taupe, 1980).

3. Rousso, *Vichy Syndrome.*

4. *Esprit* 181 (May 1992) includes contributions by Rousso, Nazi-hunter Serge Klarsfeld, Barbie prosecutor Pierre Truche, historian Jean-Pierre Azéma, and others. The quotation is taken from p.176.

5. Pascal Ory, *L'Entre-deux-mai: Histoire culturelle de la France, mai 1968–mai 1981* (Paris: Seuil, 1983), 107–48.

6. Robert O. Paxton, "Tricks of Memory," review of Rousso, *Vichy Syndrome, New York Review of Books,* 7 November 1991, 51.

7. Marguerite Duras, *L'Amant* (Paris: Minuit, 1984), published in English as *The Lover*, trans. Barbara Bray (New York: Perennial Library, 1986), and *La Douleur;* Robbe-Grillet, *Le Miroir qui revient* and *Angélique ou L'enchantement* (Paris: Minuit, 1987), published in English as *Angelique* (New York: Riverrun, 1994). Nathalie Sarraute published her memoirs as *Enfance* (Paris: Gallimard, 1983), published in English as *Childhood: An Autobiography,* trans. Barbara Wright (New York: Braziller, 1984), but she does not deal extensively with the period of the Occupation.

8. See Sigmund Freud, "From the History of an Infantile Neurosis," in *Three Case Histories* (New York: Collier, 1963), 187–316. Among the most useful further explorations of the case's ramifications, Nicolas Abraham and Maria Torok's *Wolf Man's Magic Word* (Minneapolis: U of Minnesota P, 1986) redefines the primal scene in terms of a primal word that is repeated throughout the patient's symptoms and becomes the key to deciphering them. Ned Lukacher, *Primal Scenes: Literature, Philosophy, Psychoanalysis* (Ithaca: Cornell UP, 1986), discusses the problematic real versus fictional status of the originary scene.

9. Lifton, *Death in Life,* 48–51. It is remarkable how Lifton's formulation of residual image resembles Althusser's definition of ideology in "Ideology and Ideological State Apparatuses": both attempt to theorize the mediations between events and the lived *experience* of those realities. In other words, both are useful as theories of representation.

10. Baudry, "The Apparatus," 313.

11. Metz, "The Imaginary Signifier," 63–65.

12. François Truffaut, *Le Cinéma selon François Truffaut,* ed. Anne Gillain (Paris: Flammarion, 1988), 443.

13. Don Allen, *Finally Truffaut: A Film-by-Film Guide to the Master Filmmaker's Legacy* (New York: Beaufort, 1985), 196; François Truffaut, *Truffaut by Truffaut,* ed. Dominique Rabourdin, trans. Robert Erich Wolf (New York: Harry N. Abrams, 1987), 173–74.

14. Truffaut made his film in the wake of *Le Chagrin et la pitié,* a film he greatly admired. As he says in "André Bazin, the Occupation, and I," his preface to Bazin's *French Cinema of the Occupation and Resistance: The Birth of a Critical Esthetic* (New York: Frederick Ungar, 1981), "I believe that Marcel Ophuls' film *Le Chagrin et la Pitié*—despite attacks on it from all sides, and despite the fact that French television still refuses to show it so as not to chagrin those who had been pitiless—is the film that describes with the greatest exactitude and good faith the spectrum of French behavior in the 1940–45 period" (15).

15. Truffaut, *Le Plaisir des yeux,* 176.

16. Patricia Mellencamp, "Spectacle and Spectator: Looking through the American Musical Comedy," in Burnett, *Explorations in Film Theory,* 9. Mellencamp's argument resembles Gérard Genette's analysis of the mutually interfering functions of narrative and description in "Frontières du récit," *Figures II,* 49–69. The New Novel's notorious emphasis on description over narration, as it corresponds to Truffaut's and other Nouvelle

Vague filmmakers' privileging of spectacle over plot, thus provides yet another thread linking the two groups' esthetic projects. And to the extent that history is narrative, both description and spectacle convey a distancing from historiography.

17. *La Disparue*, which refers either to a vanished or euphemistically to a dead woman, was the original title of *La Chambre verte* (see Allen, *Finally Truffaut*, 202). It is unclear whether such a play actually exists, as claimed by Mirella Jona Affron and E. Rubinstein, editors and translators of the screenplay (New Brunswick: Rutgers UP, 1985). The film calls it a new play by Karen Bergen, a Norwegian dramatist, but I have found no trace of it, and I suspect it is Truffaut's invention.

18. François Truffaut, "Pourquoi et comment *Le Dernier Métro?*" interview in *L'Avant-scène cinéma*, March 1983.

19. Truffaut, "Pourquoi," 9.

20. Gilles Jacob and Claude de Givray, eds., *François Truffaut Correspondence, 1945–1984*, trans. Gilbert Adair (New York: Noonday, 1988), 354.

21. Truffaut, "André Bazin, the Occupation, and I," 8. See also François Truffaut, interviewed by Aline Desjardins, in *Aline Desjardins s'entretient avec François Truffaut* (Paris: Ramsay, 1987), 14.

22. Colin Nettelbeck has identified *Daxiat* as one of Laubreau's aliases ("Getting the Story Right: Narratives of World War II in Post-1968 France," *Journal of European Studies* 15 [June 1985]: 116).

23. Truffaut, "André Bazin, the Occupation, and I," 18.

24. Truffaut, "André Bazin, the Occupation, and I," 22.

25. Evelyn Ehrlich, *Cinema of Paradox: French Filmmaking under the German Occupation* (New York: Columbia UP, 1985), x, 165.

26. Truffaut, "André Bazin, the Occupation, and I," 10.

27. Truffaut, "Pourquoi et comment *Le Dernier Métro?*"

28. Truffaut, "Pourquoi," 4. See also Truffaut, *Le Cinéma selon François Truffaut*, 89; and Desjardins, *Aline Desjardins s'entretient*, 22, 37 (where Truffaut suggests that 1958 was too early to make a film set during the Occupation), and esp. 39, where he recounts an incident from the film where, to excuse his absence from school, Antoine blurts out the falsehood that his mother has died. Truffaut says that "in reality as I lived it, this was a night during the Occupation," and that because of the bombings that evening, he spent the night, not in a printer's office, but in the metro.

29. Film theorists have used the term *relay* to describe the stages and complexities of spectator identification. For example, Mary Ann Doane states, "In identification, the other—whether person or image—is used as a relay, a kind of substitute to conceal the fact that the subject can never fully coincide with itself" ("Misrecognition and Identity," 20). And describing primary identification, Jean-Louis Baudry says that "the spectator identifies less with what is represented, the spectacle itself, than with what stages the spec-

tacle, makes it seen, obliging him to see what it sees; this is exactly the function taken over by the camera as a sort of relay" ("Ideological Effects of the Basic Cinematographic Apparatus," 295). Although I am describing here the ways Truffaut's biography and subjectivity are projected in the film, the mechanism and its significance are the same.

30. Truffaut, *Le Dernier Métro* (filmscript), *Avant-scène cinéma*, March 1983, 14.

31. It is, however, romantic of Truffaut to think that resistance to the Occupation and to anti-Semitism were synonymous. On the insensitivity of the Resistance to Nazi anti-Semitism, see Ted Morgan, *An Uncertain Hour: The French, the Germans, the Jews, the Klaus Barbie Trial, and the City of Lyon, 1940–1945* (New York: William Morrow, 1990); and Judith Miller, *One by One by One: Facing the Holocaust* (New York: Simon & Schuster, 1990).

32. Truffaut, "André Bazin, the Occupation, and I," 8.

33. The broadcast in *Le Dernier Métro* is based on actual radio broadcasts of the period. Alice Yaeger Kaplan discusses the importance of radio in the dissemination of Nazi propaganda in *Reproductions of Banality: Fascism, Literature, and French Intellectual Life* (Minneapolis: U of Minnesota P, 1986), 125–41.

34. Jacques Derrida, "Otobiographies: The Teaching of Nietzsche and the Politics of the Proper Name," in *The Ear of the Other: Otobiography, Transference, Translation*, ed. Christie McDonald, trans. Avital Ronell (Lincoln: U of Nebraska P, 1985), 33–35, quotation from 34. Derrida is reflecting on a quotation from Nietzsche describing the university as an umbilicus. The passage suggests circuitous connections between May 1968 and Truffaut's aural thematics. In light of my argument, the university-umbilicus connection suggests a reason why one's university is called one's alma mater. Antoine is expelled and sent away both by his mother and by the schoolmaster, and the oppressive, lifeless school in *Les Quatre Cents Coups* (1959) is evidence of the oppressive situation students wanted to overthrow in 1968. Antoine Doinel is punished, significantly, for writing his protest on the walls. The teacher shows prescience in his exasperated ejaculation: "Ah! J'ai pitié de la France dans dix ans."

35. Frank Kermode, *The Genesis of Secrecy: On the Interpretation of Narrative* (Cambridge: Harvard UP, 1979), 13. Kermode's conception of the artist's "mishearing" is very akin to Harold Bloom's description of poetic misprision in *The Anxiety of Influence: A Theory of Poetry* (New York: Oxford UP, 1973).

36. FATHER: "What that boy needs is a good thrashing." MOTHER: "That's what you think, is it? That's why he's going to be raised somewhere where you can't get at him" (*Citizen Kane*). Curiously, Truffaut claims that his memory of this film is auditory: "I noticed that I knew it by heart, but like a record rather than a film; I wasn't always certain of the image which was going to follow, but I was sure of the sound which was coming, of the quality of voice" (François Truffaut, "Citizen Kane," in *Focus on Citizen Kane*, ed. Ronald Gottesman [Englewood Cliffs: Prentice-Hall, 1971], 131).

37. But not before killing off his mother symbolically by means of one of his concocted school absence excuses. Antoine literally enacts the gesture of little Hans in *Beyond the Pleasure Principle* when he replaces abandonment and victimization with active dismissal. He also resembles the child Oskar in Volker Schlondorff's *The Tin Drum* (1979), who takes responsibility for the war-related death of everyone as a form of revenge for abandonment. The idea that he killed them is preferable to acknowledging that he has been abandoned. Significantly, he too virtually abandons speech, substituting the sound of his drum and a glass-shattering screech. Truffaut was undoubtedly familiar with this film, released the year before *Métro,* in which Heinz Bennent (Lucas Steiner) plays the role of a Nazi.

38. Desjardins, *Aline Desjardins s'entretient,* 27. Julia Phillips, "Close Encounters of the Worst Kind," *Première Magazine,* December 1990, 131–32, claims that Truffaut was not deaf at all. Although her account is vengeful and mean-spirited and her observations were clouded by cocaine, the literal truth of Truffaut's deafness is not my point. Deafness is most significant as a psychic *blessure d'origine* and as a pictorialization of the individual's central conflict in relation to the disaster (Lifton, *Death in Life*). In short, it is an autobiographical myth.

39. Truffaut, *Le Cinema selon François Truffaut,* 258.

40. Anne Frank, *The Diary of a Young Girl* (New York: Pocket Books, 1952), 103.

41. Truffaut reflects on his childhood in Desjardins, *Aline Desjardins s'entretient,* 11–12, 25, 39, 41. He characterizes his *oeuvre* as "films about a lack [*des films sur un manque*]" (44). See also Truffaut, *Le Plaisir des yeux,* 29–30.

42. See Truffaut, *Hitchcock,* 61, for an example. The dream sequence in *La Nuit américaine* is no doubt a tribute to a similar tripartite anxiety dream in Hitchcock's *Spellbound,* in which an adult man's phobias are traced to a childhood trauma.

43. Desjardins, *Aline Desjardins s'entretient,* 40.

44. Kurt Vonnegut Jr., *Slaughterhouse Five or the Children's Crusade: A Duty-Dance with Death* (New York: Dell, 1968), 73–75.

45. See, for example, Desjardins, *Aline Desjardins s'entretient,* 42. Ferrand also states as much in *La Nuit américaine.*

6. DURASIAN (PRE)OCCUPATIONS

1. Duras, *La Douleur.* Page references are to the translation: *The War: A Memoir,* trans. Barbara Bray (New York: Pantheon, 1986).

2. Duras, *Outside* (Paris: POL, 1984), 288. The piece originally appeared in 1976 in the magazine *Sorcières.* The camps reappear as a repressed memory returning in her alcoholic delirium in *La Vie materielle* (Paris: POL, 1987), 154–56.

3. A fragment of "La Douleur," the title story of *La Douleur,* appeared as "Pas mort en

déportation," in Duras, *Outside,* 288–92, where it is noted as having been published in *Sorcières* in 1976.

4. Michel Foucault and Hélène Cixous, "A propos de Marguerite Duras," *Cahiers Renaud Barrault* 89 (fall 1975): 13.

5. Carol Hofmann, *Forgetting and Marguerite Duras* (Niwot: UP of Colorado, 1991).

6. Borgomano, *L'Ecriture filmique de Marguerite Duras.*

7. Lyon, "Cinema of Lol V. Stein," 244–73, quotations from 253, 261, and 263.

8. J. LaPlanche and J.-B. Pontalis, *The Language of Psychoanalysis,* trans. Donald Nicholson-Smith (New York: W. W. Norton, 1973), 318.

9. Duras, *Le Ravissement de Lol V. Stein.*

10. LaPlanche and Pontalis, *Language of Psychoanalysis,* 317. Lyon follows LaPlanche and Pontalis in defining a fantasmatic as "that structuring activity which shapes and orders the life of the subject" ("Cinema of Lol V. Stein," 249). I follow LaPlanche and Pontalis as well as Lyon in using the spelling *fantasy* invariably (see "Cinema of Lol V. Stein," 272 n. 5).

11. Marguerite Duras, *Moderato cantabile* (Paris: Minuit, 1958). Page references are to the translation: *Moderato cantabile,* trans. Richard Seaver, in Marguerite Duras, *Four Novels* (New York: Grove Weidenfeld, 1965). *Moderato cantabile* was given a more classic cinematic adaptation by Peter Brook in 1960 in a film starring Jeanne Moreau and Jean-Paul Belmondo.

12. Resnais, "Entretien avec Alain Resnais," 215.

13. Duras, preface to *Hiroshima mon amour,* 9.

14. Lifton, *Death in Life,* 9.

15. Sharon Willis describes this as a feature of the entire Durasian *oeuvre* in *Marguerite Duras,* 59.

16. Duras, *Moderato cantabile,* 79, 90, 83.

17. Duras's biographer, Frédérique Lebelley, does speak of childhood expeditions into Saigon to see movies, but there is no mention of piano playing in movie theaters. Whether or not the pianist mother at the silent cinema is a Durasian invention, it is a wonderfully telling image of the connections linking the mother to music, silence, the inexpressible, and the Edenic.

18. Marina Warner, *Alone of All Her Sex: The Myth and Cult of the Virgin Mary* (New York: Knopf, 1976).

19. Richard Eberhart's "Brotherhood of Men," cited by Susan Gubar in "This is My Rifle, This is my Gun': World War II and the Blitz on Women," in *Behind the Lines: Gender and the Two World Wars,* ed. Margaret Randolph Higonnet, Jane Jenson, Sonya Michel, and Margaret Collins Weitz (New Haven: Yale UP, 1987), 247.

20. Julia Kristeva, "Stabat Mater," trans. Leon Roudiez, in *The Kristeva Reader,* ed. Toril Moi (New York: Columbia UP, 1986), 176.

21. Duras, *Outside,* 280–82.

22. Marguerite Duras and Michelle Porte, *Les Lieux de Marguerite Duras* (Paris: Minuit, 1977), 23.

23. Girard, *Violence and the Sacred*.

24. Rousso, *Vichy Syndrome*, 15–27.

25. Elaine Scarry, *The Body in Pain: The Making and Unmaking of the World* (New York: Oxford UP, 1985).

26. Marguerite Duras, *L'Amant de la Chine du Nord* (Paris: Gallimard, 1991), published in English as *The North China Lover*, trans. Leigh Hafrey (New York: New Press, 1992), 208–9; the page reference refers to the English-language edition. This quotation is given as it appears in the original in the epigraph to this chapter.

27. Kristeva, *Soleil noir: Dépression et mélancholie* (Paris: Gallimard, 1987), 235–38.

28. Alice Y. Kaplan, introduction to *Remembering in Vain: The Klaus Barbie Trial and Crimes against Humanity,* by Alain Finkielkraut, trans. Roxanne Lapidus with Sima Godfrey (New York: Columbia UP, 1992), xvii.

7. LOOKS THAT KILL

1. Louis Malle, *Au revoir les enfants,* trans. Anselm Hollo (New York: Grove, 1988), v. In the original screenplay, published in 1987 by Gallimard, the statement appears on the back cover. Page references are to the English translation.

2. See Françoise Audé and Jean-Pierre Jeancolas, "Entretien avec Louis Malle sur *Au revoir les enfants,*" *Positif* 320 (October 1987): 32–39; "Ce matin de janvier 44: Malle parle de *Au revoir les enfants,*" *Jeune Cinéma* 183 (October–November 1987): 34–38; and Jacques Gerstenkorn, "Malle pris aux mots," *Vertigo* 2 (April 1988): 121–35.

3. Malle may be exaggerating the boys' ignorance and injecting a note of adult irony or even of retrospective self-justification. Stanley Hoffmann finds it hard to believe that in early 1944 even sheltered schoolboys could have been so ignorant of pervasive anti-Jewish propaganda and persecutions ("Neither Hope Nor Glory: Review of *Au revoir les enfants,*" *New York Review of Books,* 12 May 1988, 21).

4. It is also possible that here and in other episodes the adult Malle is commenting ironically on the Catholic Church's failure to speak out about the persecution of the Jews. In the fatal scene when the Gestapo arrest Jean, there can be seen on the wall a portrait of Pope Pious XII, looking the other way. See Louis Malle, *Conversations avec Louis Malle* (Paris, 1993), 215.

5. Gilles Jacob, "Entretien avec louis malle (à propos de lacombe lucien)," *Positif* 157 (March 1974): 34. In an earlier version of the filmscript, Lucien, fired from his job for stealing, denounces his former employer to the Gestapo. Malle states that this version was modeled closely on an event from his childhood.

6. Louis Malle, *Louis Malle par Louis Malle,* ed. Jacques Mallecot (Paris: Athanor, 1979); and Jacob, "Entretien avec Louis Malle."

7. See, for example, Jean Delmas's review in *Jeune Cinéma* 77 (March 1974): 33–35;

"*Lacombe Lucien* et L'Occupation: Louis Malle s'explique; René Andrieu conteste," *Humanité dimanche* (3–7 April 1974): 19–22; Michel Sineux, "Le Hasard, le chagrin, la nécessité, la pitié (sur *Lacombe Lucien*)," *Positif* 157 (March 1974): 25–27; and Pascal Bonitzer, "Histoire de sparadrap (*Lacombe Lucien*)," *Cahiers du cinéma* 250 (May 1974): 42–47. François Garçon reexamines the debate itself from the perspective of the 1980s in "La Fin d'un mythe," *Vertigo* 2 (April 1988): 111–18.

8. The phrase "backward turn," which appears in the epigraph to this chapter as well, is from Metz, "The Imaginary Signifier," 5.

9. Michel Foucault, for one, insinuates that Malle was a good leftist and should have known better (see "Anti-Rétro: Entretien avec Michel Foucault," *Cahiers du cinéma* 251–52 [July–August 1974]: 11).

10. Alan Morris, *Collaboration and Resistance Reviewed: Writers and the* Mode Rétro *in Post-Gaullist France* (New York: Berg, 1992), 54–65.

11. Jean-Paul Sartre, *Le Mur* (Paris: Gallimard, 1939). See also his "Qu'est-ce qu'un collaborateur?" in *Situations III* (Paris: Gallimard, 1949), 43–61.

12. For an interesting discussion of the implications of her name, see Colin W. Nettelbeck and Penelope A. Hueston, *Patrick Modiano, pièces d'identité: Ecrire l'entretemps* (Paris: Lettres Modernes, 1986). In their chapter on *Lacombe Lucien*, entitled "D'Un Clown collabo à une France juive," Nettelbeck and Hueston suggest that the choice of the young woman's name reveals her strategy of accommodation with the Occupation (with Lucien) in order to survive and also a more generalized desire for "symbolic reconciliation of Jewish and French identities" (64).

13. For evidence that the film's release in 1981 did indeed have the impact of a first shock, see Christian de la Mazière's description of the devastating effect of its belated release on his own life in "Nous, les Français de la mauvaise chance: Le Témoignage d'un volontaire de la division Charlemagne," *Paris Match,* 13 November 1981, 128.

14. See, for example, Charles de Gaulle, "General de Gaulle's Speech to the French People, Broadcast from Algiers, April 4 1944," in Charles de Gaulle, *Two Speeches by General Charles de Gaulle, President of the French Committee of National Liberation* (New York: France Forever, 1944), French text 30, English translation 31: "A few traitors [*quelques traitres*] were, are and will still be able to serve directly the enemy's interests. They are receiving or will receive the punishment they deserve. A few cowards and unreasoning persons [*quelques lâches ou quelques aveugles*] associated voluntarily and willingly with the collaborating venture of these unworthy leaders: their weakness or blindness is being punished or will be punished. A few foolish men [*quelques sots*] may try to play what is known as a 'parallel' game, which in fact ends up only in disunity; national determination will mete out justice to their absurd intrigues. But the great majority of Frenchmen, no matter what their opinions . . . are our unhappy brothers and must only be considered as fighting men gathered together to save the country which belongs to all of them.

15. Morris, *Collaboration and Resistance Reviewed*, 44.

16. Many sources document the debates, which almost prevented the trial from taking place at all. See esp. Erna Paris, *Unhealed Wounds: France and the Klaus Barbie Affair* (New York: Grove, 1985); and Morgan, *An Uncertain Hour*. On the Touvier and Bousquet cases, see "Le Dossier Bousquet" and "Touvier: Un Procès pour mémoire," *Libération*, 13 July 1993 and 17 March 1994, respectively. Translations and scholarly analyses of these two special issues of *Libération* are forthcoming from the University Press of New England in Richard J. Golsan, ed., *The Holocaust in France Today: The Touvier and Bousquet Affairs*.

17. Nick Browne, "The Spectator-in-the-Text: The Rhetoric of *Stagecoach*," in *Film Theory and Criticism*, ed. Gerald Mast, Marshall Cohen, and Leo Braudy, 4th ed. (New York: Oxford UP, 1992), 210.

18. Thus, about the three conceptions of collaboration studied in the chapters of this section, it might be said that each artist's central conflict in relation to the disaster—each artist's characteristic configuration of denial as it is combined with a will to know—is figured as a kind of maxim ("Vous connaissez le proverbe"): Truffaut's maxim would be "Hear no evil"; Duras's, "Speak no evil"; and Malle's, "See no evil."

19. André Bazin, *What Is Cinema?* trans. Hugh Gray (Berkeley: U of California P, 1971), 148. The specific Chaplin film chosen is meaningful: when the Little Tramp arrives at New York harbor, he is not allowed to disembark. It is also worth noting, in light of the thematics of silence and *le muet* in Truffaut and Duras, that *The Immigrant* is a silent film.

20. There is some debate about this. What is important, probably, is that Malle thought he was Jewish.

21. Jean-Paul Sartre, *Réflexions sur la question juive* (Paris: Gallimard, 1946), 122, 131, 124–25, 173. Sartre's inability to define the Jew except as a purely negative quality and his ignorance of Jewish history, culture, and traditions have sparked much criticism. See Susan Rubin Suleiman, "What Does It Mean to Reflect on the Jewish Question?" (public lecture, Dartmouth College, Hanover NH, 29 November 1993).

22. Gertrud Koch, "Sartre's Screen Projection of Freud," *October* 57 (summer 1991): 14.

23. Jean-Paul Sartre, *Being and Nothingness: An Essay on Phenomenological Ontology*, trans. Hazel E. Barnes (New York: Philosophical Library, 1956), 260.

24. Jean-Paul Sartre, "Black Orpheus," in *'What is Literature?' and Other Essays*, 291.

25. Geraldine Pederson-Krag, "Detective Stories and the Primal Scene," in *The Poetics of Murder: Detective Fiction and Literary Theory*, ed. Glenn W. Most and William W. Stowe (New York: Harcourt Brace Jovanovich, 1983), 13–20.

26. Geoffrey H. Hartman, "Literature High and Low: The Case of the Mystery Story," in Most and Stowe, *Poetics of Murder*, 210–29.

27. Morris, *Collaboration and Resistance Reviewed*, 82–102.

28. The term *suture* is used to describe the panoply of cinematic and narrative operations whereby the spectator is inextricably "sewn" into the scene portrayed and implicated in its power relations, its erotic forces, its drives to closure. Suture has been most thoroughly studied in examinations of subjective and point-of-view shots and in the use of shot-countershot sequences (see Jean-Pierre Oudart, "Cinema and Suture," *Screen* 18 [winter 1977–78]: 35–47; Kaja Silverman, *The Subject of Semiotics* [New York: Oxford UP, 1983]; and Stephen Heath, *Questions of Cinema* [Bloomington: Indiana UP, 1981]).

29. Baudry, "Ideological Effects of the Basic Cinematographic Apparatus," 295.

30. Metz, *The Imaginary Signifier*, 49, 96.

31. Metz, *The Imaginary Signifier*, 63–64, emphasis in the original.

32. Malle's preoccupation with racism is evident in the three films that immediately preceded *Au revoir les enfants: Alamo Bay* (1985), *God's Country* (1986), and *The Pursuit of Happiness* (1987).

33. Marie Balmary, *Psychoanalyzing Psychoanalysis: Freud and the Hidden Fault of the Father,* trans. Ned Lukacher (Baltimore: Johns Hopkins UP, 1982); Lukacher, *Primal Scenes.*

34. Even before *Au revoir les enfants,* fathers are frequently absent or lack "legitimate" sexual or political authority in Malle's films, from *Murmur of the Heart* and *Pretty Baby* to his more recent *Damage.* In *Au revoir les enfants* it is clear that this absence has political significance similar to what Thomas Elsaesser terms the "fatherless society" portrayed in German postwar cinema (see *New German Cinema,* 239–42).

35. Susan Sontag, "Fascinating Fascism," in *Under the Sign of Saturn* (New York: Farrar, Straus & Giroux, 1980); Foucault, "Anti-Rétro: Entretien avec Michel Foucault"; Saul Friedlander, *Reflections of Nazism: An Essay on Kitsch and Death,* trans. Thomas Weyr (New York: Harper & Row, 1984).

36. White, *Metahistory.*

37. Duras, *The War: A Memoir,* 3.

38. Amy Lawrence, *Echo and Narcissus: Women's Voices in Classical Hollywood Cinema* (Berkeley: U of California P, 1991), 170. Lawrence makes this statement in the context of a discussion of *To Kill a Mockingbird,* where she is expanding on a similar point made by Kaja Silverman in *The Acoustic Mirror: The Female Voice in Psychoanalysis and Cinema* (Bloomington: Indiana UP, 1988), 52–53. Silverman focuses on the regression to the past in autobiographical texts, however, and Lawrence on the shape the text takes in the present because of the character's past trauma.

39. As I noted earlier, several critics have linked postwar writing to incomplete, delayed, or repressed mourning: see Hofmann, *Forgetting and Marguerite Duras;* Elsaesser, *New German Cinema;* and Rousso, *Vichy Syndrome.*

40. Doane, "Misrecognition and Identity," 16, 19.

1. "New New Novelist" Jean Ricardou, in his only piece of fiction that evokes historical events, inscribes the aftermath of 1968 by describing a scene of graffiti being sandblasted from a wall ("Incident," in *Révolutions minuscules* [Paris: Gallimard, 1971]). The short story originally appeared in 1970; see my discussion of it in Lynn A. Higgins, *Parables of Theory: Jean Ricardou's Metafiction* (Birmingham: Summa, 1984), 147–50.

2. Ophuls, *Le Chagrin et la pitié*, 20.

3. The title highlights a line in the film: although their personal life and their work could hardly be worse, Montand reassures Fonda on the phone that "tout va bien." The title may also evoke another popular song, in which a marquise calls home for a report on the household, only to learn from her retainers that a series of disasters, each more horrifying than the one before, has befallen her (her horse has died, her château has burned to the ground, the marquis has killed himself), while a refrain reassures her that aside from all that, "tout va très bien, Madame."

4. For further evidence of connections between World War II and the revolts of 1968, see Lynn A. Higgins, "Unfinished Business: Reflections on the Occupation and May '68," *L'Esprit créateur* 33 (spring 1993): 105–10 (special issue, "The Occupation in French Literature and Film, 1940–1992").

5. Cohn-Bendit and Cohn-Bendit, *Obsolete Communism*, 34.

6. Laplanche and Pontalis, *Language of Psychoanalysis*, 113.

7. The filmscript was published by Patrick Rotman and Bertrand Tavernier as *La Guerre sans nom: Les Appelés d'Algérie* 54–62 (Paris: Seuil, 1992).

8. Patrick Modiano, *Les Boulevards de ceinture* (Paris: Minuit, 1972).

9. Michel Foucault, *L'Ordre du discours* (Paris: Gallimard, 1971).

10. Britton, *Nouveau Roman*, 192–203.

11. Robbe-Grillet, *Ghosts in the Mirror*, 5. Godard, for one, has yet to write or film his autobiography, but his *Introduction à une véritable histoire du cinéma* (Paris: Albatross, 1980) is very autobiographical.

12. During the period of hyperformalist experimentation sometimes called the New New Novel, Simon published *La Bataille de Pharsale* (1969), *Orion aveugle* (1970, incorporated into *Les Corps conducteurs*, 1971), *Triptyque* (1973), and *Leçon de choses* (1975). Not coincidentally, most of these works were written within what Rousso calls the period of repressions."

13. Ory, *L'Entre-deux-mai*, 113. See also Hayward, who remarks that the 1980s were dominated by a "culture of nostalgia" (*French National Cinema*, 247).

14. In other words, I beg to differ with those who claim that the *mode rétro* and the New Novel are categorically incompatible. For example, Alan Morris states in *Collaboration and Resistance Reviewed* that the demythifiers of the 1970s "unfailingly reject [. . .] the revolutionary approach to narrative pioneered by the *nouveaux romanciers*," and he claims

that "those who sought to demythify saw *content,* and not *form,* as the means to secure their objective" (66, 70, emphasis in the original). Like Patrick Combes's study of the fictions of May 1968 (*La Littérature et le mouvement de mai 68*), however, Morris's statement more accurately describes his own choice of corpus, since he only selected works whose content aims explicitly to demythify.

15. Robbe-Grillet, *Un Régicide* (Paris: J'ai lu, 1978).

16. Pierre Nora, ed., *Les Lieux de mémoire,* vol. 1, *La République* (Paris: Gallimard, 1984), vii.

17. Alain Duhamel, *Les Peurs françaises* (Paris: Flammarion, 1993), 243–47.

Index

In the Stages series